MAGGOTS, MU

MEMORIES AND REFLECTIONS

OF A FORENSIC ENTOMOLOGIST

MAGGOTS, MURDER AND MEN

MEMORIES AND REFLECTIONS OF A

FORENSIC ENTOMOLOGIST

ZAKARIA

ERZINÇLIOĞLU

HARLEY
BOOKS

Harley Books (B.H. & A. Harley Ltd)
Martins, Great Horkesley,
Colchester, Essex CO6 4AH, England

Text designed and set in Galliard Carter Cone
by Peter and Alison Guy
Text printed by St Edmundsbury Press Ltd,
Bury St Edmunds, Suffolk
Bound by Woolnoughs Bookbinders Ltd,
Irthlingborough, Northants

Maggots, Murder and Men –
memories and reflections of a forensic entomologist
Published by Harley Books, 2000
Second impression, 2003

British Library Catalogue-in-Publication Data applied for

ISBN 0 946589 65 8

FOR

LEWIS DAVIES,

HENRY DISNEY

AND

IAN GAULD

THE THREE
ENTOMOLOGISTS
WHO MOST
INFLUENCED
MY CAREER

Contents

Foreword

The alliterative title of Dr Erzinçlioğlu's book is very apt indeed, for it displays the three essential elements of his fascinating memoirs, which are mixed in a way which holds the attention throughout.

The author is known with considerable respect – and some affection – as 'Dr Zak' by every police force in the country and I have had the privilege of knowing him for many years. Some of the cases we have shared appear in these pages and I especially remember Karen Price, 'the body in the carpet', probably the most forensically-satisfying investigation of my own career. Others included the tragic double shooting on the Pembrokeshire cliffs – and the body in the West Country barley-field where Zak's opinion threw the rest of us into confusion, until an unusual scientific solution calmed the troubled waters!

This book is no mere recital of half a life-time's case-work – the pages are laced through with scientific fact, philosophical debate, historical asides and political campaigning – as far as the legal system is concerned.

It is typical of the author himself, for Dr Zak is a big man – large in body, mind and soul, with a commanding presence. I occasionally felt that he was born a few hundred years too late, as he reminded me of those seventeenth-century Royal Society polymaths, with his wide-ranging interests in so many subjects. His book brings this out perfectly, with its compelling amalgam of entomology, criminology, history and – as important as the science – *humanity*, for he succeeds in bridging what would appear to be an unbridgeable gap between blue-bottle maggots and a social conscience! Yet along with details of the house-fly's life-cycle, he remembers to describe the frequent squalor of the sordid premises so familiar to all forensic specialists that have to attend scenes of death – and where, as Dr Zak so eloquently points out, human beings have to survive alongside the flies.

It might seem rather odd that a world expert on the blow-fly should write a book that is informative, intriguing, astonishing and yet show such compassion and not a little anger at deprivation and injustice – yet, for those who know Dr Zak, it is no real surprise at all.

Bernard Knight, CBE,
Emeritus Professor of Forensic Pathology,
University of Wales

Author's acknowledgements

I particularly wish to mention the late Professors Cedric Keith Simpson and Alan Usher. These two distinguished pathologists were responsible for my entry into the world of forensic science and my gratitude to them is immense. Of the many other forensic pathologists who have done everything they could to support my work, I would like to thank Professors Anthony Busuttil, David Gee, Michael Green, Austin Gresham, Bernard Knight and Peter Vanezis, and Dr Basil Purdue.

I also wish to give special thanks to Mr Alex Carlile, Q.C., formerly Member of Parliament for Montgomery and now Lord Carlile of Berriew, for his staunch support and encouragement over many years.

My thanks are also due to Lord Ferrers, formerly Minister of State at the Home Office, for his help in securing Home Office funding for my work and for his unfailing personal courtesy.

For the development of the entomological aspects of my career, I am greatly in the debt of Drs Lewis Davies, Henry Disney and Ian Gauld who, more than any of the many other entomologists I know, have supported me and over the years put up with my eccentricities. I know that, on occasion, I have tried them sorely.

Specifically in the realm of forensic entomology, I would like to thank Professor Bernard Greenberg and Mr Ken Smith for their friendship and advice.

My colleagues at the Forensic Science Service are too numerous to mention individually, but I would like to give special thanks to Dr Trevor Rothwell, Mr Peter Lamb, Mr Philip Toates, Dr Ann Davies, Mr Graham Craddock, Mrs Elizabeth Wilson and Mr Frank Gore.

Much of my career was spent working at the Department of Zoology, University of Cambridge, and, in this connection, I would like to thank, and acknowledge gratefully the support of, Professor Gabriel Horn, Professor Malcolm Burrows, Dr Ken Joysey, Professor Patrick Bateson and Dr William Foster. Of the very many other members of that large and bustling department who made my time there both pleasant and intellectually rewarding, I would like to give special thanks to Professor Michael Bate, Professor Simon Laughlin, Dr Helen Skaer and Mr Dennis Unwin, all of whom took a kind interest in my work.

With regard to my concerns about the role of forensic science in the administration of justice, I wish to acknowledge with gratitude the time and patience with which the late Lord Dainton considered my views.

I also thank Lord Lewis for listening to my concerns in this area and for his great personal courtesy.

I wish to thank Jonathan Clowes Ltd for permission to reproduce extracts from Sir Arthur Conan Doyle's Sherlock Holmes stories.

I thank Dr Michael Roberts for preparing the imaginative illustrations, which so enhance the book's appearance. My thanks also to Annette and Basil Harley, who went through the text with a fine-toothed comb, curbing my natural verbosity and saving me from making a number of embarrassing errors. I also thank Dr Susan Leech for preparing the index.

My wife, Sharon, and my children, Tanya, Larissa and Aksel, have all encouraged me during the writing of the book and their delight at its completion was my greatest reward. I particularly wish to thank my wife for her painstaking efforts in editing the book; and my children for doing their share of the work.

CHAPTER I

A very simple clue

'Who saw him die?'
'I', said the Fly
'With my little eye,
I saw him die.'
  Anon., *'Who killed Cock Robin?'*

Viewed dispassionately, a dead human body is a magnificent and highly nutritious resource. Such a resource, suddenly made available in Nature, will be rapidly colonized by various insects as well as other invertebrate animals. As time passes and decomposition progresses, different insect species will be attracted to the body at different stages of decay. Bluebottles and greenbottles will arrive to lay their eggs which hatch into maggots that feed voraciously on the tissues. Beetles will arrive, not only to feed upon the tissues, but also upon the maggots. Minute wasps will arrive to parasitize the maggots. Tiny flies, whose very existence remains unguessed by most people, will similarly arrive at various stages of decay and will leave tell-tale signs of their visits. Myriads of other creatures will arrive at various times, each to leave its mark for future interpretation by those who look into such things. On the basis of the fact that anything that changes with time can be used as a clock, the succession of insects occurring on a dead body can, in principle, be exploited as a measure of time since death.

This intriguing idea has an important application, for it can help to answer one of the most basic questions asked during a murder investigation: 'When was the crime committed?' Although this is one of the commonest questions a policeman is likely to ask himself when investigating a murder, it is also one of the most difficult to answer. Contrary to popular belief, based on so many crime stories and whodunnits, the doctor who attends the scene is usually quite unable to say anything very useful about time of death, except in certain special circumstances. The whodunnit medico, who says things like: 'Inspector, the murder took place at a quarter to two on the morning of Tuesday 23rd March', is a totally fictitious character.

In real life, forensic pathologists (medics whose expertise lies primarily in the determination of *cause* of death) can offer an opinion on time of death only during the first three days or so after a crime is committed. Forensic pathologists exploit three natural phenomena to help them answer the question of time of death. These are the onset and passing away of rigor mortis; the time taken for the temperature of the body to drop to that of the surrounding air; and the order in which the various organs start to decompose. All these changes take place and are over within two or three days of death; beyond that time there is no easily measurable pathological change that can be used to determine when the victim died.

But it is not only in the matter of time of death that insects can help in criminal investigations. They can also help us to discover the *site* of the crime and *how* it was committed. They can tell us whether someone was a victim of blackmail; whether a crime was committed with malice aforethought; and whether someone's death was a suicide. They can shed light on crimes involving the smuggling of drugs; they can lead us to the home town of a murder victim; they can help us to identify a rapist; and many other things besides.

Curiously, the use of insects in the investigation of crime is a relatively new subject. Like most of forensic science, it began to take shape during the second half of the nineteenth century but, even today, very few people, including some police officers, know that it exists at all.

Sir Arthur Conan Doyle, the creator of Sherlock Holmes and Dr Watson, was a pioneer forensic scientist. It was he who introduced the idea of taking plaster casts of footprints. His Sherlock Holmes stories, which emphasize the central importance of physical evidence in criminal investigations, were actually used as instruction manuals by the Chinese and Egyptian police forces for many years, and the French

Sûreté named their great forensic laboratory at Lyon after him. He transformed the very way criminal investigators thought about their work. We owe him a great debt of gratitude.

For a long time I believed that Conan Doyle, in spite of his great understanding of forensic matters, overlooked the evidence of the ever-present insects. In one of his short stories, *Black Peter*, in which a sailor, Captain Peter Carey, is murdered with a harpoon and pinned to the wall, Conan Doyle has Inspector Stanley Hopkins describe the scene of the murder to Sherlock Holmes in the following way:

> 'Well, I have fairly steady nerves, as you know, Mr Holmes, but I give you my word that I got a shake when I put my head into that little house. It was droning like a harmonium with the flies and bluebottles, and the floor and walls were like a slaughterhouse ... And there in the middle was the man himself, his face twisted like a lost soul in torment, and his great brindled beard stuck upwards in his agony. Right through his broad breast a steel harpoon had been driven, and it had sunk deep into the wood of the wall behind him. He was pinned like a beetle on a card. Of course, he was quite dead.'

In the conversation that follows, Holmes rebukes the young inspector for failing to notice any footmarks, saying, 'My good Hopkins, I have investigated many crimes, but I have never yet seen one which was committed by a flying creature.' Hopkins is contrite but, if he had had his wits about him, he might have retorted that although no flying creatures committed the crime they certainly arrived to bear witness to the event. For Sherlock Holmes totally ignores the presence of the flies and bluebottles, which were clearly inserted by Conan Doyle purely for dramatic purposes, not as evidence that could have been used to solve the mystery.

Ever since I first read this story many years ago, I have wondered whether Conan Doyle really could have overlooked the significance of the flies. Although Sherlock Holmes does not discuss them as evidence in Captain Carey's murder, their presence confirms the account of events given by various characters in the story. In fact, the description of the scene is so uncannily realistic that I have to conclude that Conan Doyle must have known something about the habits of flies. Let me explain.

At about 2 o'clock in the morning, Captain Carey's wife and daughter heard a loud bellow coming from the Captain's hut in the garden. They thought nothing of it, since the Captain often roared and bellowed when drunk. It was only at noon that someone went to the hut to investigate, since the Captain could be very violent when under the influence of alcohol, and it was then that his dead body was discovered, with the flies swarming around it. Within the hour, Inspector Hopkins was at the scene.

Ten or eleven hours had elapsed since the murder, which must have taken place when the Captain uttered his 'fearful yell' in the night. Under the prevailing conditions – it was the height of summer and the murder had taken place at night – the swarms of flies and bluebottles witnessed by Inspector Hopkins at about 1 o'clock in the afternoon are exactly what one would expect to see. The time delay is quite accurate. Furthermore, Hopkins told Holmes that he had followed the master detective's methods and made a thorough examination. Yet he reported no fly eggs on the body; again, this is exactly what one would expect after the given period that had elapsed since death. This is because flies will be attracted to a body, but not lay eggs on it until the conditions of decomposition and temperature are exactly right. The flies would probably have been just about ready to lay their eggs.

Flies are not normally active at night, not because it is dark but because the temperature is low. It is only during the day, when the air temperature rises, that they become active. Flies also avoid laying eggs on a body whose temperature has not dropped to a certain acceptable level. Finally, the odours of decomposition that attract flies take some hours to emanate from the body. Conan Doyle's description of the murder scene is convincing in every detail.

Flies and bluebottles are among the very first arrivals at the scene of a murder. If, like King Solomon, we could talk to insects and other animals, flies, as well as their maggots (so often found in the body of a murder victim), would be the most valuable of witnesses. Alas, we cannot talk to them, but we can do the next best thing, which is to study their habits, allowing us to draw conclusions based on our understanding of their nature.

The very simple fact that bluebottles and other blowflies will so often lay their eggs on the bodies of murder victims has very useful consequences in murder investigations. When the maggots hatch from the eggs and start feeding on the tissues of the body, they will, of course, grow and change as they age. If the age of the maggots in a body can be determined, this will give a very good idea of time of death, since the maggot cannot have been alive for a longer period than the body has been dead. Of course, the murder victim may have died some time before the flies arrived to lay their eggs, so the age of the maggot will give us a *minimum* time since death, not an actual time of death. In other words, it can give us a time *by which* death had occurred. However, this does not mean that we cannot often give an estimate of the actual time of death, based on evidence other than the age of the maggot alone.

There is much more truth in the rhyme about Cock Robin than the anonymous author ever knew, but I am convinced that the early arrival of flies at a dead body must have inspired that first verse.

I have practised in the field of forensic entomology – the application of insect biology to the investigation of crime – for over twenty five years.* I have many memories of those years, some pleasant, others not. Nevertheless, the general experience I gained has taught me a great deal about humanity, justice, science, law and, of course, insects. The world of flies, maggots, beetles and bugs opened up a much wider and more human world.

I am often asked what it is like to be a forensic scientist. The question carries with it an assumption that the forensic science profession is one that can be described as 'glamorous'. In truth, I have not found it so. However, I have always felt that the scientific investigation of crime is very interesting work, but being interesting is not its only attribute. As a forensic scientist one has to visit the seediest of dwellings at the most unsocial of hours. Often, one finds oneself trudging across a muddy field early on a cold, wet morning or carrying out a post-mortem examination late at night. Waiting for interminable hours at police stations; being ferociously cross-examined by hostile barristers in court; dropping everything at a moment's notice to go to the scene of a crime; all these things have their interesting aspects, but they are

* Entomology is the study of insects. The word 'forensic' originally meant 'of the forum', i.e. of matters concerned with public debate or the law courts. Forensic science has come to mean, not public science, but science as applied to legal problems.

usually not immediately apparent.

In spite of these somewhat negative features, forensic science is often very exciting, even exhilarating. The interesting scientific discoveries that can be made, the knowledge one gains, the insights that help with future investigations, make it all well worthwhile. But the greatest reward is the knowledge that one's findings have actually made a difference, that they enabled justice to prevail. It is a great pleasure to be told, at the end of a trial, that one's testimony was crucial to the understanding of the case.

But one must not forget the ever-present possibility of failure, that one may be mistaken. The very thought that one might have given incorrect interpretations of the evidence, however honestly, is a haunting one. I remember one occasion, early in my career, when I lay awake all night, worrying that I might have misled the jury. I went over and over the evidence in my mind, trying to reassure myself that I had said nothing that could have led to a miscarriage of justice. The next day I travelled north to meet the pathologist in the case and go over my conclusions with him, just to make sure that I had been as rigorous and objective as possible. I need not have worried, since all the other evidence confirmed my conclusions but, despite the ugliness of the thought of error, it is a concern that should never be far from the mind of the forensic scientist. Oliver Cromwell's exhortation – 'I beseech you, in the bowels of Christ, think it possible you may be mistaken' – is very wise and should be engraved on the hearts of all who are involved with the administration of justice.

My forensic work has brought me into contact with other forensic scientists, with police officers, barristers and solicitors. Some were good, some bad, some indifferent, but I must express my gratitude to them all, without exception, for I have learnt something from the best and from the worst of them. Many have shown me great kindness and it is on this more positive aspect that I will concentrate in the following pages. My name not being of a kind that is easily articulated by the English tongue, I have become known to the police (sinister expression!) as Dr Zak. But the highest accolade I have ever received from them came from Superintendent Clive Jones of the Dyfed-Powys Police, who dubbed me 'the Maggotologist'. When I came to hear of this he asked me whether I minded being so called. I said that I certainly did not and was in fact immensely flattered. As far as I know, I am the world's only holder of this august title!

Nevertheless, my experiences have shown me that there are great deficiencies within the criminal justice system, the police and the practice of forensic science. It is not possible to be involved in the investigation of crime and remain unaware of and unaffected by these flaws. It follows that a book like this cannot be complete without some comment on these matters.

Let us go back to insects, those wonderful creatures that form the connecting thread of this book. How can they help us to solve crimes? To many people, the very idea that insects can contribute to a murder investigation seems absurd. I was once told about a conversation that took place in a pub near which a murder had been committed. I had been involved in the investigation. One of the wags in the pub told the others that word was going around that 'they' had found out when the murder took place by asking a maggot! Worse still, many people seemed to believe the story! This chap could not believe how gullible people could be. He was quite dumbfounded when he was told that the story, in essence, was true!

Insects can help us to understand what happened in criminal cases because they are found almost everywhere, with the exception of the sea, where only a few species occur. On land and in freshwater, insects are the most abundant of animals, forming over eighty-five per cent of the world's known species. Well over one million species are known and new species are discovered almost every day. The total number may well be somewhere between ten and fifty million species. One witty Oxford professor once said that, as a rough approximation, all animals are insects!

Insects are found on every continent, including Antarctica. It is their ubiquity and large numbers, both in terms of species and individuals, that make them so useful in forensic investigations. The best way to explain why this is so is to invite you for a walk through a garden in spring.

As you walk along the path, looking at the flowers in the borders, you will see a number of different kinds of bumble-bee. Some are small and yellow, others are large and black with red tails, while others have white tails, and so on. You move on and come to an apple tree. Buzzing around the apple-blossom are various insects, most of which look like bees, but a closer examination will reveal that some are wasps and others are delicate black-and-yellow flies. You make your way down to the bottom of the garden where there is a compost heap;

prodding it with the toe of your shoe, a swarm of minute, nondescript flies rises into the air. All these little black or grey flies look much the same to you but, in all probability, there will be several different species in that small swarm.

What does all this have to do with forensic investigations? When you walked around the garden, what you saw was a large number of insects exploiting particular sources of nourishment. The bees on the flowers, the various insects on the apple tree, the small flies in the compost heap. Several species were all trying to exploit the same resource. Now, classic ecological theory suggests that no two species do exactly the same thing in nature because, if they did, they would inevitably have to compete with one another to the detriment of both. Therefore, species that are very similar and closely related tend to evolve life-styles that are slightly different from one another. The different bumble-bees visiting the flowers in the border were attracted to different flowers or to different parts of the same flower; the insects on the apple tree were feeding on the apples themselves or on the tree's sap; and the little flies in the compost heap were each breeding or feeding on different components of the rotting vegetation, or even parasitizing different creatures living in the mound.

One important thing follows from all this: if you should find a particular insect species in the course of a forensic investigation, it will tell you something very specific about the events that took place prior to your arrival. To take a simple example, let us suppose that you find a small insect crushed inside someone's shirt pocket. If the species in question turns out to be a kind of midge that breeds only in certain types of lake, you will have cause to look with suspicion upon the owner of the shirt if he tells you that he has never been near such a lake, near which a crime had occurred. A very similar, but different, species would not have connected the individual with that type of lake. The discovery of the first midge species would have been strong evidence against the man's account of events. It would have been a very simple, yet very powerful, clue.

Of course, this was a deliberately simple example, but it explains the essence of forensic entomology. The species, stage of development and general physiological condition of insects found during a forensic inquiry will often furnish clues that will help in reconstructing past events, which is the purpose of much of forensic science.

Forensic entomology is not a well-known field. Few forensic scientists have any involvement with it and there are very few practitioners of it worldwide. The reason for this is that entomology is a vast subject that is not easy to include within the armoury of general forensic scientists, who have to deal with so many kinds of evidence. Forensic entomologists are usually, like myself, entomologists who have turned to forensic science, rather than forensic scientists who have turned to entomology. The finding of an insect may give the criminal investigator a very simple clue, though a good deal of knowledge is required, not only to interpret it, but also to recognize it as *being* a clue in the first place.

Although this book is mainly about criminal investigation, I will allow myself some digressions. From time to time, I will make forays into related forensic but non-entomological matters on the one hand, and into related entomological but non-forensic matters on the other. I hope these excursions will both set the main subject-matter in context and be of interest in their own right.

CHAPTER 2

The Nature of Evidence

Some circumstantial evidence is very strong, as
when you find a trout in the milk.
Henry Thoreau, *Walden*

There are many paths to the truth. Many non-scientists, as well as a few scientists, believe in a thing called the Scientific Method, the application of which will automatically lead one to the truth. This is a baffling claim, since I have never been able to discover the nature of this mysterious method and have concluded that it is a notion akin to the Philosopher's Stone, beloved of the alchemists of long ago. It will be remembered that it was believed that the discovery of this Stone would enable its possessor to turn base metals into gold.

Unhappily, there is no Philosopher's Stone, either actual or metaphorical. There is no one, simple formula by which we can turn ordinary facts into the golden truth that we are seeking. The workaday facts gathered during a criminal investigation cannot be placed in a magic crucible, there to be transformed into the solution of the crime. There is no substitute for deep thought, hard work and imagination.

So, how does one set about finding out the truth about a crime? How does one search for clues? What does one do with the evidence when one finds it? How can all the evidence be fitted together in order to make sense of the case? These are some of the questions that students and others wishing to become forensic scientists often ask me. In fact, where does one begin in a situation that is usually best described as a mess?

Consider the following, fairly typical, scenario. A murder has been committed and the police arrive at the scene – a private dwelling in a deprived area of London. After an initial assessment of the situation, the policemen call for help; a pathologist, various forensic scientists, a photographer, a scenes-of-crime officer and others arrive and make their contributions. This early stage in a case investigation is usually a bit chaotic and it often happens, as in this instance, that I am among the last to arrive, largely because my own specialism is not yet one of the standard and well-known aspects of forensic science. My attendance is usually suggested by the pathologist, or sometimes by a police officer with whom I have worked before, if an estimate of the time of death is required.

When I arrive I am met with a scene of great bustle and activity. Outside in the street two uniformed officers are on guard. Inside, the old house is dirty and neglected. There is refuse of all kinds on the floor. The kitchen is littered with rotting food; empty and broken bottles lie on the table; the dustbin overflows with rubbish. Policemen are going up and down the stairs; the pathologist is talking urgently to his assistant; the photographer is struggling to move his cameras into the house; gloved, white-coated forensic scientists are busy examining the walls and taking samples. The officer in charge welcomes me and helps me to carry my case and the necessary tools of the trade up the stairs and into the room where the body is lying – the 'scene' in police terminology. As I enter the room and stand surveying the wreckage, the officer gives me the basic facts of the case.

As an aside, let me say that I have never witnessed a murder scene like those so often described in detective stories or featured in murder mystery films. The pristine, orderly appearance, the conveniently arranged pieces of evidence, the general cleanliness of the surroundings of what is usually a genteel abode – all these are outside my experience. I have never been to the scene of a murder in a grand or well-ordered house of any kind.

To return to our narrative. I am now standing in the room in which the victim, an old man, is lying on the bed. I used the word 'wreckage', because the room is in a dreadful state. The body is decomposing; everywhere there is congealed blood as well as other, less mentionable, body fluids and products. The stench is offensive and overpowering, even though the window is open. It is dark, there being only one dim lamp hanging from the ceiling and the photographer is requested to arrange some of his powerful bulbs in the room to shed light on the mystery.

Where does one begin? When a forensic scientist visits a scene, he must always remember that other scientists have to carry out their own examinations and that his own work must not be conducted in such a way that would hinder others or destroy evidence of interest to other specialists. Often, a certain amount of damage will have been done before his arrival; policemen may have trodden heavily around the room, unwittingly destroying what could have been good evidence. This is unavoidable, since it is quite impossible to arrive at a murder scene without damaging something that, with hindsight, could have been useful.

The first thing I do is to ask to speak to the pathologist, who gives me his initial impressions of the cause of death. 'It looks like a case of stabbing', he says, but his detailed conclusions must wait until the post-mortem examination. Meanwhile, the other forensic scientists have made their way upstairs. I ask them whether there is anything they do not want me to touch. They tell me which parts of the room they have examined and which they would rather we examined together, because they have not yet gone over them in detail.

I put on protective clothing, gloves and a mask and approach the body. It is infested with maggots, and flies are buzzing about in the room. There are maggots among the bedclothes and all over the floor. I take the temperature of the body and of the air in the room. I examine the position of the body; I ask whether the window was already open when the police arrived; I search the bedclothes and the floor for maggots and other entomological evidence. All the time I am taking samples and placing them in tubes which have to be accurately labelled and given identification numbers; I also take copious notes. Meanwhile, the photographer is busy; I ask him to take two or three more photographs of this or that object from this or that angle.

At last, after two or three hours, all that can be done in the house has been done and the time is a little after midnight. But the work is far from over. The body has to be moved to the mortuary. The police, having stood aside to allow the specialists to do their work, take over the 'scene' once again. The corpse is placed in a body-bag and taken downstairs out into the waiting ambulance. The pathologist and I follow in a police car. At the mortuary there is some delay, but the body is eventually brought into the building and placed on a special bench; the post-mortem examination can now begin. The pathologist asks whether I would like to start the examination, since he knows that his incisions may destroy some of the evidence I seek. I accept his offer. Having donned new protective clothing, I affix a magnifying lens to my spectacles and, armed with a pair of forceps, I search the body for clues. More tubes are needed, as well as more preservative fluid. Further samples are taken; further notes; further labelling. Throughout my examination, I provide a running commentary for the benefit of the pathologist and the police officers present. The photographer takes photographs which he will develop and print as soon as possible once the examination is over, and he will send me a full set.

I have now examined everything on the surface of the body and ask the pathologist to join in the examination. The scalpels and other paraphernalia of the medic come out and are put to work. Incisions are made and the pathologist's own commentary begins. From time to time I ask to have a look and take further samples. The hours pass and, as dawn begins to break, the work is done. We are all very tired, but a voice asks: 'Would you like a cup of tea, doctor?' It is a welcome offer, gratefully accepted. The pathologist, the investigating officer and I sit down and drink the tea which has arrived from I know not where. We talk for a while about the case and each gives his initial tentative conclusions, but we know that it is 'early days yet' and that there is still a great deal to be done. For now, it is time to go home. A policeman tells me that the car to take me there should be at the door in five minutes. I take my leave of the inspector and the pathologist and go outside. I am glad to be in the open air again; the atmosphere inside was not pleasant. In a few minutes the young police driver arrives; he does not look tired, for he is just beginning his day. I get into the car and we drive away in silence. I arrive at my home as others are beginning to leave theirs.

The mass of physical evidence collected – by me, by the pathologist and by the other forensic scientists – was not gathered haphazardly. Every sample was taken for a good reason, yet not everything that *could* have been collected was collected. How does one decide what to collect and what to leave behind?

Speaking very generally, we do not 'see' the things we are not looking for. Of course, if you are walking along the street in a city you have never visited before, you will notice the huge cathedral that looms up in front of you, even if you had been previously unaware that there was a cathedral in the vicinity. The very size of the building will impose itself upon your notice. But when one looks at a complex scene, with vast numbers of small objects in it, the human mind will notice only those things with which it is familiar. The rest will make no sense and will be ignored. Although you might well see everything, you will fail to 'see' many things, in the sense that you will not recognize them as being anything in particular and your mind will filter them out. It is the same with other sensory information; we are usually oblivious to the sound of the ticking clock in the room or the touch of the clothes on our skin.

Look, for example, at this sketch. It shows an enlargement of a black object measuring a fraction of a millimetre, scarcely larger than any of the full stops on this page. This was found on the bedsheets at the scene described above. I suspect you have no idea what it is and there is no reason why you should. In fact it is a broken part of a maggot's skeletal apparatus, the hard parts to which some of the muscles attach. If you had come across it during an examination of the murder scene, you would not have collected it, simply because it would have meant nothing to you. Similarly, if I had attempted to do the work of another forensic specialist, I would have failed to notice those things which he would have looked for and which he would have instantly recognized. We each have our own search pattern, as psychologists would say.

Let us take another example. I was once discussing the work of an archaeological laboratory with its director. The laboratory specialized in the retrieval and analysis of faunal and floral remains from archaeological sites and I asked whether the staff, during their searches, ever came across fly puparia – the pupal cases that are left behind by flies when they have completed their metamorphosis and emerged as adults. The director told me that, to his knowledge, no such finds had been made in his laboratory. I found this surprising, since puparia are very durable structures and are often found in archaeological deposits. He also said that I was welcome to come and have a look at the samples myself. I took him up on his offer and went to his laboratory. I looked at the first sample of debris from a grave site and instantly saw dozens of puparia in the Petri dish under the microscope. I pointed these out to my colleague, who said that he had not realized that these objects were of any value and had assumed that they were of mineral origin. Once I showed his staff what they were, they found large numbers of them in the samples they subsequently collected. I do not tell this little story in a critical spirit, but to show that it is not possible to attach any importance to things whose appearance or very existence is unknown to us.

Searching for clues and collecting physical evidence depends, to a great extent, on our preconceptions and expectations, which are themselves refined with experience. Knowing *how* to look is one thing; knowing *where* to look is another. Early in my career I became involved in the investigation of a murder in which the perpetrator concealed the victim's body under the floorboards of his house. At the time, I thought this a most bizarre hiding place, but my experience since then has shown me that this is a very frequent hiding place for murdered bodies. People who commit murder seem to think that the last place a criminal investigator is likely to look is under the floorboards; in fact, it is one of the first places the police check. There are, then, no fixed rules about how and where to look; only our knowledge of the subject, continually honed by experience, can guide us in these matters.

However open-minded one is determined to be when searching for clues, one usually has a general expectation of what one will find. To counter this narrowing tendency, I have found it useful to tell myself, quite consciously, that I could well find something that is out of the ordinary. It is what one does not expect to find that is often most revealing; it is Thoreau's trout in the milk.

I remember a case from Yorkshire some years ago that makes this point well. The murder of a young girl had taken me up north. I examined the evidence, which seemed to suggest that the victim had died about two weeks before her body was discovered. It was early spring and the bluebottle maggots in the body had developed slowly in the prevailing low temperatures. It was possible to conclude that a minimum of two weeks had elapsed since death. But there were other insects present, of a kind rarely found in forensic cases. They were the larvae of winter gnats, obscure insects that hardly anybody notices. In fact, they ought to be more noticeable than they are, for they are active during the winter, a time when most people do not expect to see any insects at all. If you stand in a garden on a sunny winter afternoon before dusk, you might notice a swarm of minute gnats hovering above some large object such as a garden chair, a dustbin or a large flowerpot. Although very small, the reflection of the sun off their silvery wings attracts attention. These are winter gnats, insects that normally breed in compost heaps and other rotting vegetation.

Many years before, when I was researching the habits of insects in winter, I had found the larvae of winter gnats in my experimental animal carcasses. This had surprised me for, until that time, the presence of these insects in carrion was unknown. Interestingly, I discovered later that another researcher, Elcy Broadhead of Leeds University, had found them on a human corpse at roughly the same time as I was conducting my experiments. We each wrote scientific papers on our discoveries, totally oblivious of what the other was doing!

In the Yorkshire case, the discovery of the larval winter gnats in the body told an interesting story. Death had not occurred in the spring, but during the winter. My researches on the development of these larvae enabled me to interpret the evidence in this case. So, while the absence of winter gnat larvae would not have resulted in an incorrect supposition – that death had occurred at least two weeks before discovery, their presence allowed me to arrive at much more helpful conclusions. Still, their occurrence in the case was unexpected since, my animal experiments apart, I had known them to occur in human corpses in only a very few cases.

Another case, similar in many ways to the last, took place in the far north of England. One Monday evening in early summer, I received a telephone call from a police inspector, who told me a most unusual story. Apparently, some young boys had been having an illicit party in a fairly remote spot in the country on the previous Saturday. They had taken large amounts of drink and cigarettes to a crater-like depression, where they had lit a bonfire and started carousing. The bonfire soon died down, so the boys collected sticks and twigs to revive it. The crater was thick with vegetation and, during their searches, some of the boys found a rolled-up carpet lying in the undergrowth. They took it to the bonfire and threw it on. The fire began to splutter back to life very satisfyingly. The boys were pleased with the result. But then, something very unusual happened. As the carpet burned, it became clear that something was concealed inside it. The boys watched anxiously and were soon horrified to see a human skull drop out of the carpet and roll on to the ground. The illicit party came to an abrupt end.

To their credit, the boys rushed to the nearest police station and reported their discovery. The police officer on duty, doubtless with tight lips and beetling brow, asked them what they were doing in the crater in the first place. Crestfallen and not a little afraid, they confessed their misdeeds. But, since they had subsequently behaved very correctly and responsibly, I hope their sins were forgiven.

The inspector asked whether I could come to help with the investigation the following day. I could, and took an early train north in the morning. When I arrived, I was immediately taken to the crater. There was, in fact, little to be gained from the visit, since the police had cleared the place of all its vegetation, with the exception of some old hawthorn trees growing in that strange depression, the largest and thickest-trunked of their kind that I had ever seen – veritable giants. Imagining what the crater must have looked like before the vegetation was cleared, I could see why it was chosen as a hiding place; had it not been for the boys and their party, the body would probably never have been discovered.

The body was now in the police mortuary in town. I went there with the officers and we unfolded the carpet and began the examination. It was a total mess. The body was in an advanced state of decomposition, to use one of the clinical euphemisms of science, and there was no shortage of clues. It was a matter of getting down on one's knees and searching painstakingly through the congealed mass of what was once a human being – in this case an early middle-aged man. It was many hours before the examination was complete and all the samples bottled, preserved and labelled.

I studied the samples at leisure when I returned to Cambridge. I knew from my examination at the mortuary that this was an unusual case. The body had been teeming with life and very many insect species were present; but I had found no blowfly maggots, which I would have expected in abundance at that time of year. I could not wait to start my laboratory work. There were vast numbers of scuttle flies, so named by Dr Henry Disney, because of their 'scuttling' gait. These minute insects, unknown to most people, are among the most remarkable of creatures. It is quite possible that, when the entire number of their species is discovered and described, they will turn out to be among the largest groups of animals on Earth. They exploit every biological niche on land and many in freshwater, and may well be the most biologically diverse group of land animals known. They are known as parasites of spiders' eggs, as breeders in mushrooms, as inhabitants of the liquid within carnivorous pitcher-plants and as internal parasites of human beings. Some have even been found to breed in boot-polish!

The scuttle flies in this case belonged to species known to favour breeding in corpses and animal carcasses that are concealed or buried. They did not take the investigation any further, since the position of the body when discovered was of course known. The most interesting find was the presence of large numbers of the larvae of an insect named *Scatopse notata*.* Unlike winter gnats, *Scatopse* breeds during most of the year (other than winter), but its season starts earlier and ends later than that of most fly species, including bluebottles and other blowflies.

What then did their presence, taken together with the absence of blowfly maggots, signify? The conclusion had to be that death had occurred at a time when *Scatopse* was active but when blowflies were

* There is no common name for this insect. Throughout the book I have given common names where they exist and have used scientific names only when there is no vernacular equivalent.

not. If the victim had died during the summer, the body would have been infested with blowfly maggots, not because *Scatopse* was absent but because it would not have been able to compete with the more efficient blowflies. It restricts its corpse- or carcass-feeding habits to those seasons in which blowflies are not active. For this reason, it was possible to arrive at a time of death in the spring, not in the summer.

Like so much of forensic science, forensic entomology is an historical subject, concerned with reconstructing the past. We have seen that time of death is usually left to the forensic entomologist to determine. This is much easier said than done. Although a succession of insects will occur on a dead body that is lying exposed for any length of time, it is almost impossible to predict what that succession will be. This is because the succession will depend on such factors as season, locality, interference by humans or other animals (like dogs, foxes and crows), or even chance. However, this does not mean that the phenomenon of insect succession is not useful; it simply means that it is a phenomenon about which we are not yet in a position to generalize too widely. It also means that succession is a phenomenon that can be used very effectively to reconstruct and interpret past events, but which cannot and is not intended to be used as a predictive tool.

It may seem puzzling to say that a phenomenon that cannot be predicted can still be useful for reconstructing past events. How can something that is so incompletely understood be exploited as a scientific technique with which to draw conclusions in such serious matters as criminal cases?

Before we answer this question it should be understood that the forensic scientist, like the archaeologist and the palaeontologist (a fossil specialist), is not concerned with predicting the future, but with reconstructing the past. The archaeologist is concerned with the reconstruction of events that have occurred hundreds or thousands of years ago and the palaeontologist may have to reconstruct events that took place millions of years earlier, whereas the forensic scientist is usually concerned with events that occurred days, weeks, months or, at most, a few years prior to the discovery of a crime. (To all intents and purposes, events that have taken place more than seventy years previously are of no legal interest and thus lie outside the remit of the forensic scientist).

Nevertheless, the kind of reasoning used by all three specialists is essentially the same. Indeed, many of the techniques that are developed in any one of these subjects are usually put to good use in the others.

Another point that should be understood is that any scientific investigator of past events is hampered by one major problem: there is little or no possibility of laboratory experimentation in the classic sense. To those accustomed to thinking of forensic investigators as white-coated scientists looking down microscopes and pouring coloured liquids into test-tubes, this may sound like a very odd statement. Of course, forensic scientists do work in laboratories and do conduct experiments and make use of all the usual paraphernalia used by other scientists, but their intellectual approach to the work is somewhat different. Normally, a scientist conducts an experiment under a set of controlled conditions and then notes the results, which he then tries to interpret in the light of the known conditions of the experiment. By contrast, what a forensic scientist is required to do is to make sense of an already existing situation that has resulted from a series of events that are unknown to him. He has to collect the results of that event (the 'experiment', so to speak) and try to reconstruct the conditions that led up to it.

These two answers to our question have not addressed the problem fully, for they do not tell us how we can reconstruct events by invoking an imperfectly understood natural phenomenon. However, I hope that I have shown that the aims of forensic science are rather different from those of the majority of science, which means that the methods used by forensic scientists must also be different. Let us now return to the problem of reconstruction. Let us say that you leave your workplace at lunchtime to do some shopping. When you return, you find that the briefcase of one of your male colleagues is lying in the office though it had not been there before lunch. This enables you to conclude that he arrived after you left. You might not have been able to predict that your friend would arrive at lunchtime or, if you happened to know beforehand that he was due to arrive at the office then, you might not have been able to predict that his briefcase would be the clue that would allow you to conclude that he had arrived, since he could have left his jacket or any other object known to belong to him. Here, the evidence you found enabled you to draw the correct conclusion, although you would not have been able to predict the course of events.

Now let us look at an actual forensic case. One day at the very end of October, the proprietor of a small corner shop in South Yorkshire, while going about his business, detected a strange and offensive smell which appeared to come from the house next door. He went out and knocked on his neighbour's door, but there was no answer. It suddenly struck him that it had been some time since he had last seen the old woman who lived alone in that house. He had assumed that she had gone away, but the unpleasant odour alarmed him and he decided to telephone the police.

Some time later, a policeman arrived. Taken aback by the smell, he peered through the heavily lace-curtained windows and saw legions of very small flies 'jumping up and down', as he later put it, on the window-sill. Clearly, something was very wrong. The policeman alerted his superiors and more officers arrived at the scene. The front door was broken down and the house searched. There was no sign of the old woman, and the stench that pervaded the whole house was clearly coming from the foot of the stairs. The police tore up the floorboards there and made a grisly discovery: a black plastic bin-liner containing, it became clear when they tried to lift it, a large and very heavy object. They knew what to expect. Opening the bag carefully, the policemen were greeted by swarms of small flies that flew up into their faces. Inside was the body of the woman, wrapped in several layers of blankets and bedspreads. During the post-mortem examination the pathologist, Professor Usher, collected large numbers of flies, maggots and pupae which he sent to me.

An examination of these insects revealed the presence of a number of species of very small flies, often known as lesser dung flies. These insects are much smaller than the more familiar houseflies and bluebottles. Five species were represented in all, of which one, *Leptocera caenosa*, was present as living adults, larvae and pupae. This species is known to continue breeding until quite late in the year, especially in human dwellings, so its presence indoors in October was not surprising. No living stages of the other four species were found, only their pupal cases which are left behind when the adult fly emerges. Although these cases, or puparia, are rather uniform in appearance, examination under the scanning electron microscope will reveal many distinguishing details by which they can be identified. In this case, such an examination showed that the puparia belonged to species that were active during June and July. This suggested that the woman must have died during the early summer, considerably earlier than was originally supposed. Although the woman had last been seen by the shopkeeper in the summer, the pathological evidence could not confirm that she had died at that time. It was the entomological evidence that corroborated the shopkeeper's story. In fact, it did rather more than that.

The old woman had no family, nor, it would seem, did she have any relations who visited her. However, she was known to have employed a young man to do odd jobs for her. He was married and had children, but had no formal employment and earned money by doing all kinds of jobs for various people. The old woman made unreasonable demands on his time and expected him to give priority to her concerns, treating the young fellow as an autocratic mother would her son. Having no family of her own, she made the fatal mistake of telling him that when she died she would leave her house and money to him. Unhappily, the young man did not look upon her as a mother, simply as a source of income and, although her domineering manner annoyed him, he put up with it in order to make money. Once he knew how much he stood to gain by her death, he murdered her. He himself disappeared in early summer, round about the time the old woman disappeared; it later transpired that he had gone into hiding in Scotland. The entomological evidence showed that the woman had died at that time and the police interpreted this as meaning that the young man left Yorkshire just after he killed her in order to avoid suspicion.

This case shows how knowledge of insect seasonality enables us to reconstruct the events of the past once the evidence has been found, although it would not have been possible to predict which species would arrive at the body. This does not mean however that there are no situations in which it is possible to be fairly confident that certain species will occur, but more of that later.

What exactly does a forensic scientist conclude from his findings? I am often asked whether my work enables me to identify the guilty party or whether I was ever instrumental in sending someone to prison. Of course, as a forensic scientist, it is not my role to identify the guilty person; that is the role of the jury in the courtroom. Nor, in most cases, can I say whether my evidence was the crucial factor in sending someone to prison, since the evidence is assessed as a whole and, in any case, juries cannot be asked how they arrived at their verdict.

It is of supreme importance that a forensic scientist should restrict his conclusions to matters that are within his competence. It is so easy to be tempted into giving opinions that lie outside one's expertise, but it is a temptation that must be resisted at all costs. Complete objectivity is essential. When I am asked to give an opinion on the time of death, I am obliged to give such an opinion solely on the basis of an analysis of any evidence that comes within my area of knowledge. That is why it is best, initially at least, for the forensic specialist to work on his own, without reference to the work of others engaged in closely related fields. Only after they have all arrived at their main conclusions should the specialists compare notes. Of course it is possible that a specialist may, in the light of the findings of others, modify his conclusions, but he must not start his own analysis with any preconceptions based on the conclusions of others, or on hearsay or eyewitness evidence.

Inevitably, forensic scientists do pick up a certain amount of information about the case – information that is not within their field of expertise but is, nevertheless, relevant to it. By way of example, let us say that a murder has been committed and an estimate of the time of death is required. In the case of entomology, the information needed relates to the insects found on the body, the physical conditions obtaining at the scene and various other specific pieces of information. Of course, one might come to know that a witness has come forward to say that he had seen the deceased alive and well at work on a certain day, and that the police believe him. This is evidence relating to time of death, but it should not be taken into account by the forensic scientist since such evidence is notoriously unreliable, it being very likely that someone else will come forward saying that the deceased was 'nowhere to be seen' at his workplace on that day. In any case, it is not information of the kind that can be evaluated specifically by a specialist in insect biology, so it should not be allowed to influence one's thinking.

An admittedly extreme example of how a forensic scientist can fall into the trap of over-reaching himself occurred in a murder investigation in an English coastal town. I had examined the evidence and written my report, giving my conclusions regarding the minimum time since death. These were interpreted – perfectly reasonably – by the police as supporting their belief that a particular individual was guilty of the crime. Some time later the prosecution released my report to the defence, who engaged their own specialist. This man then produced his report, disagreeing very forcibly with my conclusions, but for reasons that were scientifically insupportable.

I was asked by the prosecution to write another report commenting on the defence specialist's report. I did so, explaining in greater detail how I had arrived at my conclusions and why I believed the defence's man was wrong. I would like to be able to say that what happened next was extraordinary but, unfortunately, it is common enough. The defence specialist wrote another report in which he stated that I was incompetent; that a first year university student could do much better;

and that, if he had been the editor of a scientific journal, he would have declined to publish any of my scientific work. Finally, he said that my attempt to deprive an innocent man of his liberty was 'reprehensible'.

His personal attack upon me was most unfortunate and ill-advised but that is beside the point, which is that he had made up his mind about the defendant's innocence, a matter that was totally outside his competence. My own conclusions could be seen as evidence against the defendant, but they could not prove that he was guilty. The conclusions of the defence's man could be seen as evidence in favour of the defendant's innocence but, again, they could not prove it. It was clear that the consultant for the defence was determined to argue the case for the man's innocence, rather than present objective evidence, the significance of which others could assess.

The forensic scientist is usually asked very specific questions, such as 'When did death occur?', or 'What was the cause of death?', or 'To which blood-group does this blood-stain belong?' He is never asked, nor should he ever offer an opinion on, matters of guilt or innocence. Even a psychologist, asked for his opinion on whether a man is lying or not, should answer that question and go no further, such as suggesting that since the man lied he must be guilty. It is therefore most important to understand what conclusions may or may not be drawn from the evidence. If I give an opinion on time of death, I must also explain as clearly as I can *how* I arrived at that conclusion on the basis of my scientific expertise. It is no use my standing up in court and saying that my examination of the developmental stage and physiological conditions of the maggots removed from the corpse indicated such-and-such a time of death and that, anyway, I heard Joe Bloggs in the corridor say that he saw the defendant leaving the scene with blood on his hands at exactly the same time as I had concluded death had occurred. No one needs a forensic scientist to interpret Joe Bloggs' evidence; furthermore, the forensic scientist is in no better position to interpret that evidence than anyone else.

This point can be made more clearly by presenting the opposite scenario. What if I had concluded that death had occurred seven days before the body was found, but that I had overheard Joe Bloggs say that he had seen the defendant leave the scene four days prior to discovery? What am I to do then? Am I to agree with our friend Bloggs and deny my own evidence, or am I to stick to my own conclusions and ignore Bloggs? Clearly I must do the latter, since that is why my opinion was sought in the first place. Apart from these considerations, Bloggs may have been lying. There is no alternative to the complete adherence to one's own conclusions when giving evidence, even though they may not necessarily always be right. No scientific subject or technique is infallible and all subjects are continuously developing.

I remember a case from the West Country that demonstrates this fact very powerfully. A man was walking his dog along the edge of a barley field one afternoon in June, when the dog suddenly ran off and started burrowing and pulling at something at the edge of the field. Following it, the man saw what had interested his dog; it was the half-buried body of a woman. The police were alerted. They excavated the 'grave' and removed the body. A pathologist carried out a post-mortem examination during which numerous blowfly maggots were collected. I was not present, but the police subsequently sent me the samples for analysis.

The stage of larval development showed that at least ten days had elapsed since death, which could not have taken place before May. I wrote my report and sent it to the police, who were considerably disturbed. I received a telephone call from the inspector in charge, who sounded agitated. My conclusions were most definitely wrong, he said, since they had identified the body as that of a young woman who had disappeared the previous December. All the clothes on the body were known to belong to the person in question, including a distinctive necklace. In December her car had been found with its interior splattered with blood. There could be no doubt that she had died in December and that my conclusions were incorrect, the inspector insisted. I told him that, as far as my own knowledge and expertise allowed, I was confident that death could not have occurred before May, and I asked him whether the pathologist had expressed an opinion on the matter. He said that, as far as the pathologist was concerned, the condition of the body was consistent with both scenarios – death in May or December. But the inspector was adamant. How could I be so sure, he demanded? The age of the maggots was clearly a red herring, since the body had been buried for a long time and it was only when parts of it were exposed above the surface, possibly as a result of the activities of animals, that the flies could reach it and lay their eggs. How could I possibly give a *maximum* time since death, when I always insisted that the maggot's age, on its own, could only give a *minimum* time since death?

What is one to do in such a circumstance? Naturally, I stuck to my guns. My study of the maggots had revealed that, under the prevailing conditions, their age could not have been more than ten days, so death could not have occurred before the beginning of May. Flies are attracted to dead bodies by their highly developed sense of smell. When a body begins to decompose it releases volatile compounds with particular chemical compositions. These are the odours that attract a fly to a corpse. When death occurs, either in winter or in summer, these odours (which are, of course, highly repellent to the human nose) are given off and dissipate within a few weeks of death. This will happen whether a body is buried or not. So, although the inspector was right when he said that the flies would not have had access to the body until parts of it were exposed above the surface of the soil, it is also true that they would not have been attracted to such a body in May if death had, indeed, occurred in December, since the volatile compounds would not have been there to attract the flies. The insects would simply have ignored the body; of this I was very sure.

When the inspector realized that I was not going to change my mind, he suggested that he and I should have a conference, together with the barrister and the other forensic scientists involved in the case. The conference was held at the Chepstow Laboratory of the Home Office Forensic Science Service. During the somewhat tense discussion, someone asked why the murderer had chosen that particular part of the field, so close to the edge, where the body was likely to be discovered. A police officer replied that the ground was rather soft at that spot, because it had clearly been recently ploughed by the farmer. I asked how he knew this and he said that the 'grave' was full of lime which the farmer must have put there; there was a large mound of lime at the edge of the field and he must have used some of that.

The interesting thing is that no one had thought of asking the farmer whether he had, in fact, done this. I asked the police officers whether the lime had been examined. No, it had not. Were they sure it was lime? 'Well, yes, what else could it be?' they replied; 'you see, there was a mound of lime by the edge ...' All this was a little odd. The photographs of the scene certainly showed a large amount of white substance in the soil, but that substance had not been subjected to any kind of analysis. I suggested as a first step a chemical test, followed by a microscopical examination. These were carried out. It was not lime.

The white substance turned out to be a rare soil fungus, present in unusually large amounts. I recommended that samples be submitted to a mycologist – a fungus specialist – for identification and advice. When the report was eventually received, the conundrum was resolved. This particular fungus grows upon animal (including human) remains in the soil and, as it develops, it releases volatiles similar to those given off during the early stages of corpse decomposition. Normally this would not have affected the flies' behaviour, since this fungus species was not known to occur in amounts large enough to make a difference. In this case, for some unknown reason, the fungus was present in such abundance as to render the soil white, deceiving the police into believing that it was lime. Clearly, it also deceived the flies.

So, my conclusions were wrong but, I like to think, for the right reasons. The net result of what was a baffling and difficult experience was that our knowledge was increased and no loose ends were left. To have conceded that the entomological conclusions were wrong simply because all the other evidence went against them would have done neither, and the investigation as well as our scientific understanding would have been the poorer.

Physical evidence – the actual objects one finds and the conditions one measures, such as temperature and humidity – means nothing on its own. All clues have to be interpreted or, to put it another way, one must attach some logical significance to them. Once, at a forensic science symposium some years ago, I sat listening to a lecture by a scientist who was assessing the respective roles of the different practitioners in a criminal investigation – those of the police officer, the solicitor, the barrister, the forensic scientist, the jury member and the judge. To my astonishment he concluded that, while all these people played an important part in handling the evidence, none of them, with the exception of the forensic scientist, was engaged in its interpretation. I was even more astonished to hear, after the lecture, that this opinion was hailed as being profound and full of insight.

But it is not true. We are all continually interpreting evidence. Take a look at this picture. Is it a duck or a rabbit? It could be either. The picture itself is a fact; what you think it depicts is an interpretation and my interpretation may well differ from yours. Consider how many times you have misunderstood what somebody has said to you. Expressions like 'Oh, I see what you mean' or 'He got hold of the wrong end of the stick' are common, everyday exclamations which reveal how often we misinterpret things. How many times have you thought you have seen, say, a small spider on the carpet but, on closer examination, have discovered it to be nothing but a piece of thread or a small scrap of paper?

A policeman at the scene has to interpret the facts facing him before he can decide whether they suggest foul play. The scenes-of-crime offi-cer has to decide what kinds of evidence need to be collected, itself an interpretation of the situation as a whole. The solicitor and the barris-ter must interpret the facts of the case before they can decide whether they have a case at all. The jury must interpret the facts presented in court before deciding whether they indicate guilt or innocence. Finally, the judge must guide the jury on the very question of how the facts are to be interpreted.

So, we all interpret what we see. It does not necessarily follow from this fact that we always act upon our interpretations in a rational man-ner. When I am approached by a police officer with a request to assist with an investigation, I am usually asked a very specific question, such as 'When was the body buried?' or 'Did death occur indoors?' The police, finding that their investigation has raised a particular question, seek out someone who they believe will be able to help them on that point. This is perfectly reasonable and it is how an investigation should be conducted.

Surprisingly, matters are not always handled in this fashion. I have sometimes been approached by police officers urgently asking for my help, but having no idea what they want me to do; or, alternatively, saying that they have found large amounts of insect evidence associated with the crime and can I help them, please? When I ask them to tell me what the question is to which they need an answer, they will say they do not know, but that they have heard that I deal with insect evidence! If I ask why an examination of the entomological evidence is required, they will look at one another helplessly, then say that the inspector told them to contact me. 'Do you want an opinion on time of death?' I might ask. 'No,' they will reply 'we know exactly when the victim died.' 'Place of death, then?' Again, no; and so on. Of course, when no rea-son is given for conducting the examination, I inform the officers that there is, in fact, no point in consulting me at all. In my experience, I have found that this situation is by no means rare and I have often wondered how much of the police's resources are wasted in this way. I regret to say that some forensic scientists exploit this state of affairs, as I shall explain later.

I remember a case that must be regarded as a classic in the annals of the uncritical examination of evidence. Some officers came to see me about a murder that had occurred in the Midlands. The victim's body, with its associated insect fauna, had been found under the floorboards of his house during the summer. As usual I was asked to assist and, as usual, I asked what problem they wanted me to solve. They did not know, but one of them said that they had been told that I often gave opinions about time of death. 'Was that what they wanted to know', I asked. 'No, no', they said, they already knew that, since the watch on the victim's wrist had stopped at a certain hour and date. It also transpired that the man had not been to his work-place since that date, and that newspapers had begun to accumulate inside the door from that time. Various other pieces of evidence showed beyond any reasonable doubt that the date on the watch was, indeed, the date of death.

When I pointed out that there was no need for my assistance in this case, the officers responded by asking me whether there was anything else I could do with the insect evidence. Again, I had to explain that, if they had a specific question, I would gladly help them to answer it. 'Was the place of death an issue in this case?' I asked. 'No'. 'Was there a problem about manner of death?' 'No'. We discussed every possibility in this way until, in the end, I had to tell them that there was nothing I could do to assist. They left, looking rather crestfallen and somewhat resentful. The next day I received a telephone call from their superior, telling me, in a disapproving tone, that he was very sorry to hear that I had declined to help his force in this case. Did this mean that I no longer wished to carry out investigations for his constabulary? It took me some time to bring the point home to him.

Every contact leaves a trace. This statement is one of the basic tenets of forensic science and its classic expression is the well-known fact that, when one picks up an object with one's hand, one leaves one's fingerprints on it. I need hardly point out how useful this fact has proved to be in detective work.

If you should ask a policeman what he thinks is the most useful kind of forensic technique, he will most probably answer: 'in detective work, anything that helps to connect a person to the scene of a crime'. One of the most effective such tools, developed in Holland but inexplicably not used to any extent in other countries, is the exploitation of the simple fact that a person's odour will remain in any locality he has visited. In theory, it is possible to 'extract' these odours from the atmosphere, especially if the locality is an enclosed place like a room in a house. In practice, the Dutch police routinely extract the odours of possible perpetrators of crimes from objects they may have handled.

For example, if someone is knifed during a burglary and the knife is dropped at the scene, the odour of whoever handled the knife can be extracted using specially treated pieces of cloth. These are then presented to dogs, who 'identify' an individual in an identity parade by comparing the odour on the cloth with the odour of the individual. Although some research on this idea has been carried out in Britain, it has not yet been perfected into a practical forensic tool. However, if this research is taken further, it should be possible for the chemical profile of the odour on the cloth to be compared directly with the odour from the individual.

In my own field of forensic science, the fact that every contact leaves a trace is best expressed when a body has been moved after a murder. Murderers rarely leave their victims in the position in which they fell but usually try to conceal the body in some way. The body, in its original position, will have been in contact with an environment other than the one in which it was discovered and that original environment will have left its mark. Sometimes a murderer will bury the body but may exhume it later and place it elsewhere. The soil organisms found on the body, the kind of vegetation and fungal growth and, of course, the presence of residual traces of the soil itself will all afford clues that suggest not only that the body has been moved, but also the kind of place from which it was exhumed. I will describe later how powerful this kind of evidence can be.

Another forensic principle states that, while two objects may be indistinguishable, no two objects are identical. For example, we may not be able to distinguish easily between two apparently identical knives but we should, in principle, be able to find a means of telling them apart.

Explained in this way the apparent self-contradiction of the principle may seem to disappear; in fact, it raises another self-contradiction. If no two objects are identical, then two sets of fingerprints from the same person are also not identical. Two prints of the same photograph of the same person would not be identical and so forth. What matters, however, is the *way* in which the objects differ. The two photographs may differ, but not in a way that affects our belief in the congruence of the identities of the individual in each picture. One picture may be darker, the other lighter; one may be slightly torn, the other not; one may be larger, the other smaller; one may be marked by a pen, the other not; and so on. The point is that these differences do not affect our ability to connect the two objects in a meaningful way – they do not affect our belief that the photographs are of the same individual. Similarly, the two sets of fingerprints may differ in the degree to which particular lines or rings are clearly visible – they may be perfectly clear in one set, but ill-defined in the other. Nevertheless, we are able to attribute them to the same person. To put it succinctly, two objects may be distinguishable, yet remain clearly referable to a unique object; in the case of the photographs and the fingerprints, that 'object' is a unique human being.

Can we tell one individual maggot from another or one individual fly from another? Does such a bizarre necessity ever arise in detective work? It does sometimes, albeit not in the way in which one would want to tell one person from another. I was once called to a case in which a young man had failed to appear at his place of work and there was concern that he might have died. His house was locked from the inside; the police could see the key still in the hole. Since many days had elapsed since he had last been seen, it was thought that entomological evidence might be found.

It was, in abundance. The police broke down the door and we entered. There was no trace of anyone downstairs, so we went upstairs. As we ascended, I could hear a humming noise coming from one of the bedrooms and it got louder as we approached. One of the police officers opened the door, then immediately fell back, colliding with the inspector behind him. A great cloud of flies emerged from the room; there must have been thousands of them. The room was very hot; the floor was covered with maggots; and the stench – a mixture of a rotting smell and ammonia (the excretory product of maggots) – was overpowering. We all retreated and closed the door.

Masks and protective clothing were obtained and donned and we entered the room once again. Lying face down on the bed was the maggot-infested body of the young man. We approached, crunching maggots underfoot, and two of the police officers tried to turn the body over. Immediately, steam arose from the bed, for the feeding activity of maggots can raise the temperature considerably. Very large numbers of flies were still buzzing in the room. The pathologist made a preliminary examination and I set about collecting samples from around the room. The developmental state of the maggots would give me a minimum time since death, but I wanted to perfect this further by also collecting samples of the flies.

What I needed to establish was whether at least some of the flies present were insects that had been attracted to the body or whether they had developed as maggots within the body and had emerged as flies inside the room. If some flies had come from the body, I could arrive at a longer minimum time since death which would be more helpful to the police.

As one fly looks much like any other of the same species, how can one tell whether an individual fly has developed in a body or not? When female flies emerge from pupation they have incompletely developed ovaries; there are no developed eggs in them. In order to develop their eggs, flies have to take a protein meal, which is usually obtained from feeding at an animal carcass. After such a meal, some time elapses before the ovaries 'mature' and eggs can be laid.

I took my samples back to the laboratory, dissected and examined them, and found that they all had undeveloped ovaries. This could mean either that they were flies that had recently emerged from the body, or that they were flies that had just arrived from outside to have a protein meal. However, I had taken very large samples and none of the flies had mature ovaries. This suggested that they all probably derived from the body, since it would have been unlikely that no flies with developed ovaries had come from outside to lay their already matured eggs on the body. Still, this was only a general indication and not proof that the flies had emerged from the body. However, some of the flies were not fully pigmented; full pigmentation takes about a day to complete after a fly emerges. The full expansion of the wings also takes a certain period of time to complete. Present in the samples were flies with incompletely extended wings which, being unable to fly, could not possibly have arrived from outside.

The case was resolved satisfactorily. It was not a murder, but a case of suspicious death;* the young man had been a drug addict and died as a result of his addiction. The estimated minimum time of death was corroborated by the other known facts in the case.

Very little evidence is perfect. By 'perfect' I mean evidence that admits of only one explanation and no other. Indeed, it is very difficult to think of anything that can be described as perfect evidence, as defined in this way. If you see smoke, you may conclude that there is a fire, yet there may be doubt as to whether what you saw was smoke – it could have been steam or dust or even a distant cloud of midges! Only if you are certain that what you saw (and what you smelt and what stung your eyes) was smoke can you be certain that there was a fire. This is

* Any sudden, unexpected or inexplicable death is initially treated by the police as a suspicious death; that of a young person is almost automatically treated as such.

the kind of situation that comes closest to the notion of perfect evidence but, in practice, it is very rare.

Let us say you visit the scene of a crime and find a man's body lying on the ground. The head shows signs of a terrible blow and beside the body you find a piece of a broken, blood-encrusted stick. Fragments of wood from the skull of the deceased are found to be of the same kind of wood as the stick and the blood on the stick matches the blood of the deceased. Later, you find another piece of broken stick in the possession of someone who hated the deceased and stood to gain very substantially from his death. He has no alibi. You take his piece of broken stick and compare it with the one you found at the scene. The two broken ends match so perfectly that you have no doubt that they formed one whole stick. You conclude that the possessor of the second half-stick killed the victim by hitting him over the head with the stick so forcibly that it broke in two. The evidence of the blood and the stick, together with the presence of motive and absence of alibi, lead you to believe that there is no doubt about his guilt.

Yet there is always doubt. The broken half-stick might have been planted in the house of the accused by the real murderer. The fact that your man hated the victim and stood to gain from his death may appear less incriminating when you discover that many other people hated him and stood to gain from his death, one way or another. The absence of an alibi, in itself, means nothing, since you had no alibi either.

What I am trying to say is simply this: evidence hardly ever proves anything *beyond doubt*, which is why the Law requires criminal cases to be proved 'beyond *reasonable* doubt'.* In practice, whether one is dealing with scientific, legal, historical or any other matter, one is not dealing with absolute certainties but with probabilities. In the above hypothetical case, the jury may conclude that the balance of probability is so overwhelmingly in favour of guilt that it will return a 'guilty' verdict. Thus, in a criminal investigation, the forensic scientist must evaluate the evidence on the basis of probability.

For instance, I am sometimes asked by police officers whether the accused's story is likely to be true in view of the evidence that I have collected and analysed. This is back to front. The question should rather be whether the evidence I found was likely in view of the story of the accused. As a forensic scientist, what I should be evaluating is the probability of the evidence if the proposed scenario is true, not the probability of the proposed scenario being true if I find certain evidence.

This is not as pedantic as it may appear. Let us say I find a knife at

* Civil cases do not require proof beyond reasonable doubt; the most likely explanation of an event is the one that is accepted.

the scene of a crime. If a policeman asks me how likely it is that the knife's owner is the murderer, my answer would have to be that it was likely. However, this question would not give me any opportunity to comment on the probability of anyone else being the murderer. If, on the other hand, he had asked me how important the presence of the knife would have been in evaluating a number of suspects, I would have been able to assess the probability of each person's guilt. It is clear that the first question would not have allowed me to consider more than one possible answer. Since it would not have been possible to say that the person in question could not have been the murderer, we are no further forward. The second question allows me to consider which one of a number of possibilities is the most likely.

An actual forensic example should make my meaning clear. I was once asked to assist in the investigation of a case of murder that had one distinctive feature: there was no evidence; at least, no evidence of the kind that I am qualified to examine. Or, to put it another way, the evidence was that there was no evidence.

One day a single, middle-aged man, who lived alone, disappeared. He failed to appear at work and all police enquiries failed to discover his whereabouts. Eventually the case was closed. About a year later the case was reopened, partly because the police realized that there was one loose end that could be resolved by further enquiries. Many of the people who were questioned about the missing man responded that he had probably run off with a blonde woman, although the police could not find out who she was. However, they did notice that the source of this story was one particular individual, a plumber, from whom all the other people had heard it, either at first or second hand. Believing that he might have more sinister information about the matter, the police arrested him.

The plumber, an ex-SAS man, initially denied any knowledge of the missing man's whereabouts, but after police questioning he admitted that he had killed him. It was an accident, he said. They had both been watching television but had argued about which channel to watch. In the dispute that followed the plumber pushed his friend who fell heavily to the ground, cracked his skull and died. Overcome with remorse and not knowing what to do, he had taken the body to the house of one of his customers (he had a key so that he could let himself in to carry out some plumbing jobs when the owner was at work). Ripping up the floorboards, he had placed the body under them on the concrete base that lay about two feet below. This allegedly took place at the end of May. The culprit claimed that he had left the body in that position during the whole of June and July and the first week of August. The owner of the house then went on holiday. The plumber returned to the house, ripped up the floorboards again, broke through the concrete base, dug a hole in the soil beneath, buried the body, replaced the soil, laid new concrete above it and replaced the floorboards as before.

The police did not believe his story. They suspected that no accident was involved and that their man had, in fact, committed a premeditated murder. The body was indeed found in a shallow grave beneath the floorboards but the police believed that the plumber had dug the hole before he killed his victim and that he had buried the body *under the concrete base* soon after the murder, i.e. at the end of May, not in August. The police asked me for an opinion: did the man bury the body in May or in August? The body showed no signs of maggot activity which was rather odd because one would expect flies to have laid their eggs on the body during the summer, assuming that it had been placed in a position that would have allowed them access.

Together with the police inspector and some of his officers, I paid a visit to the scene. I asked some of the officers to remove the floorboards so that I could examine the area beneath. While they were engaged in their work, I left the house and prowled about outside looking for any entry points to the space between the floorboards and the concrete base through which flies might have gained access. There were a number of air-bricks, several of which were clear and free of debris. Re-entering the house, I examined the floorboards around the central-heating pipes. The holes in the wood around the pipes were quite large. It was clear that there were at least two potential entry points for flies; one from the outside, the air-bricks; and one from the inside, the holes in the floorboards.

By now the officers had finished pulling up the floorboards. I sat down on the edge and lowered myself into the gap. With the inspector's help, I swept the entire surface of the concrete, but I failed to find what I was looking for, namely a large number of pupal cases. Next, I sieved large amounts of soil from the area of the 'grave'; again nothing. Had the body been lying in that space during June, July and part of August, I would have expected flies to have detected its presence and entered to lay their eggs on it. The resulting maggots, after feeding on the body, would have left it to pupate on the concrete base. I sieved the soil because the pupal cases might have been swept into the hole, together with the body, when the latter was supposedly placed there in August. I concluded that the body was far more likely to have been buried in May than in August.

That was the conclusion, but the question I had to address was 'What was the probability of finding no evidence of maggot activity, if burial had taken place in May, and what was the probability of finding no such evidence, had burial taken place in August?' *not* 'What was the probability of burial having taken place in August, in view of the lack of evidence of any maggot activity?' If I had attempted to answer the second question, I would have had to say that it was unlikely to be true, but I could equally well have said that about a number of other scenarios that could have been suggested.

Answering the first question allowed me to consider that other hypothetical situations were possible. The answer I gave was that it was highly improbable that there would have been no evidence of maggot activity if burial had taken place in August, and that the lack of puparia would have been much more probable had burial occurred in May. A piece of evidence, on its own, cannot tell us whether a particular scenario is true or not; it can only help us to distinguish between two or more explanations. In the end, evidence must be seen as something that either strengthens or weakens one's belief in one of them.

It may be argued that sometimes there is no explicit choice between hypotheses. For example, one may validly be asked a question like 'When did death occur?'. When the question is asked there may be no specific alternatives to consider, but when the evidence is examined it may become clear that there are a number. As the investigation progresses, these can be whittled down until one is left with very few or sometimes only one.

To conclude the story, the blonde woman with whom the victim was supposed to have absconded never existed; she was introduced by the murderer to explain his unfortunate victim's disappearance. He was a very inventive murderer, having gone to the trouble of buying women's clothes and draping them around the house so that he could show them to his nephew, who often helped him with his work. He also painted lipstick on the rims of tea-cups to add verisimilitude to his story. The reason for the murder was that the day before he disappeared, the victim, whom I shall call Smith, had taken out a loan for £4,000. The police were suspicious; they did not believe that Smith, a man whose financial affairs were kept in perfect order, needed to take out what was, for him, such a large loan. They decided, very shrewdly, to take the murderer, whom I shall call Jones, to the banker who organized the loan. The banker, in his innocence, made an everyday remark that utterly condemned Jones. He said: 'Hello, Mr Smith'.

I began this chapter by saying that there are many paths to the truth: many ways of approaching a problem and, through the application of reason and logic, arriving at a conclusion. It is also true to say that there are many potential clues to the solution of a crime; in practice, the number of such clues is unlimited. Let us now have a look at these clues themselves and see how nature, in its beneficence, supplies us with them in infinite variety.

CHAPTER 3

The Evidence of Nature

Speak to the Earth, and it shall teach thee.
The Bible, Job XII: 8

Where would the world of crime detection, true or fictional, be without Sherlock Holmes? The stories of Conan Doyle abound with so many examples of good detection and sound reasoning that time and again one finds oneself returning to them in order to illustrate a point. Nevertheless, many crime-writers today have turned away from the great fictional detective, feeling that he has become a cliché, almost a caricature.

I can readily see why some people feel this way, since the impact of almost any work of literature must fade after a while. But my own interest in the Baker Street sleuth has never been purely literary; rather, it has been concerned with the way Holmes looked upon the world as a place teeming with clues, and with his ability to distinguish between what was relevant and what was not. My intellectual sympathy has always been with Holmes when he rebuked Dr Watson for reducing what should have been a series of brilliant essays on the science of deduction to a set of sensational tales. (This does not mean that I do not like the way in which Conan Doyle wrote the stories; quite the contrary.) I have never lost my admiration for Sherlock Holmes and the mind that created him.

Devotees of the Holmes stories will remember the incident of Mr Henry Baker's hat in *The Blue Carbuncle*. In this story, Holmes was presented with a hat that was found in the street; it had been knocked off Mr Baker's head when he became involved in a scuffle. After examining the hat, Sherlock Holmes made some conclusions about Mr Baker's character – conclusions that startled Dr Watson a good deal.

'What can you gather from this old battered felt?' Watson asked Holmes, who replied that the hat's owner (whose identity was not known to him at that point) was highly intellectual; that he had been well-to-do but had recently fallen upon hard times; that he had foresight but less now than formerly; that he had degenerated morally, probably as a result of some evil influence such as drink; that his wife had ceased to love him; that he had had his hair cut within the last few days; that he anointed it with lime-cream; and that it was extremely unlikely that he had gas laid on in his house.

Watson's initial reaction was disbelief, until Holmes explained how he had arrived at his conclusions. Although Holmes always pretended that his deductions were perfectly obvious and simple ones, he did become annoyed when other people agreed with him on this point. In *The Red-Headed League* he enumerated to his visitor, Mr Jabez Wilson, what he called 'the obvious facts' that he had at one time done manual labour; that he took snuff; that he was a Freemason; that he had been in China; and that he had done a great deal of writing lately. Mr Wilson was astounded, but when Holmes told him how he had deduced all this, his guest laughed and said that he had thought at first that Holmes had done something clever, but that he now saw that there was nothing in it after all. Clearly annoyed, Holmes turned to Watson and said: 'I begin to think, Watson, that I make a mistake in explaining. "*Omne ignotum pro magnifico*", you know, and my poor little reputation, such as it is, will suffer shipwreck if I am so candid'.

The great detective was wrong on this occasion; his reputation did not suffer, nor need the reputations of other criminal investigators suffer when their methods are explained, even if they seem absurdly simple in the end. Most things are obvious once they are made clear.

One of the most delightful things about life is that we are surrounded by objects, animate and inanimate, that can tell us a great deal about other things. It is not difficult to teach oneself to look upon one's surroundings as a vast world of clues. This is no exaggeration. Consider a very simple, everyday situation. You visit a friend who lives some distance away. You are sitting in his living room when a child enters from the garden clutching a little bunch of cowslips. What does this tell you? That the soil in the garden, and probably in the general vicinity, is alkaline not acid. If you had an interest in insects, the sight of a particular kind of bush-cricket crawling along the window-sill would tell you that there was an oak tree very close to the house. A model of a totem pole on his mantelpiece might suggest a connection, however tenuous, with Canada. An inspection of his bookshelves would tell you a great deal about your friend's interests and character. Without consciously doing so, you will gather a great deal of information about your friend, his house, his garden and his life-style.

You might say that all this is quite ridiculously simple and that you hardly needed to have it pointed out to you. This may be true, but my point is that, while all these pieces of information about the world around us are always there, the trick, if you like, is to put them together, to establish links between them and then to make sense of the whole. The criminal investigator does no more than this. What is important to remember is that nothing exists in isolation. Any object or fact is linked to some other object or fact. If we hold this idea in our mind when we are observing our surroundings, we will find that we can collect a great deal of evidence about almost anything. If we then try to connect all the objects and facts together, it is surprising what we can conclude.

Looking at the world around us in this way is not only a useful exercise when conducting criminal investigations, it is also great fun. Remarking on Mr Henry Baker's hat, Bertrand Russell once said that anyone who could extract so much information from such an ordinary object must be a happy man. Certainly, an informed interest in the physical objects around us makes life much more interesting than it would otherwise be. This is especially true of the natural world, with its infinite variety. The entomologist, Dr Miriam Rothschild, once commented that an interest in 'green' things increases one's zest for life a good deal; 'one simply cannot live long enough', she said.

I would have liked to have been able to write that, in my forensic career, I carried out a tour-de-force similar to Sherlock Holmes' deductions about Mr Henry Baker's hat. Alas I cannot, my own knowledge being of a far more specialized and narrowly-defined sort. However, I hope I will be able to show that important conclusions can be drawn from the simplest of observations.

For instance, I was once consulted by a firm of vintners, accused of negligence by an aggrieved customer in Scotland who had found a spider in one of their bottles of wine. The vintners wanted to know whether I could determine if there had, indeed, been any negligence on their part. I identified the spider as *Clubiona diversa*, which, although widespread throughout Britain, is much more abundant in the north where it is common in moss in boggy areas. It lives in silken cells under stones and bark during the day and comes out to hunt only at night. But the most important fact about this little creature in the context of the dispute with the vintners is that it does not occur indoors.

It was difficult to see how a spider of this species could have entered the wine during bottling, a process that takes place indoors and, however negligent a manufacturer might be, under relatively stringent conditions. Moreover, the complainant lived in a marshy area of lowland Scotland. So, the most likely explanation for the presence of the spider in the wine was that it entered it after the bottle had been opened, perhaps during an evening party alfresco. The complainant accepted this explanation.

The same vintners also came to me for help in another case of alleged negligence. This time the complainant had found a fly in the wine. He had bought the bottle some ten months before he opened it, whereupon he found the fly floating in the wine. This time the species did not give any indication as to what had happened; it was a common one, frequently found indoors. Nevertheless, there was something odd about it. When the complainant removed it from the wine and allowed it to dry out, it retained its shape. This was most unusual because, unlike most other insects, flies do not have a very robust cuticle, as the toughened skin is called. This means that after a fly has been immersed for some time in an alcoholic solution, or any liquid that tends to absorb water, it becomes shrivelled and distorted when removed and dried out. This fly was not shrivelled and therefore could hardly have been in the wine for more than a few minutes. Once again it was possible to conclude that the insect entered the wine not during bottling but after the bottle had been opened.

These examples show how apparently trivial little bits of information can lead to important conclusions. If the vintners had been shown to be negligent, they might have suffered loss of business or even temporary closure of their firm. I am reminded of the occasion in *The Naval Treaty*, in which Sherlock Holmes told Dr Watson that he was about to see whether a particular liquid he held in a test-tube was acid or alkaline — if the litmus paper remained blue, all was well, but if it turned red, it meant a man's life. This statement was regarded as a bizarre exaggeration, since nobody could see a connection between the acidity or alkalinity of a liquid and a murder. However, I am sure that I would have obtained the same reaction if I had said that, if the fly were to be found shrivelled, negligence could be suspected; if not, the vintners would be cleared of blame. The same applies to the species of spider. I suspect that if I had written a novel centred around either one of these ideas it would have been regarded as very contrived and unreal.

Holmes loved to surprise Watson by breaking in on his thoughts and telling him what he had been thinking or, indeed, what he intended to do. In *The Dancing Men*, he surprised Watson by telling him that he had inferred that he did not intend to invest in South African securities. Before he explained how he had arrived at such a conclusion without Watson having said a word about it, Holmes told him how one could produce such seemingly surprising results:

> 'You see, my dear Watson, it is not really difficult to construct a series of inferences, each dependent upon its predecessor and each simple in itself. If, after doing so, one simply knocks out all the central inferences and presents one's audience with the starting-point and the conclusion, one may produce a startling, though possibly a meretricious, effect.'

It is indeed very easy to produce such an effect. Although I do not normally do this, since it is rather pompous as well as being a little unkind to the listener, I do remember one occasion in which, quite unintentionally, I produced such an effect by knocking out the 'central inferences'.

It was late winter and I was examining some evidence from a case of murder in the company of a young police officer. I was looking down the microscope, totally absorbed in what I was doing and busily making notes on a piece of paper. Eventually, I looked up and spoke. I suppose I was really talking to myself out loud. I remarked that the death of the victim had clearly taken place during late autumn and that the body had lain at the edge of a wood for some time before being concealed indoors. I also said that a wound to the chest was the probable cause of death.

I have not often seen such a look of complete astonishment – fear, almost – as I saw on the face of that young officer that day. He knew that I had been given no detailed information about the case, since he was about to give it to me as soon as I finished my preliminary examination of the evidence. I had looked at what he must have thought was some nondescript debris and had yet presented him with a reconstruction of events. As Mr Jabez Wilson might have said, it was not all that clever, and I am not affecting any kind of false modesty. It is very easy to impress with specialist knowledge. The reasoning was quite simple and straightforward and, if I had arrived at my conclusions using everyday information available to everyone, the officer would not have been unduly impressed, since he could have arrived at the same conclusions himself.

In the debris, there were remains that indicated that the maggots of a certain species of fly had developed within the body. These flies are known to be particularly active during late autumn, as well as being especially abundant on the outskirts of woodland. There was also evidence that a different species of fly, which is known to occur in houses and which would not have been active during late autumn in that part of the country, had bred within the body. The presence of this species could be explained by concluding that the corpse had lain indoors during part of the winter, since it is only inside dwellings that the temperature would have been high enough for these flies to be active at that time of year. Finally, the labels on the tubes of samples told me that the majority of specimens had been collected from the chest region; hardly any were present in any other part of the body. Flies normally lay their eggs in the natural body orifices, such as the eyes, nose, ears and mouth, because the eggs are less likely to desiccate in such places which are both moist and shaded. They will not lay eggs on the general body surface. If a body is wounded, the flies are much more likely to lay their eggs in the wound because it is usually a much moister locality than any of the natural orifices. Therefore, the presence of the maggots' remains in the chest area and their absence from other parts of the body indicated that the chest had been badly wounded.

Once explained, the conclusions appear very simple and obvious. Interestingly, Holmes once explained his methods by using a zoological example. In *The Five Orange Pips*, he told Watson: 'As Cuvier could correctly describe a whole animal by the contemplation of a single bone, so the observer who has thoroughly understood one link in a series of incidents, should be able to accurately state all the other ones, both before and after.'

It is impossible to know beforehand what the insects in or on a dead body will tell us. We have already seen how the succession of insects on a corpse can be used as a measure of the time that has elapsed since death. Apart from its usefulness in forensic investigations, faunal and floral succession is one of the most fascinating of all natural phenomena.

In November 1963, a violent volcanic eruption took place in the Atlantic Ocean off the coast of Iceland. During the next three and a half years a volcanic core built up and Surtsey, a new island one square mile in area, came into existence. When the island cooled after the volcanic

activity ceased, geologists, botanists and zoologists began a programme of study to investigate how an entirely new world would be
colonized by living things. It was a rare opportunity and full advantage
was taken of it.*

One can observe much the same kind of phenomenon in one's own
back garden. Digging a pond will create a new world for animals and
plants to colonize; even a bucket of water left in the garden will be colonized and become a miniature pond teeming with life. An animal carcass left on the grass will be colonized by insects, other invertebrates,
plants, fungi and so forth, and studies on such carcasses have provided
us with a great deal of knowledge that can be applied to forensic work.
However, there is one fundamental difference between the colonization of an island or a pond on the one hand, and the colonization of a
carcass on the other; the colonizers of the carcass will, in time, destroy
the new community which is necessarily temporary. The carcass is not
a sterile base upon which a community lives; it is the very source of
nutrients. An island or a pond, far from being destroyed by its colonizers, will actually be consolidated by them. This does not mean that
succession on a carcass is of lesser interest; to me it is of greater interest, because it expresses more about life on Earth. It shows us not only
the growth and development of a community but also its decay and
slow demise. We see the beginning, the middle and the end.

Sometimes the species of insect that provide the vital forensic clue
are quite unexpected. Some years ago, in Tennessee, a human skull was
found lying in the grass in midwinter. Inside it was a nest made by
paper wasps, so named because of the particularly delicate nature of the
material of which their nests are constructed. These insects build them
in the spring and only in sites that are clean and dry. The skull therefore must have been free of any flesh or tissues before the beginning of
spring. The evidence of the wasps' nest suggested that the murder had
been committed about eighteen months earlier. When the person's
identity was established on the basis of a comparison of the teeth in the
skull with dental records, the known time of his disappearance agreed
with the wasp evidence.

* 'Surtsey' means Surts Island, hence the usual designation, 'Surtsey Island', is tautolog-
ical. The island was named after Sutur, the fire god of Icelandic mythology.

The dramatic tale of *The Hound of the Baskervilles* begins with a conversation between Sherlock Holmes and Dr Watson about a stick that Dr James Mortimer had left in the Baker Street rooms the night before when the detective was not at home. Holmes, looking at the stick through a convex lens, remarked that the doctor possessed a dog that was larger than a terrier and smaller than a mastiff. When Watson laughed incredulously, Holmes pointed out that the marks of the dog's teeth, plainly visible in the middle of the stick, showed that the animal had a jaw that was too broad for the first and too narrow for the second. In fact, the dog turned out to be a spaniel, confirming Holmes' conclusion.

Animal teeth and their bite marks often feature in forensic investigations. Injuries inflicted on a person alleging an attack by someone's dog may be investigated by forensic odontologists, who can determine whether the wounds were caused by a dog or by some other animal or, indeed, by human agency. Nevertheless, the cause of tears in cloth are very difficult to determine, even by experienced odontologists. In the Lynne Chamberlain case in Australia, in which a baby was said to have been snatched by a dingo near Ayer's Rock, the clothes that were eventually found had a number of rents in them. Specialists disagreed with one another over whether these were caused by a dingo's teeth or by scissors, causing a great amount of confusion in the court-room. Lynne Chamberlain was found guilty of murdering her own child, partly on the basis of the belief that dingoes do not snatch babies. After Mrs Chamberlain's release from prison, following a Royal Commission of Inquiry, several incidents involving the attempted snatching of babies by dingoes were reported, as well as several attacks on adults by these animals.

A British case also demonstrates the importance of determining the real cause of damage to clothing. In a Stoke Newington graveyard a fox discovered and unearthed the body of a young girl and scattered her bones and clothes around the cemetery. These were taken to Dr Peter Vanezis, then Head of the Department of Forensic Medicine at Charing Cross Hospital,* who set about trying to determine whether they had been torn by a knife, as was suspected, or by animal teeth. There was no alternative to a direct test. Some of the cloth was wrapped around the thickened arm coverings used in training police dogs and a dog was allowed to bite it. These new tears were then compared with the originals and it was eventually concluded that some of the latter had, in fact, been caused by animals (most probably by the

---

* As a piece of incidental intelligence, Dr James Mortimer, in *The Hound of the Baskervilles*, had been a house-surgeon at Charing Cross Hospital.

fox that discovered the body) but others had been caused by a knife. The discovery of a bone that had clearly been cut with a knife clinched the matter. The girl's stepfather was found guilty of her murder and was sent to prison for life.

Of course, not only mammals have sharp teeth. In a case from Florida, the handless body of a woman was discovered floating in a freshwater canal. The coroner suspected that the hands might have been removed to prevent fingerprint identification and the problem was taken to an anthropologist, Dr William Maples. His examination showed that the hands had been broken off, not cleanly cut with a sharp instrument. He then noticed that there were grooves running across the long bone of the arm and it occurred to him that they might be the tooth-marks of a large carnivorous animal, such as an alligator. Dr Maples took the bone to the Florida Museum and compared the grooves with the teeth in alligator skulls. The teeth and the grooves matched exactly. There had been no foul play.

Carnivorous mammals' habit of interfering with the remains of murder victims has practical uses. First, the way foxes, wolves, coyotes and similar predatory animals scatter bones follows a predictable pattern, so it is possible to know whether the bones were scattered by them or by a human being. Secondly, damage to human bones caused by the teeth of carnivores may appear superficially similar to stab wounds or other injuries inflicted by man-made tools. A detailed study of such damage, however, will often reveal whether the damage was caused by an animal or not; for example, dogs and dog-like animals gnaw the ends of long bones, leaving a characteristic kind of damage.

Coyotes in the United States will take human remains to their dens and a search there by a forensic investigator may result in the discovery of the remains of a missing person. Quite small mammals like mice and voles will collect small bones and hide them in their burrows, for the purpose of gnawing them to keep their teeth in trim. Dr William Rodriguez, a forensic anthropologist, once reported the finding of a finger bone, complete with wedding ring, in a vole's burrow, a find that helped materially with the identification of the victim! On a number of occasions he also discovered bullet casings in vole-burrows close to the scene of a crime which, again, were of considerable assistance to the police.

There are even occasions when birds have helped the police to identify victims as a result of their interference with human remains. I am not referring to vultures and other birds of prey but to small birds which, while building their nests, may use the hair from the head of a corpse lying nearby. Hair can be used to identify people, and

its presence in a bird's nest may be very helpful, especially if the body
has later been removed.

Dogs' teeth are not the only aspect of these animals that figure in forensic work. In Conan Doyle's story, *Silver Blaze*, the solution of the mystery depended largely on the behaviour of a dog, a classic event in the
Sherlock Holmes canon. When asked by the police officer, Inspector
Gregory, whether he could offer some clue to the solution of the
crime, Holmes referred to 'the curious incident of the dog in the night-
time'. Puzzled, the inspector replied: 'The dog did nothing in the
night-time'. Came the answer: 'That was the curious incident'. Holmes
was drawing attention to the fact that, contrary to expectation, the dog
had not barked during the night.

Of course dogs' behaviour is important to the police mainly because
of their ability to find living people as well as dead bodies, using their
acute sense of smell. Their prowess in this regard is very well known,
but what is, perhaps, not widely appreciated is that dogs can find
drowned bodies in water, even if they are lying well over one hundred
feet below the surface. In the USA, in Lake County, Illinois, the police
use of dogs in this way is particularly well advanced. The dog – usually
a bloodhound – is taken on a boat to the lake or river in which the
deceased is thought to lie. The odour of the dead body rises through
the water and is dispersed at a height of about one foot above the surface, and it is this 'plume' of odour that the hound detects. But it does
not plunge into the water at once; it waits until it detects the greatest
concentration of smell, then leaps in. Although a bloodhound has an
extremely good sense of smell, it is not equally adept at swimming, so
it is accompanied by trained divers who help it if it should find itself in
difficulty! It almost always finds the body.

Water, whether a lake, a river or the sea, has always been used by criminals as a place in which to dispose of incriminating evidence. In *The*

Sign of Four, Sherlock Holmes' efforts to recover the stolen diamonds were frustrated by the fact that they had been tossed into the River Thames. On another occasion, the finding in the Thames of Mr Neville St Clair's coat, weighted down with coins, furnished Holmes with one of the clues that solved the mystery of *The Man with the Twisted Lip*. What most criminals do not know is that, once an object is thrown into the water, living organisms will take an interest in it of a kind that may later provide further evidence against the criminal.

An example of this is illustrated by a dramatic and most unusual case. On Anzac Day, 25th April 1935, as visitors to the Coogee Aquarium in Sydney, Australia, were watching the exhibits, a most extraordinary thing happened. One of the pools contained a fourteen-foot long shark that had been captured about a week earlier by some fishermen who had found it entangled in their nets. It was a sulky creature, refusing to eat, just swimming slowly back and forth. Then, on Anzac Day, it went berserk. It suddenly started thrashing through the water, churning it into foam, and lashing about wildly with its tail. Finally it disgorged a mass of matter, amongst which, to the horror of the spectators, was a human arm.

Naturally a police investigation began, which was made easier by the fact that the arm had a highly distinctive tattoo showing two boxers in fighting positions. Eventually, the owner of the arm was identified by his wife and brother as one James Smith. Fingerprints were taken from the hand which corroborated their testimony.

Smith had gone on a fishing expedition with a friend on 8th April, nine days before the shark was captured. Astonishingly, Mrs Smith began to worry about her husband only after he had been away for two weeks, reporting his absence to the police shortly before Anzac Day. The finding of Smith's arm did not necessarily mean that he was dead. However, a piece of rope was found tied around the wrist which clearly suggested either foul play or suicide. (Suicide by means of tying one's arms and jumping into the sea while attached to a heavy weight is not unusual.) Examination of the arm by forensic pathologists revealed that it had been cut off with a sharp instrument, not bitten off by the shark.

The police began to suspect that Smith had never gone on his fishing expedition at all because one of his associates, with whom he most probably would have gone fishing, could not account for the absence from his house of a large tin trunk that he possessed. Furthermore, a rope had gone missing from his boat. The suspicion now grew that Smith had quarrelled with this man, who had killed him, cut up his body and placed it in the trunk. The arm probably would not fit in, so it was surmised that the murderer had cut it off and tied it to the side of the trunk with the rope, before throwing the whole grisly bundle into the sea. Finally, it was thought that the shark had swallowed the exposed arm shortly before it was netted.

This crime came to light under such extraordinary circumstances that I would like to have been able to relate that the murderer, whoever he was, was brought to justice. Alas, this did not happen. On the night before the inquest, an important witness was shot in his car by someone who was almost certainly a passenger and who had chosen his time and place very well. This murder was committed beneath the Sydney Bridge and the shot was fired as a train roared overhead, drowning out the noise of the firearm. The man accused of murdering Smith was acquitted. Later, two men accused of murdering the second victim were also acquitted. The case remains a mystery.

The object most frequently tossed into water for concealment is, of course, the murder weapon. One winter some years ago, a knife suspected of having been used in a murder was found in an English canal. It was covered with the egg cocoons of leeches. These jelly-like structures remain attached to the substrate even after the young leeches have hatched. Scientists from the Natural History Museum in London were asked to investigate the knife in order to determine whether or not it was the weapon. The murder had taken place in October, but these freshwater leeches lay their eggs during the summer which indicated that the knife had been in the water since long before the murder had occurred and was therefore unconnected.

It is a strange fact that most disease-carrying insects (like mosquitoes, horseflies, biting midges and so forth) breed in water, and I am often asked whether these bloodsucking insects are significant in forensic investigations. Their predominant role in the dissemination of disease suggests that they might be expected to play an important part in criminal investigations. Indeed, they sometimes do, but they have not yet been fully exploited in this way. Nevertheless, there are indications that they may indeed soon join the arsenal of the forensic entomologist in a most novel manner. An idea, as yet untested in any actual forensic case, is that bloodsucking insects could be used to identify the perpetrators of crimes. This was first suggested in the United States, where biting flies are much more abundant than in Britain. If a murderer, thief, rapist or any other criminal should be bitten by, say, a mosquito, its stomach will contain his blood. If this could be extracted, a DNA profile of the perpetrator could be prepared. Of course, such a technique could only be used in cases in which the crime was discovered very soon after it was committed, otherwise the blood would have been digested. If the DNA were that of the victim, this could be established immediately. If the DNA in the blood-meal had come from an innocent person who happened to be nearby, then other evidence would clear them.

It is worth emphasizing at this point that evidence in a criminal enquiry is cumulative, and that forensic evidence is essentially the same as any other kind of evidence. In other words, simply because a DNA match is found, this does not mean that a person will automatically be accused of a crime; a great deal of evidence is required to demonstrate guilt and there would have to be a *prima facie* case against an individual in the first place.

The notion of using DNA from the stomach of a mosquito will remind some readers of the story, *Jurassic Park*, and thus give the impression that the idea has science fiction undertones. This would be misleading, since *Jurassic Park* deals with the re-creation of whole organisms from the DNA in the gut of the mosquito, whereas the forensic technique under consideration is simply concerned with producing a DNA profile, a perfectly valid and attainable goal. Such human DNA profiles from mosquito blood-meals have already been produced, but the technique has yet to be applied in a forensic case.

Other biting flies sometimes feature in forensic cases. Blackflies are notorious bloodsuckers, occurring in most parts of the world, including Britain, Europe, the United States and especially in the Tropics. The aptly-named *Simulium damnosum* is an African species that transmits the terrible nematode-worm disease known as onchocerciasis or river blindness, sufferers from which are truly damned.

Blackflies are quite extraordinary insects. Measuring from 1.2 to 6.0 mm long, these minute flies have astonishing egg-laying habits. Like mosquitoes, blackflies lay their eggs in water but, unlike them, they frequent fast-flowing streams and rivers and even mountain torrents. When ready to lay her eggs, the females of many species will submerge themselves in the water and attach their eggs to objects such as stones or aquatic plants. The fly will then emerge from the fast-flowing water with apparent ease. When the larvae hatch, they attach themselves to the substrate, which is usually a stone, although some species will seek out a specific living carrier such as a freshwater crab or prawn, or a mayfly nymph. Blackfly larvae and pupae can breathe the oxygen dissolved in the water. This is possible only in highly oxygenated, fast-flowing water, which is why blackflies cannot breed in still water. Mosquitoes, of course, breed in stagnant water but, as their larvae and pupae are unable to breathe in such a relatively oxygen-deficient environment, they have to come to the surface to do so.

Some years ago a car was found submerged in a river in Illinois. The body of a drowned woman was found in it. Her husband told the police that he had last seen his wife alive in June, a few weeks before the car was discovered. However, an examination of the car revealed the presence of considerable numbers of blackfly pupae on it. Since in that part of the United States blackflies lay their eggs in April, the car must have entered the water in the spring at the latest, which showed that the husband was lying. It eventually transpired that he had murdered his wife and pushed her car, with her body inside it, into the river.

Insects that lay their eggs in water sometimes mistake the shiny surfaces of some cars for the surface of a lake or pond and will lay their eggs on them. Mayflies and midges have been seen doing this. In the heat of the sun, the eggs are baked hard on to the surface and the paint may flake off leaving distinctive circular marks.

The presence of other, non-water-breeding insects on a vehicle has sometimes been used to trace its movements. Small insects will often become trapped in the tyre-treads or other parts of a car encased in mud; many insects will burst on impact on a windscreen and their remains may be identifiable. In the southern United States, a kind of fly known as the Lovebug is present in great abundance in some localities during May and September. They can become smashed against car windscreens in large numbers and can even clog up radiators, causing cars to overheat. This phenomenon provided evidence in a Florida murder case to determine the place frequented by a suspect. The honeydew from aphids on trees overhead will stick to parked cars and is likewise of forensic value.

One of the most bizarre cases involving an aquatic creature was told me by my friend Dr Basil Purdue of the University of Edinburgh. Apparently a fisherman went to his doctor complaining of an unpleasant rash on his leg. When the doctor examined the man's leg, he was puzzled to find that a large area of the skin was bright red. No immediate diagnosis could be made, but subsequent laboratory analysis of samples taken from the skin revealed that the discoloration was caused by a strain of bacteria known to occur among the scales of marine fish. The fisherman then remembered that during an argument with his wife she had struck him on his naked leg with a fish – a herring, to be precise. Thus the initial confusion was resolved; the answer was a red herring!

All natural bodies of water, whether fresh or marine, teem with large numbers of microscopic algae called diatoms. These single-celled plants have cell walls made of finely-sculptured silica which are distinctively patterned and unique to each species, enabling the specialist investigator to identify them. The range of patterns is very large, there being more than 9,000 known species. The widespread occurrence of diatoms, together with the fact that every water-body has a distinctive mixture of species, means that they are often used in criminal investigations.

One such case concerned a man found drowned in a car that was submerged in a lake in the south of England. The owner of the car, a known friend of the dead man, was arrested and questioned, but he denied that he had ever been near the lake. The police did not believe him. A pair of trousers belonging to the suspect, which appeared to have been thoroughly wetted at some stage, were submitted to Dr Anthony Peabody, a diatom specialist at the Metropolitan Police Forensic Science Laboratory in London. He rinsed out the garment and extracted from it large numbers of diatoms. Examining these, together with samples from the lake, he found that the diatom profile of the lake exactly matched that of the trousers. The accused was lying. He had been guilty of reckless driving which resulted in the death of his friend. He was sent down for five years.

Even fossil diatoms have been known to help the police catch criminals. Diatoms from ancient deposits are used in match-heads, where their hard and abrasive silica coats make them ideal for striking. Each brand has a different and highly distinctive mixture of diatoms which remains identifiable even after the match has been struck. In a criminal case, much can turn on the identification of a match.

Again, because of their abrasive nature fossil diatoms are used in the manufacture of car polish, each brand having a unique mixture. In at least one case, a thief was caught out by diatom evidence. He had stolen the hub-caps of a car and attached them to his own. A comparison of the diatoms on the stolen hub-caps with those on the rest of his car revealed that the composition was very different, but it exactly matched that on the car from which the hub-caps had been stolen.

Plants, of course, exist in great abundance on land as well as in water, and their nature and condition in criminal investigations are often of great relevance to police work. In *The Five Orange Pips*, Sherlock Holmes explained to Dr Watson that the Ku Klux Klan used plants as symbols of threat; sometimes they would send their enemies a sprig of oak leaves, sometimes melon seeds and sometimes five orange pips. The use of plants in this way is deadly enough, but they are often employed in more directly fatal ways. Since time immemorial, they have been, and continue to be, a source of poisons. Even some of the most familiar plants contain powerful toxins; for example, cyanide exists in almonds and apple pips, although not usually in quantities that could deliver a fatal dose. The seeds of the castor oil plant are very poisonous and were used in 1981 to murder Georgi Markov, a Bulgarian dissident, who was killed in London by an agent of the Bulgarian Government using a poisoned umbrella tip. Poisons from mistletoe may also have been included in the toxic mixture.

It is often supposed that scientists and the police have at their disposal tests with which any poison can be detected. Sadly, this is very far from the truth, since there is no known test for most poisons. In *The Devil's Foot*, Sherlock Holmes discovered that a murder had been committed using an African poison previously unknown in Europe. According to Holmes, *Radix pedis diaboli*, a root shaped like a foot, half human and half goatlike, had never entered the pharmacopœia or the literature of toxicology and, apart from the sample in the story, only one other existed in Europe, in a laboratory at Buda. Although no such thing as the *Radix pedis diaboli* is known to exist, Holmes' remarks reflect a general truth, namely, that poisons from obscure or unknown plants have been used for murderous purposes in England. There is evidence that a number of suspicious deaths within the Asian community were the result of either deliberate or accidental ingestion of certain Indian seeds that are normally used for making necklaces. No diagnostic tests for these poisons are known.

While plant poisons are frequently used as murder weapons, plants themselves can often help us to catch a criminal. This was demonstrated particularly well in a case of rape that took place in Florida. One night, a man abducted a young girl at knife-point and drove her to a deserted spot where he raped her on a blanket he took from his car. Some days later, the girl recognized her assailant's car in the street. She immediately told the police who arrested the car's owner. A search of the car produced a blanket covered with seeds, twigs and other pieces of vegetation, but the man said that he only used the blanket for picnics in his garden and a neighbouring park. The blanket was taken to a botanist, Dr David Hall, who extracted millions of plant fragments and analysed them. He found seeds and twigs of many plants: beardgrass, dog fennel, creeping beggarweed, Spanish moss, sandspur and beakrush. Three of these species were common everywhere. However, several species were not found in the man's garden or in the park, but were common where the rape occurred. Moreover, although the three widespread species were found in the garden and park, they were not in a sufficiently developed state to produce seeds, whereas in the locality of the rape they were. The jury found the botanical testimony compelling. As Dr Hall put it: 'The rapist was sentenced to eighty-eight years on the evidence of a seedy blanket'!

It is quite remarkable how a plant will retain its identity despite being subjected to the destructive attentions of human beings. We have seen how diatoms can still be identified, even after the match in which they are found has been lit. Sawdust, which is, in effect, powdered wood, can be identified in the same way, in that it is possible to determine from which species of tree it came. This fact has been put to good police use in a rather unexpected fashion. Until relatively recently, gaps inside the doors of metal safes were filled with sawdust as an insulator. The type used by each manufacturer was constant and there are cases on record in which safe-breakers have been incriminated by this evidence. In one case a thief blew open a safe, showering everything including himself with sawdust. Identification of that from the safe and a comparison with dust from the thief's clothes showed that the content was one and the same, a fact that formed part of the evidence against the culprit.

An entire tree can sometimes 'give' evidence. I know of a case in which a man was found hanged with a rope around his neck, but the tree to which the rope was attached had subsequently fallen down. A botanical study of the tree resulted in an estimate of the time the tree fell, giving an approximate date for the time of the suicide, since, clearly, the tree would have had to have been upright when the man hanged himself.

In another case I came across, the murderer actually encouraged a tree to give evidence against him, in a manner of speaking. He had murdered a woman and decided to bury her at the base of an old tree. Whilst digging the grave, he accidentally damaged the tree's taproot in several places with his spade. The damage resulted in the development of side roots which, encouraged by the now enriched soil, grew into the body and through the skeleton. Years later, when the body was discovered, botanists were able to narrow down the time of death by measuring the roots, whose rate of growth is known, and their growth rings. The evidence helped to incriminate the killer.

These days we are accustomed to hearing about DNA profiles that help to identify individual human beings. What is, perhaps, not widely realised is that the same thing could, in principle, be done with individual plants. The first time this idea was used in a criminal case was in a murder investigation in Arizona. A man had been seen with a prostitute, whose murdered body was found dumped at the site of an abandoned factory later that day. When arrested and questioned, the man admitted that he had been with the prostitute, but denied murdering her or going anywhere near the factory site. Growing at the site in question were several blue palo verde trees, a kind of giant woody pea plant. Police investigations revealed two interesting facts in connection with these. First, one tree, which dipped low over the driveway, was found to have had its bark scraped. Secondly, two seed pods of a blue palo verde tree were found in the accused man's pick-up van. If proof could be found that the seed pods had come from that particular tree or had been knocked off when the accused man's van scraped against it, the case against the accused would be very strong. The police went to Dr Tim Helentjaris of the University of Arizona and asked him whether he could link the pods to a particular tree using DNA evidence. He agreed to try and the police supplied him with samples from every tree on the site and the tests were done as blind trials. The results showed that the DNA from the pods found in the van matched that from the scraped, bent tree. This was strong evidence, but it was not possible to attach any figures of statistical probability to it, since the number of trees sampled was small compared with the much larger samples used when human DNA profiles are assessed.

One extremely abundant kind of plant product has, curiously enough, not been fully exploited in the investigation of crime. This is pollen, the cause of so much hay-fever in the summer. There have been several attempts to use pollen as criminal evidence, but it was only relatively recently that it was put to an interesting test.

In February 1994, a grave containing the skeletons of thirty-two murdered men of unknown origin was discovered in Magdeburg, Germany. Initially, it was suggested that the remains might have belonged to Hitler and some of his associates but for various good reasons this thought was dismissed. The area in which the grave was discovered had been under the control of the Gestapo until March or April 1945, but it was subsequently occupied by Soviet forces and remained under their control for several years. For various reasons, the possible nationalities of the men were narrowed down to two hypotheses. First, the men could have been victims of the Gestapo who had been murdered in the early spring of 1945. Secondly, they could have been Soviet soldiers killed by the Soviet Secret Police following the revolt in the German Democratic Republic on 17th June 1953. It is known that some Soviet soldiers refused to take part in the suppression of the German revolt and were killed. The skeletal evidence showed that all the men were aged between eighteen and thirty when they died. Also, there was no sign of any dental work on their teeth, a fact which would have been most unusual for Germans in the mid-twentieth century but not at all unusual if they had been soldiers of humble origin from the Soviet Union. This dental evidence supported the second hypothesis.

Pollen analysts from the Otto von Guericke University were asked to examine the skulls. They found a quantity of pollen associated with them, mostly in the nasal cavities. This showed that the pollen did not come from the soil but had been breathed by the men when they were alive. When the pollen was analysed it was found to have come from plant species that emit their pollen during June and July. In particular, pollen from plantain, a plant that releases vast amounts of pollen during those months, was present in high concentrations in the nasal cavities. The findings clearly supported the belief that the victims were Soviet soldiers.

The associations between insects and plants are often a good source of evidence, since their interactions are usually strongly linked to precise times of the year. A few years ago a woman parked her car at midnight near her home in a comfortable Chicago suburb. It was midsummer. As she walked to her house, a man wearing a ski-mask emerged from the shrubbery and raped her. Although the man disappeared after the assault he had made the mistake of speaking to the woman, who identified him later during a police voice line-up. This was not strong evidence, since it is notoriously easy to make errors of identification on the basis of voice alone. Nevertheless, the police searched the man's apartment and discovered a ski-mask. The man insisted that he had not used it since the previous winter. However, attached to the mask were two cockleburs, which the police decided to take to Professor Bernard Greenberg of the University of Illinois at Chicago for forensic examination.

Protesting that he was an entomologist not a botanist, Professor

Greenberg nevertheless agreed to examine the contents of the cockleburs in search of any entomological clues. His work bore fruit, for he discovered several caterpillars belonging to the burdock seed moth, *Metzneria lappella* inside. This species has a one-year life cycle; the larvae do not hibernate but pupate within the cocklebur and the adults emerge during late summer and hibernate over the winter, so the cockleburs must have been caught up in the mask during the summer in question. It became clear that the man was lying.

Some years ago, a rather unusual moth played a prominent part in a murder investigation. Professor Pekka Nuorteva of the University of Helsinki, Finland, received from the police two branches of a rowan tree. They had been found on 8th July covering the decomposing corpse of a man in an isolated corner of a park in a Helsinki suburb. Some of the rowan leaves had been spun together into a nest by a colony of larvae of the small ermine moth, *Hyponomeuta malinellus*. These pale-coloured caterpillars can cover whole shrubs or trees and sometimes completely defoliate them. In Finland, they spin their nests at the end of May or the beginning of June, suggesting that the branches were broken off the tree at that time of year. Subsequent police investigations revealed that the victim had been knifed on 2nd June of that year.

One very dramatic near-accident was the work of leaf-cutting bees. These interesting insects normally construct nests in dead wood out of very neatly cut pieces of leaf. In this case, three aircraft were grounded because the bees had made them in the airspeed indicators, immobilizing the planes. Initially sabotage was suspected but, after Scotland Yard asked Mr Ken Smith of the Natural History Museum in London to investigate, the problem was resolved.

Among all these wonderful natural clues there is one in particular that stands out as the star of the show. Without it, or rather her, forensic entomology would not amount to very much. This paragon of an entomological clue is the female bluebottle, together with her close relations. We have already met her in the case of *Black Peter*, where Sherlock Holmes so discourteously ignored her presence. She is the most extraordinary of creatures yet so often overlooked, or even despised as an unclean insect that should be swatted at the earliest opportunity. True, it is not a good idea to allow a fly to land on your food since it could easily leave pathogenic bacteria on it. Nevertheless it is not true to say that the quality of our lives would be greatly improved if we could free the world of flies. As we shall see later, such an event would have disastrous consequences for mankind.

The life-cycle of a bluebottle is deceptively simple. It has been perfected over millions of years of evolution, with the result that this creature is one of the most successful of organisms. Dr Miriam Rothschild once commented that, if the rate of destruction of the countryside continues unchecked, by the middle of the next century biodiversity in Britain will consist of a crow and a bluebottle. The life history of a bluebottle begins when the female fly finds a dead carcass or corpse, which it can detect from a very great distance. After settling on the body, the fly seeks out the moist areas of the eyes, nose, ears or mouth, or a wound, in which to lay its eggs. This ensures that the eggs do not desiccate; in fact, the fly will not lay any eggs until its feet come into contact with free water. When it has found a suitable site, the fly will lay its eggs – up to 300 at one sitting. It can do this up to ten times during its short life of a few weeks, laying something of the order of 3,000 eggs in total.

This large number of eggs is not reflected in an equivalent increase in number of flies in the population. It is an 'insurance policy', so to speak; the dead bodies of animals and people are of interest to many other creatures, including large carnivorous mammals and birds, and very many of the fly's eggs, or the larvae that hatch from them, will be consumed by them and never reach maturity. Most of the adult flies that eventually develop will also be eaten by birds, spiders and predatory insects, or fall victim to fungal, bacterial and other diseases. The result is that the total number of flies in the environment remains roughly the same from year to year, despite the vast number of offspring produced by a single fly.

After a day or two, depending on the prevailing temperatures, the minute first-stage larvae will hatch. This is the most vulnerable stage of the life-cycle, the minute larvae being very susceptible to both desiccation and drowning, so they do their best to find the best conditions for their short lives. After another day or two, they shed their skins and turn into second-stage larvae, which themselves, after a similar period of time, moult to become third-stage larvae. These are the well-known fisherman's maggots. They will feed voraciously upon the tissues for several days and grow to many times their original size. It is usually said that insects cannot grow to any extent without shedding their skins; maggots have not heard this dictum and can grow to six or seven times their original size without moulting! When the maggots finish feeding they clear their guts of any remaining food material and leave the body to wander about for a variable period of time. Generally speaking, they move far from the corpse to pupate, often covering relatively great distances, thus avoiding the risk of being eaten by predatory animals that may take an interest in the carcass. Normally, the maggots burrow into the soil and pupate below the surface.

Once the maggot has settled into its pupation site, its skin will begin to contract, harden and darken to form a structure known as a puparium, or pupal case. Inside this shell, the tissues of the maggot begin to rearrange themselves during the process known as pupation. The pupa slowly forms and turns into the adult. The whole process takes about two weeks, at the end of which the adult fly emerges by breaking off the front end of the puparium. As it emerges underground, it starts tunnelling its way upwards to the surface of the soil. It does this by means of a blood-filled, balloon-shaped sac on its head, which pulsates inwards and outwards, acting as a battering ram.

A newly-emerged fly cannot, in fact, fly. Its wings are crumpled and take time to expand and harden, which makes this stage rather vulnerable to predation, so the insect remains hidden in nooks and crannies until the wings become functional. If it is a female, she now has to find a source of protein, usually a carcass, not in order to lay eggs but to feed. The protein meal is needed so that the eggs can develop. (It is for this reason that only female mosquitoes suck blood; they, too, need the protein in order to develop their eggs.) As soon as the eggs have developed fully, the fly seeks another carcass on which to lay them and the life-cycle begins once again.

Having spent many years of my life studying this life-cycle, I cannot expect others who have not done so to get quite as excited about it as I do, but it is a magnificent feat of evolution. Consider how it must have begun. Everything we know about insects indicates that the ancestral forms had larvae that were, essentially, miniature editions of the adults. Many insects living today, such as grasshoppers, crickets, greenfly and shieldbugs, have larvae like this, but the most successful groups of insects – amongst which are butterflies, beetles, wasps, bees and ants – have developed a larval stage that is very different in appearance and function from the adult. Nowhere, however, is this condition expressed as perfectly as it is among the flies. The maggot, which millions of years ago was a miniature fly when it emerged from the egg, is now a creature so fundamentally different from the adult of its kind as to be almost a different species. This great difference in form and function enables the maggot to exploit, as completely and efficiently as possible, the environment in which it grows. The despised, worm-shaped maggot is the reason for the great success of flies, which have plagued mankind since earliest times.

The study and practice of forensic entomology shows that the maggot is also a great leveller. Bluebottles will lay eggs on the bodies of beasts and men, without discrimination. In the words of the great French entomologist, Jean Henri Fabre:

'At the surface of the soil, exposed to the air, the hideous invasion is possible; ay, it is the invariable rule. For the melting down and remoulding of matter, man is no better, corpse for corpse, than the lowest of the brutes. Then the Fly exercises her rights and deals with us as she does with any ordinary animal refuse. Nature treats us with magnificent indifference in her great regenerating-factory: placed in her crucibles, animals and men, beggars and kings are one and all alike. There you have true equality, the only equality in this world of ours: equality in the presence of the maggot.'

I was standing on a cliff on the west coast of Wales, looking out to sea. It was a beautiful, warm Spring day. The sky was a clear blue, the sea a much deeper shade and the sun was shining brilliantly. I was not there on a professional case but on holiday with my family. Looking down the cliff, I could see the waves crashing against the rocks below; looking across the bay, I could see the craggy promontory that jutted into the sea. No other human being was present; only trees and rocks and the sounds of birds and insects. It was one of my very favourite spots in the country, one that I had visited time and again but, alas, we were due to return home the following day. I remember saying to my wife that it would be so pleasant to stay for just one more day, the scene being so peaceful, the weather so perfect. But it could not be; the demands of work were such that we could stay no longer. After watching the view for a few more minutes, I reluctantly walked back to the car.

A few months later, I revisited this scene. The sky was as clear as it had been when I was there last, the sea as blue, the sun as brilliant, but I did not admire the scene nor derive any comfort from it. This time I was not on holiday; I was back in my professional capacity and in the company of grim-faced police officers. I have never visited that place again.

It was a very hot summer. I was sitting at my desk writing a scientific paper with, I must confess, some difficulty. The heat was oppressive; I was unable to concentrate and I remember considering whether I should stop trying to write and perhaps do something else that required less thought, when release came in the form of a telephone call. The urgent Welsh voice of the police superintendent at the other end informed me that a horrific double murder had taken place and that he would like my opinion on the matter of time of death.

A couple had been on holiday near the Welsh coast, a place they had visited with their caravan year after year over a long period. One Thursday morning they had decided to return to their home in England but thought that it would be nice to have one last walk along the coast before leaving. They walked away from the caravan site at about half past nine and were never seen alive again. When they failed to reappear at their home at the weekend, their relations became anxious and informed the police. A search began, with policemen and dogs combing the sea-coast along which they had said they would walk. As they moved along the tops of the cliffs, some of the officers could see a black swarm of flies above a spot further along the path and slightly to one side of it. Hurrying over, they found an artificial screen of vegetation at the edge of the path, roughly at the point where the land began to descend sharply towards the sea. Behind the vegetation, lying on the slope, were the bodies of the missing couple.

It was no easy matter retrieving the bodies. A pathologist had joined the police and he told me afterwards that he and some of the officers were in constant danger of falling into the sea, so steep was the incline. The bodies were tied with ropes to prevent them from sliding down the cliff and, eventually, they were pulled up to level ground. The couple had been shot at very close range. Shotgun pellets were found not only in their flesh but inside their lungs. This meant that the guns had been held very close up against the faces of the victims, who inhaled deeply, probably out of sheer terror, just as the guns were fired.

The cause of death was therefore easily established, but when did the couple die? Here, a problem arose. The police speculated that the husband and wife were killed shortly after they set off on their last walk. However, the bodies of the two victims – that is, their torsos and heads – were heavily infested with maggots, but their legs were not. An examination of the legs suggested to the pathologist that death had not taken place as long ago as the day the couple were last seen alive, a week before the discovery of the bodies. It was suggested that the couple might have been abducted on the Thursday, then kept in confinement somewhere until the following Sunday, when they were killed and their bodies dumped on the edge of the cliff.

The maggots told a very different story. Their age indicated that the murder was committed very shortly after the victims were last seen alive. It was quite impossible for the maggots to have reached their stage of development in the period between Sunday and Wednesday under the prevailing conditions. The 'gut-feeling' of the police that the murder had taken place on the day of disappearance was supported by the entomological conclusions, but they wanted further corroborating evidence. I should say that the pathologist's opinion was given simply as a suggestion and he did not insist upon it.

Further evidence arrived in a most unexpected form. When news of the crime reached the media, a visitor from England, who had been travelling in the area at the time of the murder, rushed over to see the police. He said he had been walking along the beach on the Thursday morning in question, looking up at the cliff-top where the murder occurred. He raised his camera to take a photograph of the scene and, as he pressed the button, he heard several shotgun explosions. His camera was the type that recorded the date and time on the photo-graph; and the recorded time was 11.15 a.m. on Thursday. The visitor had thought nothing of the shotgun blasts at the time, believing them to be caused by a farmer shooting rabbits. It was only when he heard the horrific news that he realised what valuable evidence he had.

The crime was never solved and the murderer or murderers were never brought to justice. I attended the inquest in Wales, on a day of howling gales that flattened several buildings in the vicinity, and gave my evidence. The jury concluded that it was an unlawful killing by a person or persons unknown and that the motive of the murder was robbery, since some of the victims' belongings were missing.

I think it is fair to say that most people tend to think of evidence as facts, or interpretations of facts, that incriminate somebody. Thus, it is normally seen as a negative thing, something that one produces *against* someone else. Of course, everyone really knows that evidence can also clear someone of a crime or misdemeanour but this aspect is not usually emphasized in whodunnits.

Our friends the maggots are no exception, for they, too, can be used to demonstrate someone's innocence. One morning, a Finnish government official entered his office to find a number of large maggots crawling about underneath the edge of his carpet. Summoning the cleaning woman, he asked her when she had last cleaned the carpet. She said she had cleaned it the previous evening. The official could not believe such large 'bugs' could have developed in the carpet overnight. He accused the woman of lying and she was dismissed from her job. Some time later, the official, who had kept and preserved some of the maggots, showed them to Professor Pekka Nuorteva of the University of Helsinki, who identified them as the wandering, post-feeding stage of a particular species of greenbottle. Clearly, they had been developing in a dead rat or something similar in some other part of the building and had wandered off to find a place to pupate. Moreover, such maggots do not feed on carpets. Professor Nuorteva concluded that the maligned cleaning woman had not been lying and she was reinstated in her job. I hope the official made her a suitable apology.

CHAPTER 4

Foul, Strange and Unnatural

Murder most foul, as in the best it is;
But this most foul, strange and unnatural
Shakespeare, *Hamlet* Act I, Scene 5

'Well done, boys!'

Words pleasant enough, you might think, until you know who spoke them and to whom. Robert Black – known as 'Smelly Bob' because he never washed – had just been sentenced by Mr Justice Macpherson at Newcastle Crown Court to ten life sentences for murder, abduction and the prevention of burial. He had raped and murdered three young girls: Susan Maxwell, aged eleven; Sarah Harper, aged ten; and Caroline Hogg, aged six. Mr Justice Macpherson described him as a 'very dangerous man'. Mr Hector Clark, Deputy Chief Constable of Lothian & Borders, said he was 'the most evil of men'. Even his own barrister, Mr Ronald Thwaites, called him a 'wicked and foul pervert' in open court.

The hunt that brought Robert Black to justice took twelve years. The investigation cost £5 million, the trial another £1 million. Up to 400 police officers worked on the case, amassing twenty-two tons of paperwork in the process. Two storeys of an office block were specially rented to house the documentary evidence and the building had to be reinforced to cope with the weight. The names of 190,000 suspects and possible witnesses were screened and eliminated from enquiries. At one stage during the investigation, a blue Ford Cortina was thought to have been used by the killer (it was later shown to be a false lead) and the owners of 25,000 such cars were questioned by the police. Six police forces worked on the case. It was the biggest murder investigation in British history.

Now, at last, Robert Black stood in the dock, convicted and sentenced. When Mr Justice Macpherson pronounced sentence, he said that Black could expect to spend the rest of his life in prison. The 'most evil of men' looked round the court-room and his malevolent glare came to rest on the twenty-three police officers who had brought him to justice. '*Well done, boys!*' he said.

I never saw Robert Black. The police officers told me what happened, but I never set foot in the court-room during his twenty-four-day trial, although I had been asked to give evidence and had travelled to Newcastle for that purpose. I sat in my hotel room as the trial progressed. At intervals, a police officer, Inspector Shevas, would leave the court-room and come to the hotel to ask me to clarify some points of evidence. He would then return and explain it to the barristers. My evidence was discussed by both the prosecuting and defending barristers, who eventually agreed its significance without my having to appear in person. To have done so would have been callous in the extreme, since I would have had to answer questions that can only be described as 'horrific' under the circumstances and upsetting for the children's parents who were present in court. So after all the time I had spent assisting with the investigation of the case, I never in the end set eyes on the man who had killed the three little girls. I could not help feeling that by not seeing him, somehow, something was left unfinished. This was not morbid fascination, but a desire to tie up loose ends, a desire to make sense of the whole tragic, grisly business. Seeing him, shaken and full of remorse, would have been a fitting end to the case. But he was not shaken nor full of remorse. As one of the children's parents put it: 'There was nothing in his eyes at all'. Nothing at all, until he turned his malevolent gaze on the policemen.

Black's first victim was Susan Maxwell. She had been playing a game of tennis at a club in the Scottish Border town of Coldstream and was walking home – the first time she had been allowed to do so alone. It was a hot summer day as she crossed the bridge over the River Tweed towards her home in Cornhill, Northumberland. Raymond Wooding, who was on his way to the river to fish, heard the clip-clop of her shoes and saw her swinging her tennis racket as she walked happily along. He was the last person to see her alive. Her sexually-assaulted body was discovered 300 miles away beside a road in Staffordshire.

The second victim was Caroline Hogg. She had gone out in her best party frock to play 'for only five minutes', as her mother explained later, but she never returned. She was last seen in Portobello in Edinburgh at about 7 o'clock on a fine summer's evening. Her parents and brother began a search, scouring all the places she was likely to have visited – the promenade, the beach, the playing fields, a funfair and an amusement arcade. All to no avail; the six-year old girl had disappeared. Her sexually-assaulted body was found 300 miles away beside a road in Leicestershire.

The last victim was Sarah Harper. She was walking home with a loaf of bread from a corner shop in Morley, Leeds, when she vanished 'as though into thin air', to use the words of the prosecuting barrister, Mr John Milford, Q.C., at the trial. Her sexually-assaulted body was found floating with her hands tied behind her back in the River Trent in Nottinghamshire, twenty-four miles from the spot where Caroline Hogg's body had been found. The medical examination revealed that she was alive when she was thrown into the river. The area in which all three bodies were discovered became known to the police as the 'Midlands Triangle'.

What was the evidence that Robert Black committed these terrible crimes? To begin with, there was very little evidence against him and almost no forensic evidence, with the exception of the pathological conclusions about what happened to the bodies and my own entomological testimony.

Eight years after the murder of Susan Maxwell, the police still had no leads, no suspects. Hector Clark and his team began to despair. Clark came to believe that the investigation was doomed to fail unless an extraordinary piece of luck came his way.

Eventually, such a piece of luck, in a terrible form, did come his way. A man working in his garden saw another man bundling a child into the back of his van. He alerted the police, who immediately set up a road block and intercepted the van in the Scottish border town of Stow. Inside the van was a six-year old girl, hooded, gagged and stuffed into a sleeping bag; she was terrified, but she was alive. Although only twenty minutes had elapsed between her abduction and release, she had already been sexually assaulted. The driver of the van was Robert Black. He was immediately arrested and Hector Clark had a possible suspect. He went to see Black in his prison cell where he found him sitting with his head in his hands. Clark remembers the moment vividly. 'Slowly, he looked up at me and my gut feeling was that this was my man. I had always thought that when I saw him I would know him and every instinct told me this was the guy. I knew by his body smell and his dishevelled appearance. Except that he was bald, he was just as I expected'.

Unfortunately, a policeman's instincts, although often sound, do not amount to evidence. Black was clearly guilty of the assault on the child in Stow – he was caught in the act and he admitted his guilt – but there was still no evidence to link him with the murders of the other three girls.

Robert Black was taken to trial in Edinburgh Crown Court and found guilty. He was sentenced to life imprisonment for abducting the child in Stow. The fact that he was already serving a life sentence when he was put on trial in England four years later remained unknown to the English jury until the end of the trial.

Since Robert Black had been caught kidnapping and sexually assaulting a very young girl somewhere along the border between England and Scotland, he could reasonably be suspected of the sexual assault and murder of Susan Maxwell and Caroline Hogg. He was a professional van driver, delivering advertising posters to various parts of the country, and he often drove between England and Scotland. But how could he be linked to the murders? A painstaking police investigation to retrace his movements finally provided such a link. By examining work-logs at his base in Stamford Hill, north London, by checking depots that he visited and by studying the credit card receipts for petrol, they were able to place him in the same localities from which all three children disappeared and at the same times. He was driving along the A697, along which Susan Maxwell was also walking on the day she vanished. He was in Portobello when Caroline Hogg disappeared. He was delivering posters 150 yards from where Sarah Harper lived when she too disappeared.

When did the girls die? This is where the entomological evidence came in. I worked only on the cases of Susan Maxwell and Caroline Hogg as there was no entomological evidence in the case of Sarah Harper. The police and the prosecution wanted to know whether the times of death of the two girls coincided with the times of their disappearance. They did, which is one small mercy. They did not endure Black's attentions for long. But the prosecution barrister, Mr John Milford, wanted some other information which alas I was not able to give him. I could not tell him where Caroline Hogg died. Why did it matter? The reason had nothing to do with the case against Black as such, but with the question of whether his trial for the murder of Caroline Hogg should take place in England or in Scotland. If Caroline had died in Scotland where she was last seen alive, the trial would have had to take place in Scotland but, if she had died in England where her body was found, the trial would have had to be in England. The question did not arise with Susan Maxwell and Sarah Harper, since they were both last seen alive in England and their bodies were found in England. Although the evidence showed that Caroline died very soon after her abduction, one could not conclude that she died in Scotland, since the drive from Edinburgh to the English border would have taken a very short time. It is also very unlikely that Black would have attempted a sexual assault in Edinburgh, where he might have been discovered in the act.

It was not only the legal question of where to hold the trial that mattered. The case against Black depended on the interconnecting nature of the serial killings and Mr Milford wanted to put Black on trial for all three murders at the same time, not individually. In the end, all that could be said was that there was no evidence that Caroline Hogg had died in Scotland and, since her body was found in England, Mr Justice Macpherson, at a pre-trial hearing in Chelmsford Crown Court, ruled that Black should be put on trial in England for all three murders.

Other evidence against Black was an assault he had made on a teenaged girl in Nottingham. He tried to push her into his van, but he did not reckon with the spirited young girl's struggle to free herself; she succeeded in pushing him away and escaping. Black had also been convicted of two minor sexual offences against girls of six and seven years old, long before the murder of Susan Maxwell. He also possessed large amounts of pornographic literature and children's clothing, facts that did not help his case during the trial.

Interestingly, the trial of Robert Black was conducted in a rather unusual manner which, in my opinion, was justified under the circumstances. Mr Justice Macpherson agreed to Mr Milford's request that Black's previous offences, including the assault in Stow, be revealed to the jury. Normally this is not allowed for fear of prejudicing it against the defendant, but in some cases the *modus operandi* of earlier crimes can be seen as valid evidence in a trial. It was not so much a question of whether Black had committed sexual offences before, but *how* those offences had been committed. The random snatching of a girl from the street and then pushing her into his van, as happened in the Stow and Nottingham cases, was very similar to the reconstructed events in the murders of the three girls. Ronald Thwaites, the defending barrister, told the jury that while Robert Black was a foul pervert he was not a murderer. The jury was not persuaded.

I spent more time on the case of Robert Black than I have done on any other case in my entire career. Horrible though the case was, I do have some pleasant memories of those involved in its investigation. It was one of the most professional police investigations I have known. I would like to pay tribute to the police officers who worked on this case and to Mr Milford, whose determination to see justice done impressed me very much. There were also light-hearted, even humorous moments. It came to light while I was discussing the case with Mr Milford that he was quite an amateur entomologist, a fact that he had for some time modestly kept to himself. Inspector Shevas, a Scotsman working for the Leicestershire Police, was deputed to liaise with the Scottish police in this case because, as he put it, he could 'speak the language'!

It was a very cold, grey, damp morning in early December as I picked my way over a fallow field towards a patch of woodland at Stapleford Tawney near Ongar in Essex, taking great care not to slip and fall in the mud. My companions – police officers and forensic scientists from the Home Office – were equally careful not to slide. We were approaching the site in which the body of a teenaged boy had been found by a gamekeeper and his dog.

Earlier in the day, as I was being driven down to the field from Cambridge, Mr Peter Lamb, the Home Office forensic scientist accompanying me, told me that the boy had not yet been identified. I was somewhat surprised by this since I thought that the easiest thing to do would be to enquire about any missing children in the area. My companion smiled; yes, he said, the police did make such enquiries, of course, but it was not possible to tell which one of the fifteen young boys that were missing from that small area of East Anglia was the boy in question. Until then I had not realised the magnitude of the problem of missing children, or missing people in general. It is said that about 25,000 people go missing every year in Britain. I do not know the number of children that disappear every year, but it is only a small proportion of this figure. Since the care of children is the responsibility of adults, the disappearance of a child is considered to be a suspicious event; consequently, it is investigated with greater rigour and concern than is the disappearance of, say, a man in his prime. When an adult disappears it is not necessarily assumed that there has been foul play, although of course there might have been. The discovery of the bodies in Gloucestershire in the notorious Frederick West case demonstrated this very clearly. When a child disappears, someone must be held responsible.

As we were walking across the field, the investigating police officer who met us informed us that the boy had now been identified; he was Jason Swift, a fourteen-year-old who had been missing for some time. The body had been removed to the mortuary, but we were invited to visit the scene first to gather any evidence that might be found there. We arrived at the woodland without mishap. The police had set up posts and tape around the trees and an officer admitted us to the 'scene'. Just inside the woodland there was the remains of what had once been a large, dome-shaped thicket of brambles, nettles and ivy. It was inside this thicket that the body had lain, to be discovered by a gamekeeper who had initially thought that the boy's naked body was a pig's carcass. The temperature had been well below freezing in the preceding days but it had risen to just above zero when the body was found. What we saw now was a large area of exposed ground within the woodland, the thicket having been almost totally destroyed in order to recover the body. The ground had been trampled and rendered useless for the gathering of evidence, reminding me of Sherlock Holmes' exasperated remarks on the habits of Scotland Yard detectives who managed to destroy so much evidence before he himself arrived at the scene. Nevertheless, my forensic colleagues and I searched the area for clues as best we could. We found precious little. It was time to go to the mortuary to see the body. There we were shown into the room where it lay. I carried out the post-mortem examination in almost total silence. One police officer gave me a detailed account of the investigation in an urgent voice as I worked, but I fear I was not attending closely to what he was saying and was obliged to go over the details later. The smell of death, curiously similar to that of decaying rose petals, filled the room and I was appalled by what I saw. My examination took some time to complete but when it was over, I was more than usually eager to get out into the open air. It was about noon, and I went to lunch with Mr Lamb and the police officers, who told me what was already clear to me from my post-mortem examination. The boy had fallen victim to paedophiles.

How people can do things like this is, and I hope always will be, incomprehensible to me, as it is to most people. Later, when the investigation was over and the perpetrators of the deed had been tried and convicted, several police officers who had been deeply affected by the horror of the crime were specially debriefed to help them to cope with their experiences. Today we would say they were given counselling. It is not necessary to say any more. The murder of a child is a terrible thing. To murder a child from motives of gain or hatred is despicable enough, but this was done for pleasure. Those who killed Jason Swift killed him because they enjoyed it. The human spirit can sink to such hideous depths.

Jason Swift was unhappy at home. Although he was a likeable and popular boy of a quiet disposition – and the headmaster of his school spoke well of him – he was bullied by his family. Desperate to escape from this tyranny, he ran away and went to live with his sister. Later he ran away again, having stolen £75, and lived rough on the streets. He kept body and soul together by begging and by selling himself as a prostitute to men, services for which he was paid in cash, food or overnight shelter. Before long in the words of the prosecuting barrister, he 'would do virtually anything for money and became easy prey for men who found sexual gratification with young boys'.

Eventually, Jason fell into the clutches of a wealthy and internationally-organized paedophile ring operating from a shoe shop in Hackney, which acted as their East London headquarters. The group had recruited some sixty boys for their purposes and they produced manuals on how to entice young boys and secure their confidence in order to seduce them. Runaway boys could make a lot of money this way. As Dr David Tithers of the Methodist National Children's Home explained, Jason represented 'an all too typical picture ... In the old days, runaways used to turn to pickpocketing. Now they become rent boys or prostitutes – it pays well. And it is my belief that the problem is growing'.

And so Jason Swift ended his life in a council flat in Hackney, when four men held him face down, slowly strangling him as they raped him. It took him fifteen minutes to die, according to the medical evidence. He had been paid £5. The sum of his other worldly possessions were his clothes, 98p, a Monopoly game with his initials scratched on it that had seen better days and a tobacco tin containing his coin collection.

At the trial, Sidney Cooke and three other men were given various sentences for the killing. My evidence showed that the killing had taken place indoors and not in the woods (since the flies that had laid eggs on the body could not have been active out of doors at the low temperatures prevailing at the time); and that the body had been placed in the thicket two days before it was discovered. Cooke was sentenced to nineteen years, which was reduced to sixteen years because he had not killed the boy on his own. It was thought that this diluted his guilt. In the end, he was released after serving only nine years of his sentence.

Most people would consider the deliberate destruction of a new-born baby to be one of the most malevolent acts imaginable. I have been involved in several cases of infanticide in my time. Some were, indeed, committed with a most malicious intent, yet others, no less tragic, were committed with an aching heart and without the least trace of malice or hatred.

One case of this latter kind came my way when someone discovered a dead baby in a cardboard box at the edge of a field adjacent to a garden. The matter was reported to the police, who recovered the body and started their enquiries. They did not have to spend much time on the case, for the most obvious starting point was to call on the owners of the garden near which the baby's body had been found. The occupants of the house were a late middle-aged couple and their teenaged daughter. When told about the baby, they all denied any knowledge of where it could have come from. However, the police were not satisfied and I was asked to estimate the time of death. I carried out my examination and concluded that death had occurred about ten days prior to the discovery of the body. In fact, the police had a very shrewd idea of what had happened; they suspected that the daughter had given birth to the child, then killed it. She was a skinny, undernourished girl, the sort who would not look pregnant, even during the late stages of pregnancy. Questioned by the police, she finally broke down and confessed. Yes, she had given birth to the baby and, yes, the date of birth coincided with the estimated time of death. The whole period of the child's existence on Earth was but a few hours.

It was the old, old story. The girl had had an affair with a much older man and became pregnant. She was at her wit's end what to do. She was terrified that her parents might discover her secret and punish her. One night, when she felt that the time was drawing close, she went to her bedroom and gave birth to the child in secret. Astonishingly, the parents were not aware of what had happened. The girl kept the baby with her in bed all night long but did not attempt to feed it. She wanted it to die for fear of her parents' wrath. She dressed it in some doll's clothes but by the early morning it was dead. Heart-broken, the girl put it in a cardboard box, took it down to the bottom of the garden before her parents woke up and placed it in the field beyond. Inevitably, the truth came out as the police enquiry progressed and the parents too were heart-broken. They told their daughter that if only she had confided in them they would have supported her and helped her to look after the baby. The whole tragedy need not have happened and the police officers, who were deeply moved by the sense of loss, did not press charges.

I have known several such cases of unwanted babies abandoned to die. While one cannot possibly condone the actions of such mothers, even under the circumstances, one can understand them and see that no malice or bitterness is involved, only fear, ignorance and irresponsibility. Nevertheless, it is a monstrous thing to snuff out a life at its very beginning.

In other cases, the murder of a new-born baby cannot be so easily understood. One day around Easter time, a ten year-old girl, while playing with her friends in a garage in London, had the horrible experience of discovering the body of a baby in a black bin-liner. The police started an investigation to trace its parents or, at least, its mother, but first they had to establish the cause of death. The pathologist, Dr Peter Vanezis, concluded that the baby, a three week-old boy, had been killed by being held by the feet and swung violently against a wall, smashing his skull. The badly decomposed tissues offered no clue as to race and it was initially thought that the baby might have been black. However, analysis of the tissues revealed that he was, in fact, white.

I was asked by the police to investigate the case. I examined the garage and collected specimens there, as well as from the bag in which the body had been placed. Finally, I examined the body of the child in the mortuary. It was quite decomposed and the head had been shattered. The entomological evidence as a whole suggested that the baby had been killed six days before its body was discovered. But there was

further insect evidence suggesting other things. Among the insect fragments recovered from the bag were those of a gnat-like creature known
as the window-midge. This curious little insect has distinctive mark-
ings on its wings and is frequently found indoors, especially, as its
name suggests, on windows. It breeds in decomposing matter and its
presence in a kitchen suggests some overlooked and decaying vegetable
substance lying around. As well as the window-midges, many specimens of various fly species and other invertebrates that breed in the soil
were recovered during the post-mortem. All this suggested that the
child had been murdered six days before discovery and his body left
lying indoors for some hours; and that it had then been removed and
placed in a garden – on soil that had probably only recently been dug
– before being placed in the bag and removed to the garage.

Police investigations revealed that the time of death coincided with
the time that a local girl, known to have been pregnant, no longer gave
the appearance of carrying a child, although she had no baby to show
for it. Of course she was called in for questioning, but she denied
everything. Clearly, the matter would have to be resolved some other
way and I made the obvious suggestion of comparing DNA from the
baby with that from the putative mother. I remember leaving the police
station that day, confident that the problem would soon be solved.

It was never solved. A few days later, a police officer telephoned me
at work. He thanked me for the work I had done, but told me that the
case had been shelved. There would be no DNA fingerprinting and no
further enquiries were going to be made. Surprised, I asked him why
they had suddenly lost interest. He answered, somewhat sheepishly,
that the baby's body had disappeared. It had been stolen from the
mortuary!

In a case like this it is very difficult to believe that the mother could
be the perpetrator of the murder. Even if a mother could murder her
child, she would hardly do it in such a savage manner as this. In these
situations suspicion usually falls on the father, or on a male acquaintance who is not the father, a person euphemistically known as a
'boyfriend'. These are among the most dangerous of men. They will
prey upon the emotions of girls and young women with disastrous
results. I have known so many cases of murder involving casual 'relationships' of this kind. Often the man is very much older than the girl,
who may well be of an age to be his daughter.

Typical of such cases was one that began when a ten-year old girl,
whom I shall call Samantha,* met a young man of about thirty when
she was playing in the local park. The man spoke to her and gave her

* Her real name cannot be given for legal reasons.

sweets and when she returned home she told her unmarried mother about him. The mother did not seem very concerned. Some time later, Samantha met the man again and this time he invited her back to his house. She went with him but, apparently, nothing untoward happened. She visited him again and again, without her mother's knowledge, and the visits seemed to remain innocent. Samantha and the man, together with various of his male and female friends, used to go for walks or watch television. All in all it was a very strange, if so far harmless, relationship. Eventually, Samantha, in turn, invited the man to her house.

Samantha's mother had had a succession of 'boyfriends' and the new visitor very quickly became another. Soon after his first visit, a 'relationship' began between him and Samantha's mother. Samantha did not find this at all odd, because, by the age of ten, she herself had already had many sexual experiences with a boy of twelve. She was only following her mother's example. The inevitable, or what experience has shown to be inevitable in such households, eventually happened; the man began to have sexual relations with Samantha. Again, as is common in such households, rows between the mother and the boyfriend and Samantha and the boyfriend were frequent and often savage. At this point in dramas of this kind, violence frequently follows. Samantha disappeared. The police were alerted and, after a short search, Samantha's body was found buried under a mound of broken bricks and rubble in – of all places – the grounds of a hospital. The left side of her head had been smashed in by a savage blow from a heavy object, probably a brick or a stone. There were some very small maggots in the body and there was evidence that Samantha had been indulging in sexual intercourse.

As you may well imagine suspicion fell upon the man, who was arrested and questioned, but he denied killing the girl. My own evidence, based on the timing of death after an examination of the minute maggots and fly eggs found on the body, revealed that the murder had been committed soon after the time when the man was last seen with her. When the matter came to court, he broke down halfway through the proceedings and confessed that he had indeed committed the crime. Apparently in the middle of an argument, the girl threatened him, telling him that she would tell her mother about their amorous relations. He had panicked and silenced her. It seems that the description of how the flies and the pathology evidence incriminated him was more than he could bear.

Uncannily, a few years after Samantha's death, I had a case that was not only almost identical to hers in its general circumstances, but the girl's two first names were the same as Samantha's. Once again an older man had befriended a very young girl, then had a 'relationship' with her and her mother. This girl also disappeared soon after being seen in the company of the man.

On a warm and sunny day in early autumn I visited the scene where the body had been found – the edge of a harvested field. I had been asked to estimate the time of death. The body had long been removed, but I was searching for further evidence in the soil upon which it had lain; specifically, I was looking for blowfly puparia. Unusually for the time of year, the maggots infesting the body belonged to a species of greenbottle, flies that are usually active at the height of summer and not very much in evidence later in the year, unlike the more familiar bluebottles, whose season of activity generally begins earlier and ends later than that of greenbottles. But it had been an extremely hot summer and the autumn was very warm. The insect evidence suggested that the girl had died about three weeks before discovery, in other words, at the time she was last seen with the man. In addition, a very great deal of other evidence was gathered and examined. DNA, soil, blood and various other lines of evidence all pointed to his guilt. He was sentenced to life imprisonment. The motive once again was a desire to silence the girl before she told her mother about her own involvement.

As I have mentioned before, I could recite a number of cases from my forensic experience that would, in essence, be the same story as that of these two girls, with slight variations. Suffice it to say that such relationships are not uncommon and almost always lead to misery and degradation, if not always to murder.

I was once peripherally involved in a case of child-murder that was somewhat different from the two histories above, for in this case the victim, a nine-year old girl, was not 'involved' with the man. Miles Evans, a private soldier, was accused of murdering his step-daughter. Zoe Evans disappeared early in January and it was generally believed that she had run away from home. Her mother and stepfather immediately organized a search for her and made a television appeal for her to return home. Nevertheless, the police were suspicious and arrested both parents although the mother was very quickly eliminated from their inquiries and released.

Miles Evans remained in custody and was closely questioned. The police discovered inconsistencies in his answers and he lied several times. Before long they decided that he had killed Zoe, and they charged him with murder even before the body was found. The hunt continued and six weeks later, towards the end of February, Zoe's naked and decomposing body was found wedged head first into a badgers' sett. The pathologist's conclusion was that death was by suffocation from having her shirt stuffed into her mouth and from the inhalation of blood that had flowed into her mouth from her nose, which had been broken by a violent blow. The police also found bloodstained clothes and undergarments belonging to her stepfather.

On the basis of his lies and inconsistencies, as well as evidence of the blood-stained clothes, Evans was put on trial for murder. I was contacted by his solicitors, who asked me to determine the time of death, since they believed that this would become an important point in the case. I agreed to do so in the company of Mr Nigel Wyatt of the Natural History Museum, who had been retained by the prosecution. He and I examined the entomological evidence at the Huntingdon laboratory of the Forensic Science Service. Unfortunately, there was very little of interest, the only significant finding being the presence of winter gnat larvae on the body. This indicated that death had occurred in the winter, but this revealed nothing new, since both Zoe's disappearance and the discovery of her body had taken place in the winter. The solicitors also wished to know whether the evidence suggested that the body had been in the badgers' sett since death, or whether it had been moved from another location since death. Again, it was impossible to tell.

Although Miles Evans continued to maintain his innocence, he was found guilty of murder and sentenced to life imprisonment. Throughout the trial he behaved like a bereaved parent and, when the verdict was announced, he tried to comfort Zoe's mother, who was firmly convinced of his guilt. So convinced in fact, that she stated that only the death penalty would be suitable punishment for him.

Again, the question must be asked, 'Why did he do it?' In fact, no motive could be shown. Inevitably the suggestion was made that Evans had tried to abuse his step-daughter but there was no evidence for this, nor was there any history of Evans misbehaving in this way. In fact, all the evidence showed that he was devoted to Zoe. Yet his lies and the blood-stained clothes told against him.

'Only he knows why he did it', said a police officer working on the case, 'And now he has the ultimate terrible secret, because who can he tell?' And yet it is also possible to make another, equally valid, statement. 'Only he knows *whether* he did it'. It strikes me that the answer to the question implicit in this statement is much harder to live with, whatever that answer might be.

The violent death of young people is, of course, particularly upsetting. Terrible though the murder of a very young person by a much older one may be, there is something even more dreadful – I am tempted to say, *unnatural* – in the murder of one young person by another. An extreme case is the murder of the toddler James Bulger by two young boys. I was not involved in the investigation of that case and, since so much has been written about it, I will not comment on it further.

A case that I found especially brutal was the murder of a fifteen-year old schoolgirl by a fifteen-year old schoolboy. The facts of the case are simple enough: the boy wanted to date the girl but she was not interested, so he killed her with his bare hands. Apparently, it was as simple as that. The girl's remains were found between the rear fence of her parents' house and the railway embankment running alongside the back of the row of houses. The body was found in late July lying in a dip and covered with vegetation and other debris. When the police came to consult me about this case there were two distinct possibilities about the time of the girl's death. Specifically, I was asked whether the victim died shortly after she was last seen alive in the middle of May, or whether she had died some days or weeks later, in June or July.

There was a great deal of insect activity and remains on the body. The empty bluebottle and greenbottle puparia allowed me to conclude that death had taken place a minimum of three weeks prior to the discovery of the body. In addition to these puparia there were large numbers of cheese skippers, which are the maggots of small flies with the scientific name of *Piophila casei*. These creatures have the habit of flinging themselves high into the air to escape predators, acrobatics they accomplish by means of hooking their front ends to their back ends, then letting go suddenly. They are often found in badly tanned leather, in poorly curated museum specimens (such as stuffed animals) and, as their name implies, in cheese that has been left exposed. I understand that some French cheeses are not considered edible until they are infested with these maggots!

As well as these larvae, there were many grubs of the so-called larder beetle *Dermestes lardarius*. These dermestids are also associated with museum work, but in a beneficial way, since they are used to clean up skeletons for display purposes. Both cheese skippers and the larder beetle larvae make their first appearance on bodies about two months after death, arriving at a particular stage of protein putrefaction. Their presence, therefore, placed the minimum time of death at about the middle of May. Also on the body were large numbers of *Hister* beetles, which are predators of maggots, among other things. Although the rate of increase in *Hister* numbers on a dead body has not been measured, and consequently an accurate time of death on the basis of their presence cannot be given, nevertheless their mere presence in large numbers suggested that a period of several weeks must have elapsed since death.

The conclusion that death took place in mid-May was corroborated by later police investigations. The boy was too young to go to prison but was placed on probation.

Two young women, one aged eighteen the other twenty-nine, were walking along a wooded lane in Norfolk one pleasant autumn afternoon. They were friends, or so the younger one, Rachael, firmly believed. They were chatting amicably. Rachael was happy; she was looking forward to starting university life at Southampton later that month. She was confident and in excellent health, and life was good. Maria, in contrast, was unwashed, barefooted, unkempt and utterly miserable. She had nothing to look forward to and had been living rough for the past few days. Earlier that day Maria had telephoned Rachael, asking to meet her in that dead-end lane.

Suddenly, as Rachael was talking, Maria drew out a long knife and stabbed her unsuspecting companion. 'Maria! Maria!', shouted Rachael, raising her hands to protect herself, but Maria struck again. And again and again and again. Fifty-seven times she raised her arm and stabbed Rachael, striking with such force that her hand would often slip down the handle and on to the blade, cutting it badly. At last Rachael was dead, stabbed in the chest, throat and back. She fell face down on the fallen leaves. Maria took her by one hand and her ankles and pulled her towards a tree, covered her with leaves and other vegetation and left her.

'She had everything and I had nothing'. At her trial this was the justification given by Maria Hnatiuk for killing Rachael Lean, for she did confess to killing her. She admitted manslaughter on the grounds of diminished responsibility, but not murder. She claimed that she was under an evil influence when she committed her crime and that she could not be blamed for its commission. This evil influence was not drink or drugs. It was that of a tyrannical man whom she believed she loved. Ian Wells was described in court as a 'sadistic psychopath', who claimed to be a member of an SAS-style organization called Knox which had sent him to Cambodia. He demanded signed pledges of devotion from Maria. He beat her and threatened her. He told her that he had access to truth drugs. He told her he could harm her family, if she did not do his bidding. He made her set fire to the cottage of one of her previous boyfriends. He forbade her from seeing her family. He humiliated her and made her dress in abnormal fashions that excited him. He compelled her to bring women to his house in order to watch her perform deviant acts with them. He cut her hair, destroyed her belongings and made her look like a tramp. He drew up a list of people whom he demanded that she should kill; if she killed the first two people on the list, he would allow her to visit the gymnasium in which she had first met Rachael. If she killed all the people on the list – including Rachael – he would marry her. Finally, he threw her out and made her live rough in the countryside.

Maria remained devoted to Wells, but lost all self-respect. She wrote him letters, describing herself as a 'tart, scum and trash' and degenerated into a lost, lonely figure. Wells had told her that her future happiness depended upon her killing Rachael and she came to believe that this act would release her from her misery and win her Wells' approval. 'I feel very upset about what has happened to Rachael', she said at the trial. 'I still can't believe what happened. I don't believe in violence.' But she admitted that her intention had been to kill Rachael. She was totally obsessed by the idea. 'I had the thought going round and round in my mind. It wasn't, "I am going to do this", but Ian saying, "You've got to do it". I wasn't in a temper. She just had to die'. After the murder, for that is what the court decided it was, Maria Hnatiuk had been seen sobbing on the floor of a telephone box not far from the scene. She had been speaking to Ian Wells, who arrived and took her to Bristol to stay with her sister. Five days later, the body was discovered.

I was asked to determine the time of death. It is not necessary to go into the details, but it was possible to establish that the time of death coincided very closely with the time Rachael was last seen with Maria. During the early stages of the inquiry, these conclusions mattered greatly, since they linked Maria Hnatiuk very strongly to the crime. I was questioned repeatedly about how certain I was about my conclusions but I was quite confident that the time of death was accurate. In the end it did not matter, since Maria Hnatiuk confessed to the crime. The question the court had to decide was not whether she committed the crime but whether she was responsible for her actions.

The prosecuting barrister, Mr David Stokes, Q.C., said of Maria Hnatiuk: 'This was a wicked and calculating woman, who killed a young woman on the threshold of life, who had trusted her, and then pursued a false defence'. The jury found her guilty of murder. Police officers wept openly in court. Pronouncing the sentence of life imprisonment, Mr Justice Blofeld said: 'This chilling murder was committed by you when you clearly knew what you were doing. You deliberately chose, brutally, to end the life of Rachael Lean. She had done you no harm. She had been your friend. You killed her by repeatedly stabbing her. You then covered her body to prevent discovery and thereafter lied and lied again'. Sobbing, Maria Hnatiuk was led out of the dock.

A very ugly fact known to all criminal investigators is that it is not the most hated people who fall victim to murder, but those whom it is easiest to overcome. Murder victims are usually those who are naturally vulnerable; children, women and old people. In my experience at least, it is not Colonel Arbuthnot who is shot in his study, nor Lord Edgware who is stabbed in his mansion. It is eighty-year old Mrs Such-and-Such who lives in a damp London basement who is murdered for her few possessions, or, as we have seen, the unhappy child who runs away from an uncaring home who is murdered because it is so easy to overcome a child. I have been involved in the investigation of such cases as that of an old man who had been beaten to death 'for fun' by some hoodlums, or that of an old woman who had been raped and murdered by an unemployed and embittered youth. Such deeds, while mercifully not very common, are much more frequent than most people realize.

Racial murders are another category of horrific crimes. I remember one case in which an Indian garage proprietor was kicked to death by two youths who had robbed him of what he had in the till. They did not consider the £100 or so that they found on the premises sufficient reward for their hard work in breaking into the place, so they kicked the man to death in their rage. I attended court to give evidence in this case. I remember seeing the sad and uncomprehending faces of the deceased man's family and wondering what could be going through their minds. I also remember meeting the prosecuting barrister, Mr Roger Smith, Q.C., who was one of the kindest and most sympathetic barristers it has ever been my privilege to come across.

Another type of murderer derives pleasure from mutilating the body of his victim after death, a phenomenon known in the clinical jargon of the medical profession as post-mortem injury. An extreme example of this is manifested in the horrific injuries that the Yorkshire Ripper used to inflict on his victims – injuries that are best not described. Others appear to enjoy whipping or marking the skin of the dead body. Consequently, any repeated series of marks on a corpse – any injuries that look as though they are part of a pattern – immediately arouse police suspicion. I remember a case in which a large part of the body of a murdered prostitute was covered with repeated pairs of marks, like two dashes: - -. Initially, the police suspected some perverted activity but, when I examined the body, a thought occurred to me. It was late autumn, a time when earwigs will congregate beneath various objects such as stones or logs. The marks seemed to me to be of a shape and size that an earwig, with its opposable, biting mandibles, might produce. I mentioned this to the officer in charge, who asked the policemen who had removed the body from the rough ground in which it was found to comment. Sure enough, they said that, when they lifted the body, large numbers of earwigs scuttled away. I have also known such post-mortem injury to be inflicted by carabid ground beetles which have the same kind of mandibles as those of earwigs. In the United States, there are some cases on record in which the small, pockmark-like injuries caused by the formic acid secreted by ants initially aroused suspicion as possible post-mortem mutilation.

No-one involved in criminal investigation can remain totally unaffected by their experiences. Witnessing the consequences of horrific crimes over a period of twenty-five years inevitably leads to the formation of moral questions, opinions and attitudes towards the problem. Why do such things happen? How can they be prevented? Did such things always happen, or has the world changed in recent years? This last question is one that is very frequently asked, often in a rhetorical sense, many people believing that the world has become more wicked and that 'in the past' monstrous crimes, such as those documented in this chapter, used not to happen. Is this true? Often discussions of this question become very heated, each side being absolutely convinced of the truth of their position. It seems that people can be divided into those who believe that 'the past' was a golden age and those who believe that 'the past' was nothing but a period of barbarism. I have naturally formed my own opinions on the subject.

Not so long ago, a young girl was burnt alive by two young men who thought it was great fun. Did such things happen in the past? Yes, they did: for example, heretics were often burnt at the stake. What about the murder of children? Yes, children were often murdered in the past. So, can one conclude that nothing has changed? I do not think so. My own reading of history has taught me that, although great evil existed in the past, there was, nevertheless, a *logic* to the situation – a kind of logic that often seems to be absent today. By this I mean that, while burning someone alive at the stake because their religious beliefs differed from those of the majority is certainly a great evil, it is not on the same level as burning a young girl for fun. One may condemn burning people at the stake, but the terrible deed was done as a consequence of religious conviction, however perverted it may have been. The recent burning of the young girl could not be 'justified' by any moral belief.

Today, the destruction of property or of natural objects takes place in a manner that clearly did not take place in the past. Monuments that have stood unmolested for hundreds, sometimes thousands, of years are now frequently damaged or destroyed. The stained-glass windows of churches are smashed; crucifixes broken; standing stones sprayed with graffiti; train seats slashed; newly-planted trees cut down; graves defiled. Violent young men, finding nothing easy to hand to destroy, will now turn upon their own belongings and destroy them. These are facts of modern life and there is little to suggest that such things happened in the past. Certainly churches and monasteries were destroyed and burnt, trees were chopped down, graves desecrated and so on, but then there seemed always to be some kind of logic to what was happening. Truly dreadful things were done during the course of mediæval wars, but they were apparently carried out in accordance with certain sincerely-held beliefs. One may disapprove of Oliver Cromwell's destruction of church ornaments, but his actions can hardly be equated with those of the modern-day vandal who smashes such things simply because he derives pleasure from the distress it causes others.

Of course, abominations and meaningless violence did take place during historic times, especially when society broke down during and after a long war. What seems to be new is that such meaningless violence now occurs during times of peace and prosperity. It is widely thought that conflicts in the past were periods of unrestrained barbarity, whereas modern, enlightened humanity is much more civilized in its conduct of war. In fact this is not true. During the Middle Ages, men like St Augustine and St Thomas Aquinas believed that a resort to war should be made only when all other ways of resolving conflicts were exhausted and that, when war was waged, it had to be conducted in such a manner as to minimize the harm done to civilian populations. But it was not only saints who held such views. The fourth-century Roman military authority, Vegetius Renatus, wrote that war should be waged in order to achieve, or protect, peace. His book, *De re militari*, remained the most influential military manual for 1,000 years after his death. However, although many mediæval wars were conducted in a restrained manner and non-combatants were largely unharmed, in many other wars, such as the Hundred Years' War, civilians were treated with the most appalling ferocity, much the same as civilians were treated in the Bosnian War in our own time. As far as the conduct of war is concerned, human behaviour seems to have remained unchanged.

Let us come now to the treatment of children. Did the abominations committed by men like Sidney Cooke or Robert Black have their counterparts in times past? I do not doubt that they did, but equally I do not doubt that they were much rarer events. Men who behaved in this way in the past were dealt with in a much more uncompromising way than they are today. Serious talk about the 'rights' of paedophiles to indulge their desires is a very recent development. Alas, we live in an age in which such discussion, devoid of any moral or intellectual rationality, can take place. I have observed the effects of things done to children – things that I will not discuss here – that I would not have thought humanly possible had I not seen them myself. Nor am I alone in this; certain practices were simply outside the experience of everyone involved in criminal investigation – police officer, scientist or lawyer – until very recently. I have not the least doubt that such things are late developments in depraved human behaviour.

The welfare of children is seen by some as being a very modern, civilized concern of enlightened twentieth-century humanity. Again, let
us look at history. In 1483, men wept in the streets of London when the
Princes in the Tower were thought to have been murdered. In the wars
between the Turks and the Byzantines in the Middle Ages, the Byzantines would sometimes place children at the head of their army in order
to confuse the enemy, who would not attack while the children were
there. Whatever one might think of the ethics of such a tactic, it
showed that both sides would not move to harm a child and that each
was confident of the other side's aversion to doing so. Today, children
in the Balkans are killed by snipers and murdered for political ends.
When the murders of children make headline news, people no longer
weep in the streets.

But *why* do these things happen? Here we enter into territory that is
even more subjective than the question of whether or not certain kinds
of depravity are new, for much depends on one's moral viewpoint. I
think that no-one will disagree that the very notion of morality is
ebbing away, in the sense that there are few moral principles that can
be said to be held by more or less everyone in Britain or, for that matter, in the West, generally. Moral relativism has undoubtedly fragmented society, making it much easier for people with extreme views
to secure an audience.

Once such opinions receive a serious hearing, tolerance of them will,
to a certain extent, increase. People who speak of the 'rights' of paedophiles have become more and more strident, asserting that such people
are yet another persecuted minority. Those who like myself disagree
are forced to argue against the contentions of such activists. The result
is the illusion of a debate – that there *is* something to discuss. In the
end, the alleged 'rights' of paedophiles will come to be seen as equal to
the true rights of children and the matter will be discussed in the same
spirit as a dispute over wages between an employer and an employee.

It seems to me that when we no longer regard certain matters as
sacrosanct and inviolable, chaos is bound to follow.

CHAPTER 5

Broken Lives

If you have tears, prepare to shed them now.
Shakespeare, *Julius Caesar*, Act III, Scene 2

'I have been in prison for eight years for a crime I am totally innocent of committing ...'

Thus began a letter from a man serving a life sentence for murder; he was asking me to look at the evidence afresh and demonstrate his innocence.

'I felt compelled to write to you as I strongly believe that I am one of the victims of injustice caused by an unscrupulous forensic expert ...', was the *cri de cœur* of another prisoner, convicted of arson and murder.

I often receive such letters, most of which strike me as being quite sincere. It is one thing simply to protest one's innocence; quite another to ask for a new and independent look at the evidence. I usually reply to such letters by saying that I would be glad to examine the evidence and give an opinion. I also send a copy of the letter to an organization known as *Justice*, which is the British Section of the International Commission of Jurists. Among other things, its aim is to investigate cases of possible miscarriage of justice.

Being sent to prison must be one of the most horrible fates that can befall a human being, although I hasten to add that I do not speak from experience. Being sent to prison, knowing that one is innocent, must be heart-breaking. Contrary to popular belief, it is no easy matter to protest one's innocence once one has been convicted, for such protestation is seen as a refusal to repent. It is considered bad behaviour to claim that one is innocent after conviction, and early release on the grounds of good behaviour becomes impossible. Therefore, those who insist, year after year, that they are innocent have a certain credibility, for why persist if this would lengthen, or at least not shorten, the period of time spent in prison?

Of course, some prisoners may gamble in the hope that they might just succeed in convincing the authorities that they are truly innocent, when they are actually guilty. In the letters that I receive the constant refrain is a variant of 'please look at the evidence again'. This indicates an objectivity of outlook that, in itself, argues the case for innocence. Many of those who have written to me have taken a great deal of trouble to instruct themselves in the aspects of forensic evidence that led to their conviction, acquiring a quite astonishing depth of knowledge. In almost all cases I have found that the evidence had been misinterpreted or, at any rate, admitted of more than one interpretation.

Prison is a dreadful punishment, affecting both mental and physical health. While many people can easily imagine the mental anguish that prisoners must experience, it is, perhaps, less widely appreciated that physical harm may also follow. Michael Sams, the murderer of Julie Dart, on whose case I spent a considerable amount of time, developed cancer in prison and his leg was amputated. Another criminal I came across was a severe diabetic who feared that his condition would get worse in prison, which it almost certainly did. These two people were guilty of their crimes, but consider the harm done to the innocent. Patrick Nichols was convicted of a crime he did not commit and which, moreover, was subsequently found not to have been committed at all. The old woman he was supposed to have murdered had, in fact, died of natural causes, but the forensic evidence was interpreted in a manner that resulted in his imprisonment for more than twenty years. Nichols went to prison a healthy man; he left it in a wheelchair.

Nothing is infallible and one could say, philosophically, that miscarriages of justice are bound to happen. This may be true, but general human infallibility is not always the cause of injustice being done. Sometimes it is the result of malpractice by forensic scientists, for there are some whose desire for payment and wish to ingratiate themselves with the side that pays them overrides their concern for justice. We shall return to this matter in the last chapter of this book.

One of the most memorable cases on which I worked with *Justice* was that of William Funnell. Mr Funnell was a carpenter. He lived with his wife and three sons in Dover, on an estate that was perched on top of one of the white cliffs. One day his wife, Anne, went missing and he made enquiries to find out where she had gone. He asked his sons and his neighbours, but no one seemed to know her whereabouts. Eleven days after her disappearance her body was found among some bushes at the edge of a green that was used by people to walk their dogs. The children from the estate played there and many people walked to work on a path that ran along one side of it and past the bushes behind which the body was found. Mr Funnell was arrested and made a full confession: he said he had murdered his wife.

But did Mr Funnell really murder his wife? There was so much evidence to suggest that he was innocent, but most of this was not heard in court. The problem, as so often in murder cases, was that there was a *prima facie* case against Mr Funnell; he had quarrelled with his wife before her disappearance.

At the trial, Mr Justice (now Lord) Woolf said that it was the old story of the Eternal Triangle. Mrs Funnell worked as a barmaid in a local public house and soon became friendly with a man named Peter Brown. They were often seen embracing. Mr Funnell seemed not to suspect that there was anything seriously wrong until one Friday night when he went to bed before his wife returned from the pub. At 3 o'clock in the morning he woke up to the sound of a car's engine and, looking out of the window, he saw Brown's van. He then saw his wife get out of the van and walk into the house. He confronted her and asked her what was going on and she told him she had been visiting the home of an old school friend. Knowing that she was lying, Mr Funnell became angry and an argument ensued during which Mrs Funnell admitted that she had been having an affair with Brown, but she also said that the affair was now over and that she would not see Brown again. The next day, Mrs Funnell changed her mind and said that she would leave and take the boys with her. Her attitude changed several times over the next few days. Then, on the Tuesday, she disappeared. When Mrs Funnell's body was discovered eleven days later, Mr Funnell was arrested and, after forty hours in police custody, he produced a full written confession to the crime, in which he stated that he had had an argument with his wife on Tuesday and that he had taken her by the throat. Apparently, she did not struggle but simply fell to the floor. He said he left her lying on the floor until dark, when he lifted her over his shoulders, carried her downstairs and out into the street. He walked along the street in front of the estate, turned left at the green, went up the path and, finally, deposited her among the bushes. As a result of his confession, Mr Funnell was sentenced to life imprisonment.

One day, I received a telephone call from Mr John Smithson of the BBC. He told me that he produced a series of television programmes called *Rough Justice*, which told the stories of people who might have been victims of miscarriages of justice. He wanted to come to Cambridge to discuss the case of William Funnell. When he arrived some days later, he told me the whole story and said that some maggot evidence had been preserved. Would I be willing to examine this evidence and comment on the probability of Mrs Funnell's body having lain behind the bushes unnoticed for eleven days? Of course I said I would be happy to do so, and that I would like to visit the spot where the body had been found.

A few days later Mr Smithson and I, together with his colleague, Mr Bob Duffield, and Mr Peter Ashman from *Justice*, drove down to Dover. It was bright and sunny when we arrived at the top of the white cliffs. We parked the car near Mr Funnell's house and walked the 170 yards to the end of the estate. On our right, dropping sheer to the sea, was the white cliff; to our left was the housing estate. In spite of the sombre circumstances of our visit, I could not help thinking that it must be wonderful to wake up to such a view of the sea.

One hundred and seventy yards is a very short distance to walk – if one is not carrying someone else across one's shoulders. We arrived at the end of the estate and turned left on to the path that ran beside the green. It sloped upwards. Just before we arrived at the bushes, the slope suddenly became much steeper and Mr Smithson kindly lent me his shoulder to lean on so that I could climb to the top. On the right were the bushes. The dominant vegetation was Alexanders (*Smyrnium olusatrum*), a common plant in coastal areas. I examined the area in detail and satisfied myself that there was no reason why a maggot infestation could not have taken place in a body lying in that locality and position. We walked back to the car and drove into Dover for lunch.

Afterwards, we went to the police station in Maidstone to watch a video recording of the removal of the body and the post-mortem examination. The police officers who met us were extremely courteous, but were adamant that Mr Smithson and Mr Duffield should remain outside. I watched the video with Mr Ashman and the pathologist assisting *Justice*. We watched the general activities of the police and the forensic scientists at the scene; the preparations, the equipment, the clearing of the vegetation, the removal of the body ... at this point I asked the police officer to stop the video and wind it back a minute or so. Something was not quite right. Again we watched the body as it was lifted up. I asked the assembled company whether they had noticed anything out of the ordinary. They hadn't. 'Rewind again ... Stop'. The still frame now showed the body suspended in mid-air by several police officers. The vegetation beneath the body was bright green. Perhaps it was my experience in examining forensic scenes that made me notice it. It was certainly not a matter of intelligence. Place a spade or a plank of wood on your lawn for two or three days and, when you remove it, the grass will be discoloured and yellow. But the vegetation beneath Anne Funnell's body, which was supposed to have lain in that spot for eleven days, had not discoloured. It seemed highly unlikely that the body could have been lying on that patch of vegetation for that period of time. I suggested to Mr Ashman that a plant biochemist be consulted on the matter so that the period required for the leaves of the plant in question to discolour when under an object could be established beyond doubt.

Professor David Walker of the Institute of Photosynthesis at Sheffield University carried out the necessary experiments. Taking some Alexanders' leaves, he placed them between two sterile panels held firmly together. This placed the leaves in darkness and applied physical pressure upon them, the same conditions that they would have experienced had they been lying beneath the body. After two or three days the leaves had discoloured. I can add one further point to Professor Walker's conclusions. A decomposing body releases many toxic compounds into the soil beneath it, resulting in a much faster rate of discoloration of plant leaves. The body could certainly not have lain among the bushes for eleven days.

Back in Cambridge, I examined the maggot evidence. This, too, was most unusual. It was possible to sort the maggots into two groups; one consisted of very old maggots, the other of very young, newly-hatched maggots. There was no gradation in the age of the maggots, such as one usually finds on an infested body. The findings suggested that the body had been exposed to fly activity soon after death, concealed, and then exposed once more. Again, this supported the belief that the body could not have lain among the bushes for the full eleven days. The age of the oldest maggots indicated that death had occurred within hours of Mrs Funnell's disappearance.

Almost every detail of Mr Funnell's confession is extremely unlikely to have happened. He was well-known and well-liked by the people of the estate. Nobody who knew him could believe that he had committed the murder, including his wife's relations. Returning to the question of how long the body lay among the bushes, there is a great deal of other evidence that suggests that it could not have lain there for any length of time. Dogs being walked on the green would certainly have detected it. The boys playing football who often had to retrieve their ball from the bushes would also have noticed it. Builders repairing the house adjacent to the path and who went among the bushes would have noticed it too. The father who went searching for his child's missing spectacles among the bushes during the critical eleven days would certainly have seen it. These and many others had been past or into the bushes since the disappearance of Mrs Funnell; it is not credible that such people could have failed to see a body. In fact, it was discovered by a young lad who had already been into the bushes a few days earlier.

If Funnell murdered his wife on Tuesday, what did he do with the body until darkness fell? In his statement he said that he left her lying on the bedroom floor. When the boys returned from school, Mr Funnell did not ask them not to enter any particular room. In fact, the eldest son, Stephen, did enter his parents' bedroom to remove a television set, but he did not see his mother's body. It could not have been concealed under the bed, because the bed was too low. The head injuries observed and described by the pathologist, Dr Peter Vanezis, during the post-mortem did not tally with Mr Funnell's account of what happened. Severe head injuries had been sustained; the consequent profuse bleeding would have left much of the bedroom bloodstained, but this was not found to be the case when the room was examined, nor was there any evidence to show that the carpet, the walls or the bed had been washed or cleaned to remove blood. In fact one small bloodstain was found on the wallpaper, but tests showed that this could easily have come from one of the boys who was prone to nose-bleeds and would often come into his parents' bedroom for treatment.

And Mr Funnell's midnight walk to the green with his wife's dead body across his shoulders – could that have happened? Consider what would have had to happen if this story were true. Mr Funnell would have picked up his wife's body and placed it across his shoulders; carried it downstairs, past the bedroom in which his brother Jack was staying; past Mrs Funnell's dog, which everyone said would bark at anything; out into the garden and past the tent in which his sons were camping for the night; along the 170 yards of cliff-top walk, up the slope and, finally, into the bushes.

Mr Funnell was no bigger than his wife and not much heavier. The task he claimed to have accomplished would be no easy one. A subsequent experiment conducted by Birmingham University showed that a fireman was able to perform the task of lifting and carrying a weight equivalent to Mrs Funnell's on his shoulders along the route from the house to the bushes only with difficulty. Firemen are accustomed to carrying people over their shoulders, whereas Mr Funnell was not. All the evidence demonstrated clearly that Mr Funnell did not murder his wife.

Why then did he confess to the murder? First, it has to be understood that false confessions are not rare or unusual; there are all kinds of reasons that make people confess to crimes they did not in fact commit. In the case of Mr Funnell, he was told by the police that if he had not committed the crime, then it was clear that his eldest son Stephen had. This suggestion was, of course, outrageous and unfounded, but Mr Funnell, in order to protect his son and spare his family further agony, confessed to a crime that he did not commit. He had hoped and believed that, once his case came to court, the truth would come out at the trial.

In spite of the results of the investigation by *Justice* and the BBC programme, Mr Funnell was not set free, but was eventually released on licence many years after the programme was shown.

The victims of murder are so often people whose lives are already broken and who live in despair. No-one is near to comfort or advise them, there is no promise of a glimmer of light at the end of the tunnel, no happy memories or pride of achievement to look back upon, no hope of future happiness or prosperity, no likelihood of being remembered when they are gone. It is difficult for more privileged people to understand this state of existence. Many of my forensic cases have given me an insight into the way such people live – unwanted people, readily dispensable. Often the crime is committed by a person equally lacking in hope or happiness.

One of the saddest cases I have known concerned the murder of a mentally-retarded young man. He was looked upon as a figure of fun by his 'mates' and one day he was set upon and killed, his body dumped beside a river. The horror is that those who committed this deed may have felt, genuinely, that this man's life did not have quite the same value as that of other people. I have known several murders of this kind.

One Thursday in early summer, I received a telephone call from the police. The officer told me that a man in his sixties had been murdered – stabbed in the chest several times. He had been found lying on his bed after his wife, also in her sixties, telephoned the police to say that she had killed him. She had rung them the previous morning, Wednesday, and they had called at her house later that day. She told them that she had stabbed her husband to death at around 9 o'clock on the evening before – Tuesday.

An initial pathologist's examination of the body had been carried out on the Wednesday at about 4 o'clock, when a large number of maggots were removed and preserved. The police wanted me to examine this evidence to establish the time of death beyond doubt and they intended to bring me the preserved specimens after the more extended post-mortem examination, to be carried out on the Friday.

When the scenes-of-crime officer arrived on Friday afternoon, he had a strange tale to tell. Apparently, the woman could not have murdered her husband, as the post-mortem showed that the 'stab wounds' were only very superficial cuts on the skin, none of which had penetrated deeply enough to cause serious injury or death. The matter of time of death now assumed greater importance since any further evidence might shed light on this intriguing mystery.

As soon as the officer left, I began my examination of the maggots. They belonged to a species known as the false stable fly (*Muscina pabulorum*), resembling as it does the true stable fly (*Stomoxys calcitrans*), a blood-sucking insect often found in farmyards. The false stable fly does not suck blood but lays its eggs on blood, even in the absence of a body. The maggots were at a relatively advanced stage of development and it was quite out of the question that the eggs from which they hatched had been laid only on Tuesday evening. Eggs laid on Tuesday would not have had enough time to hatch before the first post-mortem examination on Wednesday.

Clearly, the woman was lying, but why? I wrote my report, concluding that death or at least bleeding must have taken place on Sunday at the latest. Of course, it is possible that the woman might have inflicted injuries on her husband on several occasions, the last one being at 9 o'clock on Tuesday, but this last assault cannot have been the first one and bleeding from an earlier attack must be invoked to explain the stage of development of the maggots. If it was not the first attack then the man must have been infested with maggots some time before he died which is extremely unlikely.

What then was going on? Was there some complex mystery behind this charade? The answer was nothing so dramatic or sinister, merely apathy, ignorance and confusion. Both husband and wife had been unemployed for many years; he spent his time watching football on television and drinking beer; she spent hers drinking vodka in large quantities and telling her husband to stop watching football. Their house was dirty and strewn with empty vodka bottles and beer cans. Although they drank a great deal, they ate hardly anything. It was a home devoid of hope or cheer, and the woman, apparently bored sick by the constant television, went for her husband in a 'fit of irritation'. Note that I say *irritation* not rage – she was too apathetic to experience such a powerful emotion. It seems clear that she attacked him with a knife on the Sunday, inflicting a few minor scratches. At the coroner's inquest, I gave evidence that it was highly unlikely that death occurred on the Tuesday. The pathologist testified that his examination had revealed that the deceased had a serious heart condition and that he had suffered from heart attacks. It was eventually concluded that the woman must have attacked her husband in the bedroom on the Sunday and that he had suffered a heart attack, which was the cause of death. She then left him dead on the bed until Wednesday morning, when she thought of telephoning the police. She was drunk when the police arrived and they believed, on the basis of what appeared to be recently opened vodka bottles, that she had been drinking solidly since Sunday. Where she slept during those days is a mystery.

The verdict was death by misadventure. No action was taken against the woman who returned to her home and her drinking.

While murder is a dreadful fate to befall anyone, dying alone and neglected, knowing that no-one is aware of one's impending fate, must also be a horrible and tragic end for a human being. One day in early September, I received a somewhat unsettling telephone call from the police. The officer's voice sounded concerned and he was ill at ease as he gave me the details of the case. As I listened, I knew exactly what I wanted the conclusion of the investigation to be; never, before or since, had I wished that the evidence would give me the particular answer I wanted.

The dead body of an old man had been discovered on 31st August in a house that had been boarded up. He was lying in bed. His body was infested with maggots. He had no family or friends. Nobody knew anything about him. I knew what I was about to be asked to do. 'Doctor, can you tell us whether he died before or after the house was boarded up?' The thought of an old, clearly sick man lying helpless in his house, unable to do anything for himself or even to cry out as his house was being sealed in darkness from the outside world, was haunting.

The police officer had to take a flight from the north to bring me the entomological specimens from the body, so it was not until the following day that I had an opportunity to see them. When he arrived and handed me the tubes of specimens, I took a quick look at the maggots through the clear plastic of the tubes. They were relatively young maggots. I asked the officer for the date on which the house had been boarded up. 'The fourteenth of August', was the reply. I could have given him my answer there and then, but I did not. I asked to see the photographs taken during the post-mortem examination; I asked for the Meteorological Office's climatic data and their reconstructed temperatures in the house for the month of August; I wrote down the officer's detailed description of the house. I looked at all this with dismay. I told the officer that I would conduct a full examination of the evidence and send him my report.

I set to work on the specimens at once. The maggots belonged to a greenbottle species, flies that do not usually enter dark buildings, unless attracted by the strong scent of decomposition. Having dissected and slide-mounted the maggots, studied the temperature measurements, and considered the fact that the house had a number of points of entry through which flies could have reached the body with ease, I had to conclude that the old man had died *after* the house was boarded up. Not only that, but he had died at least a week after he was shut away from the world. Never have I wished my conclusions were other than they were. I wrote my report and sent it to the police. They telephoned to thank me, but, of course, nothing further happened. No crime had been committed, only a most tragic error.

A similar case in some respects to this one was when the police discovered an old man lying dead in a caravan in which he lived alone. The body was maggot-infested but the caravan had not been sealed; the door had been forced shut with an iron bar that had been planted in the ground outside and wedged under the handle of the door. The victim was found lying on the floor, as though he had fallen over. The date the door was barricaded was unknown, as was the identity of whoever had done it. It was not even possible to determine whether foul play had taken place, since the door could have been wedged closed after the man's death and it may have been an innocent act. The case was never solved.

Very soon after the caravan case, I became involved in the investigation of a murder of an old man in Wales. He had lived alone in a most odd-looking house; it was white-washed, but the window and door frames were painted bright red, giving it the appearance of an astonished human face. The yard in front of the house was littered with junk of all kinds – old wash-basins, broken chairs and tables, tyres, pots and pans, steering wheels, cardboard boxes, furniture with torn upholstery and many other things. Amid this wreckage lay the old man's body. He had been beaten with the utmost savagery.

There was very little entomological evidence on the body, except for some fly eggs around the man's eyes. These were removed, some being placed in liquid preservative and some kept alive and allowed to hatch. The maggots that hatched enabled me to determine the fly species; the preserved eggs allowed me to determine their age at the time of preservation. I was therefore able to conclude that death must have occurred at least twenty-four hours prior to the discovery of the body. In fact, taking the evidence as a whole, I concluded that in this case the minimum time of death was also the actual time of death.

I was very pleased with the results of my investigation, since I felt that the determination of time of death was particularly accurate. I sent my report to the police, only to discover later that it was greeted with disappointment; 'Is that all you can say?', was the response. The investigating officer felt that my estimate of time of death was far too vague and had expected an actual time, such as 2.43 p.m.; my conclusion of approximately 3.0 p.m. was not considered to be sufficiently exact.

I mention this not in a spirit of pique but to show how some police officers regard scientific evidence as being something akin to magic, endowed with a precision that is totally uncompromising. It is often said that lawyers demand that evidence should be presented in black and white, no shades of grey being permitted. In my experience, I have found this attitude to be much more prevalent among police officers than among lawyers.

The eggs of flies are fragile and delicate things and their ephemeral existence suggests that they are unlikely to be of great use as evidence. In fact, a number of cases have been solved on the basis of an examination of such evidence. Here, I cannot resist the temptation of retelling a case from Hungary, which illustrates this point particularly well.

The body of a postmaster was discovered on board a ferry some time after 6.0 p.m. one September evening. The captain had arrived at the ferry at 6 o'clock and was suspected of the murder, although he swore his innocence. At 4 o'clock the following evening a post-mortem examination of the body was carried out and a number of fly eggs and newly hatched maggots were found. However, no account of this evidence was taken at the trial and the captain was convicted and sent to prison.

Eight years later, the case was reopened and a new trial began. This time, however, the evidence of the fly eggs and newly hatched larvae was discussed. An entomologist, Dr Mihalyi of the Budapest Natural History Museum, gave evidence, saying that no corpse-breeding flies were active in September after 6.0 p.m., the temperature being too low to allow fly activity. In other words, the eggs had to have been laid either before 6 o'clock on the day of the murder or some time during the day of the post-mortem. The latter scenario was impossible because the eggs and larvae were at a far too advanced stage. The conclusion had to be that the flies had laid their eggs before 6 o'clock on the day of the murder, in other words, before the captain arrived at the ferry. On the basis of this and other evidence, the captain was released from prison.

As I have mentioned earlier, thousands of people go missing every year in most countries and what becomes of the majority is never discovered. Some such people are found, dead or alive, by accident. For example, some forty years ago, the body of a woman, who appeared not to have been missed, was discovered in July on Mt Tokusawa in Japan, 3,000 metres above sea level. The feet were covered with snow, but the rest of the body was exposed. Flies of various species were seen laying eggs on these exposed parts and there were egg masses as well as maggots of the blowfly species *Triceratopyga calliphoroides* – a wonderful name which sounds as though it ought to be that of a dinosaur! The pattern of infestation suggested that the head must have been exposed (i.e. free of snow cover) for about five days and the upper part of the trunk for two days. The absence of maggots from the feet and the absence of snow beneath the body indicated that death had occurred some time in September, before the first snow fell. Other evidence corroborated these conclusions.

It may seem strange to think of flies laying eggs while snow is lying on the ground but this, in fact, happens quite commonly if the air temperature is high enough. I have seen maggots feeding under a layer of snow in February in experimental rabbit carcasses that I had put out in the Cambridge University Botanic Garden. Often, in certain parts of the country flies will become active on warm, sunny days in winter and may lay eggs.

Rain too may play an important part in blowfly behaviour. It is said that some species can fly better than others in the rain, although many of these statements are based upon anecdotal evidence. Fleshflies, those large grey, chequered flies often seen basking on stone paths on hot summer days, are said to be particularly efficient at flying in the rain and, under such conditions, may well be the first to arrive at a corpse.

Saturday, 8th November 1862 was a cold, wet, miserable day in the little community of Hugglepitt at the edge of the village of Clovelly in Devon. Two little girls aged ten and two left their cottage and went for a walk in the woods. They were never seen alive again.

Eliza and Ellen were poor children. Their father, James Lee, was a farm labourer in the employ of the Lord of the Manor, Colonel Henry Hamlyn-Fane. James' wife, Mary, was Ellen's mother, but she was the stepmother of the older girl, Eliza. The Lees also had two sons, Billy and Charles. When James returned home on Saturday evening, his wife told him that the girls had left home earlier in the hope of meeting him on the way back from work, but James had not seen them. They did not return home that night and, strangely, no search was carried out.

When the children failed to return the following day, Sunday, the parents raised a limited hue and cry and began a search, with the help of other villagers, of all the places the children would have been likely to go, including the woods that lay to the north of Hugglepitt and stretched towards the sea. But they did not find the children that day.

The following day, Monday, James Lee took a day off work and reported the matter to the police. P.C. Richard Nicholls took charge of the case and immediately organized a further search with the help of other police officers, as well as local villagers. The searchers ranged far and wide, but they concentrated on the woods between Hugglepitt and the sea as being the most likely place to find the children, again without success.

On the Tuesday, P.C. Nicholls organized yet another search. This time he divided the search-party into four groups: one searched the woods to the north-west; a second, the woods to the north-east; a third, the cliff-tops by the sea; and a fourth, the beach between tides. There was still no sign of the children.

At this point, rumours began to circulate that the parents had murdered their children. Although there was no foundation for these allegations, *The North Devon Journal* asserted:

'The parents ... who should feel the deepest interest and manifest the greatest anxiety in the matter, shew almost a brutal indifference as to their [i.e. the children's] fate – an indifference that can only be accounted for by the demoralising effect of their dissolute habits'.

Further malicious rumours sprang up. The wicked stepmother, who was expecting another child, had murdered her stepdaughter (and presumably her own daughter, as well). Perhaps the children had been 'foully dealt with' by their parents and had been buried in the garden or thrown over a cliff. In view of these rumours, P.C. Nicholls felt obliged to question the parents. He even had the Lees' garden dug up, but he found no evidence of foul play.

As the frantic and unsuccessful searches continued, Henry Jenkins, a nineteen-year old ploughman, said that he had seen the children on the day of their disappearance. On Tuesday, 18th November, ten days after the children's disappearance, The Bideford Gazette reported the news in the following way:

'On Saturday se'ennight, about 5 o'clock, as Col. Fane's ploughman was about to leave work, he saw two children lying down under the hedge of a field; a girl about nine years of age and a younger child about two years old. They were asleep; the younger lying in the elder's arms. He aroused them and sent them towards their home and saw no more of them, nor have they been seen since. They were the children of a man named Lee, Col. Fane's waggoner. Hundreds of feeling hearted people were searching for them throughout Sunday and since but no tidings have yet come to hand. Five or six policemen have been there every day since and searched all the woods and cliffs and on Tuesday all the villagers turned out and made a thorough search'.

At noon on Thursday, 20th November, twelve days after the children went missing, P.C. Nicholls found their bodies in the woods to the north-east of Hugglepitt, fifty feet from the track. Eliza was lying on her back on the steep hillside. Close by, Ellen too was lying on her back but with her head downwards.

An inquest was held on the following day, Friday. The coroner, John Henry Toller, called four witnesses to give evidence, the first of whom was Henry Jenkins.

His evidence confirmed the observations of *The Bideford Gazette*, but he had much more to say. As well as seeing the girls at about a quarter to five, he had also seen them earlier in the day, at about ten minutes past two, on his return to the field after lunch. He said that Eliza had been collecting firewood and Ellen was standing by the pile already collected. Eliza told him that she was not going to collect any more wood until her brothers came, whereupon Jenkins said that, when the boys came, he would give Billy a penny to go and get some tobacco for him. Eliza said that she would get him the tobacco and, carrying her sister, left for the shop which was about half a mile distant. When she returned, Jenkins gave her a penny for her trouble. A little while later, he lost sight of the children, only to come across them again at a quarter to five. He then picked up Ellen and went back to his plough with Eliza walking beside him. He then told the girls to go home; Eliza made no reply, but taking Ellen in her arms, she went away.

The second witness was Elizabeth Bartlett, the farmer's wife from Hugglepitt Farm and the Lees' neighbour. She testified to the fact that Mr and Mrs Lee always treated the children well and that they were well fed.

P.C. Nicholls was the third witness. He gave an account of the searches and of the eventual finding of the bodies. He also said that Eliza had gone missing from home twice before. Finally, he said that he had no doubt that all the rumours about the parents were untrue.

Last of all came Dr W. H. Ackland, the medical examiner. He had conducted an external examination of the bodies, but not an internal one. He said that Eliza's legs had shown lividity on the front; that her eyes and mouth were wide open; that her throat was fuller than natural; that there were many scratches and abrasions on the body; and that her belly was flat. Regarding Ellen, Dr Ackland reported that her eyes and mouth were wide open; that there were scratches on the body; and that there were some maggots in the right eye and on the body. He said that he saw no signs of external violence on either body and that 'the putrefaction being decidedly influenced by the temperature of the air, it was very much retarded'. He concluded:

'I consider that death was produced by cold, accelerated by moisture in the form of sleet and rain. Sensibility under such circumstances speedily disappears and a state of torpor ensues, followed by profound sleep. In this state of lethargy the vital functions gradually cease and death takes place'.

A juryman asked the doctor whether he had any doubt that the children died on the night of their disappearance, but no reply is recorded. The jury did not retire to consider the evidence but returned an immediate verdict: 'Found dead in West Wood through exposure to the cold and inclemency of the weather'.

One hundred and thirty years passed. One evening, as I sat in my living room reading a book, the telephone rang. It was Mr Harry Clement, formerly a career detective at Scotland Yard, but now retired and living in his home village of Clovelly. He told me that he was researching the history of the disappearance and death of Eliza and Ellen, known locally as 'the Babes in the Wood', as he was dissatisfied with the verdict. He could not believe that the girls died on the night of their disappearance, and suspected that there might have been foul play. With the diligence practised during twenty-eight years of police detective work, he set about examining the evidence and reconstructing the most probable course of events. He contacted me because he wanted to know the significance of the maggots found on Ellen's body, but he first explained the reasons for his doubts about the jury's conclusion.

The most baffling aspect of the case was the fact that the bodies of the children were not found until twelve days after their disappearance, despite many painstaking searches of the woods. How could hundreds of villagers and several policemen, searching daily for twelve days, have failed to find them? Also, the girls were found only fifty feet inside the woods from the track, which meant that they could have been seen very easily by anyone almost as soon as they entered the woods. The bodies were discovered less than three-quarters of a mile from their home. The girls knew the area very well and frequently walked back and forth across it and it is highly unlikely that they could have lost their way.

The medical evidence too was curious. The flatness of Eliza's belly, even allowing for retarded putrefaction, is incompatible with death having taken place twelve days earlier. The belly would have been distended. Marks of lividity, such as those observed by Dr Ackland on the front of Eliza's legs, are caused by the action of gravity on the blood after death and occur on that part of the body lying closest to the ground; in other words, such marks should have been on the backs of Eliza's legs, unless the position of the body was changed after death. The fullness of Eliza's throat and the wide open mouths and eyes of both girls suggest foul play, possibly manual strangulation.

The absence of any sign of interference with the bodies by wild animals was also puzzling, especially after twelve days at a cold time of year when creatures such as foxes, crows and rats would be expected to have fed upon them. Moreover, the position of Ellen's body was most unusual, since one would not normally go to sleep on a hillside with one's feet higher up the slope than one's head. The evidence seemed to suggest that the girls had not died on the night of their disappearance but later, possibly on the night of 19th/20th November when their bodies were placed in the woods.

I listened with great interest to Mr Clement's arguments and felt sure he had a compelling case against the jury's verdict.* He then asked me what the presence of the maggots implied and whether it supported his point of view.

The weather during the twelve days in question was described in contemporary accounts as being cold and windy, with rain and sleet. According to the Devon Record Office, the average temperature for November in Devon is about 6.2°C. The chill factor of wind, sleet and rain would have lowered the temperature still further. No British fly species known to breed in carrion will lay eggs at such temperatures. The conclusion is that the bodies must have lain in a building of some sort, such as a barn or stable, in which flies might have been active in the warm straw usually found there. In a field bordering the part of the wood in which the bodies were found was just such a building. If death had been due to exposure to cold and rain, then flies would not have been active at the time. The inescapable conclusion towards which one is drawn is that the girls were abducted, kept somewhere for most of the twelve days, then killed and subsequently deposited in the woods.

The obvious question leaps to mind – who did it? Mr Clement entertained the possibility that Jenkins might have committed the crime, perhaps because he had attempted to assault Eliza sexually. Whether he failed or succeeded in his attempt, both girls would have had to be silenced. Mr Clement supported this theory by drawing

* Mr Clement has since written a book about this and other cases. Please see references.

attention to the fact that a penny was a very large sum of money for a ploughman to give to a young girl merely for buying some tobacco. On this point, it is not possible to know the truth on the basis of the available evidence. We can, however, be reasonably sure that the children did not die of exposure, but were murdered.

So after 130 years a case of murder has come to light, though it must be said that even back in 1862 there appear to have been some doubts and yet no action was taken. Commenting on the results of the inquest, *The Western Morning News* wrote:

> 'The melancholy fate of the two poor unfortunate children is one of the most painful that we have had to record for some time ... perishing in the woods within half-a-mile of their home ... It is quite clear that they did not miss their way in the woods, as their bodies were found close to the road – a road which the elder girl knew very well ... It is astonishing that the bodies should have remained so long undiscovered, in spite of the efforts made by the policemen, Nicholls, Dunsford and Brimacombe to recover the bodies, and when found they were not in a state of decomposition, and yet the medical opinion is they died the first night'.

Today, a visitor to the woods near Hugglepitt will find a stone memorial to the two girls, commemorating the spot where their bodies were found. Inexplicably, it is not in the right place but some way to the north of the true site. The date of discovery is given, also incorrectly, as 19th November. A flawed memorial, but a memorial nevertheless; the inquest and the verdict were flawed too, so there is a sad symmetry to it all.

I was crawling on my hands and knees over a mound of sacks in a house that was filled with sacking from the floor to half-way to the ceiling. It was the only way of reaching the inner room where the body of a woman had been discovered. The house was filthy; it was infested with rats, the smell was offensive and it was very hot.

As is often the case in forensic work, the telephone call that had brought me here came late at night. It was an officer from a north of England constabulary – could I come early the following morning to assist with the investigation of a suspicious death? He offered to send a car to fetch me at 6 a.m. The car duly arrived in Cambridge at the appointed hour and I reached my destination before mid-day.

The house in which the body had been found was situated on the outskirts of a village. When I arrived I found that the natural curiosity of the villagers had got the better of them, for the police were having some difficulty in keeping the small crowd away from the door so that police and forensic work could proceed unhampered. The house, although now in a quite dilapidated state, must have been a rather fine residence earlier in its history. I remember seeing fine wood carvings on the staircase and around the door-frames, and the rooms were large with high ceilings. Now, it was used simply as a storehouse for cloth sacks and its owner lived elsewhere.

When I reached the inner room, I found it teeming with huge numbers of small moths and caterpillars and in the middle of the room, seated upon a pile of sacking, was Professor Alan Usher, the pathologist. The body was lying under a metal table, so firmly wedged between its legs and their connecting bars that it could not be moved without damage. The body, of course, had to be kept intact until the post-mortem examination. As the problem of how to extract it was being pondered, I ventured to suggest that what we needed was a metal saw to dismantle the table. Miraculously, such an implement was produced almost immediately and the task of sawing the table apart began. While the dismantling was in progress, I turned my attention to the rest of the room and began gathering specimens. The number of moths and their caterpillars was truly vast and, as I was busy collecting, preserving and labelling, a blue object lying in a corner of the room caught my eye. I could not help smiling as I picked it up and showed it round the assembled company, to their great amusement. The police photographer insisted on taking a photograph of me holding the amusing article. One witty officer said that here was a case for prosecution under the Trade Descriptions Act – the cause of the mirth was a book of carpet samples labelled 'Guaranteed Moth-Proof'!

Meanwhile, the area around the table and the body was being cleared of sacking. Suddenly, one of the officers called out, not loudly but in an urgent tone of voice. We all looked at him. He held in his hand a piece of sacking which he placed to one side, then slowly picked up two objects with his gloved hands. They were a cup and a small plate that had been used as a saucer – strange things to find in such a place lying beside a dead body. Their significance was soon to become apparent, although I suspect that most people present had already guessed it.

The work of recovering the body was long and tedious but when it was over we did not leave immediately. It was hot and uncomfortable in that dingy place and it was suggested that a cold drink was in order. Someone went away and returned some minutes later with a tray laden with glasses. So, the work over for the moment, we all drank cold orange juice in those grisly surroundings.

The remains were eventually placed in a body-bag and taken swiftly to the ambulance, which left for the mortuary. We all emerged into the sunlight, having removed our white overalls, gloves, masks and other protective clothing. It was time for lunch.

Later, the post-mortem took place and I conducted my examination. Together with samples I collected at the scene, I was able to recover no fewer than thirteen moth species, all small and of the 'clothes-moth' kind. The caterpillars of these insects can survive for long periods without water, being able to metabolize water by breaking certain chemical bonds in keratin, the substance that forms such structures as hair and fingernails. Their presence suggested death some years earlier; indeed, such a conclusion was already obvious, as the body was quite desiccated; in fact, it was almost mummified. Before finishing my examination, I discovered that another kind of insect had visited the body. There were several puparia of a blowfly species known as *Phormia terraenovae*, which favours northern and upland areas, and colder places generally. Where it is found, it is usually the first blowfly to appear as the weather becomes warmer and its discovery in this case suggested that death had occurred in the spring.

When the police investigation was complete, it was found that death had, indeed, occurred in the spring, four years earlier. It was a sad case, not of murder, but of something that was, in a way, even more tragic. The young woman, who was identified by her clothing, was known to have had periods of extreme depression. In the end, she could no longer bear living. She went to the cloth-sack house, which belonged to her father, and lay down among the sacks. Alone, she committed suicide, using the cup to take the poison. Four years later, her father found her body.

Suicide is the ultimate act of despair. To most people, it may seem to be a rare event but, unhappily, it is common enough. It is said that most suicides are committed around Christmas time when unhappy, lonely people feel their unhappiness and loneliness most acutely.

I have been involved in the investigation of only a few cases of suicide, but insect evidence is often very useful in them. Maggots have the remarkable ability to store in their tissues many of the chemical compounds that have been ingested by a person before death, a fact that has been exploited very effectively in many cases. Where the tissues of a corpse have been largely consumed by maggots, to the extent that there is little tissue for a toxicologist to analyse, the maggots themselves can be tested to see whether they have fed upon a compound poisonous to humans. For example, there are cases in which the tissues of the maggots were analysed and showed that the ingestion of barbital was the cause of death. Even when there is enough human tissue for toxicological analysis, it is also advisable to analyse the tissues of the maggots because the victim's tissues, being in the process of decomposition, may well give misleading results. It is better by far to analyse living tissues than dead ones. Nevertheless, maggots that have developed in the corpses of people who have taken large quantities of poison or drugs must be examined with care since some drugs, such as heroin, may shorten the time of development of the maggots of many species. Curiously, this is not the case with all fly species, some being apparently totally unaffected by such drugs.

A particularly apt example is a case in Germany that was investigated by Dr Mark Benecke. One day, a woman known to have been a heroin addict committed suicide by laying her neck on a rail in the path of a moving train. The headless body, when found, was infested with cheese skippers, whose age was determined on the basis of knowledge acquired from studies of the development under more normal conditions, i.e. in tissues not containing heroin. The known date of her disappearance fitted well with the time expected for the larvae to reach the stage in which they were found, so it would seem that heroin has no effect on the developmental rate of cheese skippers.

Another of Dr Benecke's cases illustrates the fact that bacteria can also be picked up by the maggots and may reveal that the victim was diseased. Puparia removed from the body had a distinctive red colour, which suggested the presence of the bacterium, *Serratia marcescens*, which is known to be pathogenic in people whose immune system is not functioning well. The victim in this case was known to have been in poor health.

The presence of certain compounds or elements in the human body and their accumulation by maggots has other applications in forensic entomology. The following case from Finland shows how the analysis of maggot tissues can help ascertain the normal place of residence of a murder victim. An unidentified young female hitch-hiker was murdered in July and the police set to work trying to establish her identity. As some parts of Finland are heavily mercury-polluted and others not, the police took maggots from the body to Dr Erkki Häsänen of the Reactor Laboratory in Otaniemi and asked him to establish the concentration of mercury in the body. Normal levels do not exceed 0.2 parts per million but Dr Häsänen found that the concentration of mercury in the girl's body was only between 0.12 and 0.15 parts per million. In other words, she almost certainly did not reside in an area with high levels of mercury pollution. Eventually, when the girl's identity was established, she was found to have been a resident of Turku, a city devoid of mercury pollution.

It is said that most serious crime today is related in some way to addictive drugs. Undoubtedly, most police officers believe this to be so. A robbery is committed to acquire funds for purchasing drugs; a murder is committed to dispose of a rival drug 'pusher'; life and property are destroyed whilst the criminal is under the influence of the drug itself. There can be no doubt that drug abuse and drug trafficking are among the world's greatest curses. In the United States, about one-eighth of the population has used drugs at one time or another – a figure of some thirty million people, equal to half the population of the United Kingdom. The role of drugs in destroying people's lives cannot possibly be overstated.

It may be nothing but a commonplace to say to oneself *What a waste!* on beholding the wretched state of a drug addict and knowing that, whatever happens, his future life will be lived in the shadow of his indulgence. Health, spirit and reputation will have been sacrificed for nothing. Observations such as these have come to be seen as trite, simply because they have been repeated so often. Repetition, however, does not weaken the truth of a statement. Perhaps most people have not seen the full horror of the effects of drugs on young men and women.

If my own experience can be considered representative, most drug addicts are young. At any rate, I have not known a case involving an old drug addict. It was sad to deal with the murder of a young Frenchman who came to England to attend a 'festival', only to be stabbed to death during an argument about drugs; or with the case of a young girl dying of her addiction in a public lavatory in London; or with the case of a young student choking on his vomit while taking drugs.

I have had several cases of murder in which both the victim and the perpetrator were drug addicts or drug 'pushers' or both. Most of these were quite straightforward, but a few were noteworthy for various reasons. It was during one such case that I became aware of the full extent of the readiness of some barristers to use quite extraordinary ploys to win their cases. This particular one concerned the killing of one drug addict by another, the victim's body having been discovered in a wood. About two weeks before the trial, I had gone over the evidence with the prosecuting barrister, a distinguished Q.C., and it seemed an open-and-shut case. However, on the day of the trial the Q.C. fell seriously ill and his junior, a very young man, had to appear in court in his place. The young prosecutor was nervous and unsure of himself and seemed awed by the presence of the older, more experienced, barrister for the defence. I went into the witness box and stood, waiting to be examined. The young barrister also stood silently for a while, seeming to collect his thoughts before starting his examination. Almost every time he asked me a question, the defence Q.C. would cough; or utter a low, contemptuous-sounding laugh; or look at the jury and smile indulgently, as if to indicate that the young fellow did not know what he was doing. The effect on the young barrister was clearly unsettling. He stammered; he repeated his questions; he got in a muddle; all of which made the senior man redouble his efforts to undermine him. The prosecution lost the case.

Many drug murders have an international dimension. Often, the very manner in which the crime is committed reveals its international character. Firearm murders, other than by shotguns, are rare in Britain, but are much commoner in the United States. In Britain, most murders are committed using a knife, a blunt instrument or bare hands, although shotguns are sometimes used in rural areas where such weapons are close at hand. Murder by handgun is very unusual so when one comes across such a case, an international, or at least foreign, dimension must be entertained.

Some years ago, at the height of summer, a known American drug-dealer in his thirties was found shot dead in his flat in the Midlands. The windows of several rooms were open and flies would have had no difficulty in entering the flat. The body itself was heavily maggot-infested and the deceased's girlfriend had the horrible experience of discovering it. When she arrived at the flat, to which she had a key, she found him seated in an armchair. Thinking he was asleep, she came closer and removed a cushion that was lying on the body, only to be met with the horrific sight. She was hysterical for several days after-wards. The case was indeed one of international drug-dealing and its investigation took the police to New York, among other places. It is interesting to note that the case might not have been so easy to inves-tigate had the victim been killed in a more British fashion!

It was possible to determine the time of death with a high degree of accuracy, but the maggot infestation did not follow the usual pattern as it was not distributed around the body in the manner one would normally expect. We have already seen that flies normally lay their eggs in the ears, eyes and other moist orifices where the eggs are less likely to dry out. The hatching maggots move from these areas to the rest of the body, usually as one great mass. In this case, the maggots were found mainly around the waist and the neck, although many were in the face. This odd distribution was explained by the presence of bullet wounds in the body – wounds that would produce the same conditions as a normal egg-laying site. Indeed, they would be more attractive to the flies, since they would be particularly moist and would give off more powerfully attractive odours.

The odd distribution of the maggots did not tell us anything that was not already known, since the presence of the bullets revealed the manner of death. However, in cases where the victim had been stabbed with a knife in, say, the chest, the abnormal distribution of the mag-gots would indicate that death had occurred in such a way, especially if the tissues around the wound had been consumed by the maggots, leaving no recognizable wound for the medical examiner to diagnose as such. In such cases, of course, the instrument of death would not be embedded in the body or the background, so the manner of death would not be discoverable by direct evidence.

One spring day a man walking his dog came upon a shallow grave in the woods. Parts of a man's body were protruding above the surface of the soil. Both feet, part of the left leg, the left hand and part of the left forearm had been eaten by animals. The body was excavated under the supervision of Professor John Hunter, a forensic archaeologist, whose expertise enables him to reconstruct the manner in which a body has been buried. He concluded that the burial could not have taken place earlier than late the previous year, since there was an absence of leaf-mould upon the area of disturbance on and around the burial site. The body must have been buried after all the leaves had fallen. The pathologist's conclusions supported this view. In addition, the post-mortem revealed that the man had been strangled to death with bare hands.

As the time of death was an important facet of the case, the police invited me to join the investigation. The insect fauna on the body was surprisingly rich, especially in the light of the paucity of fauna in that woodland's soil. The larvae of a small fly called a heleomyzid were present in some numbers on the body, suggesting that the burial probably took place at the end of winter or in early spring because eggs laid before winter would not have survived to produce larvae. It may be argued that the body might have been *in situ* for some time earlier and that the flies only laid their eggs when the climatic conditions became favourable. This however could not have happened because, had death occurred earlier, the body would not have been attractive to the flies when the air temperature rose since the volatile compounds (i.e. the odours) that attract these flies to the body for egg-laying would have disappeared and the flies would not have laid eggs. Consequently, there would have been no larvae present had the body been buried much earlier.

An interesting fact about these heleomyzid flies is that they will often lay their eggs on the surface of the soil above a buried body. Unlike most other corpse-breeding flies, the hatching larvae will burrow into the soil to reach and feed upon the body, which explains their presence underground. In other words, their presence does not necessarily mean that the body must have lain exposed for some time before burial, a conclusion one would have been forced to arrive at had certain other fly species been involved. Other insects, mainly beetles predatory upon maggots, were present on the corpse; there were also species that fed upon tree roots, which were near the burial spot.

The burial must have taken place earlier in the year of discovery, not during the previous year. The entomological conclusions supported both the pathological and archaeological ones. But who was the victim? This was a truly international case. The man was a drug-dealer, who was wanted for trafficking, robbery and murder in half a dozen countries. A diary found in his jacket pocket contained the names, addresses and telephone numbers of his contacts and associates. It was a great gift to the investigating CID officer.

The strong association that many insects have with specific host plants in different parts of the world has been exploited as a method of identifying the geographical origin of such plants. A particularly important forensic application of this link is the identification of the place of cultivation of drug plants such as cannabis. In such cases, the raw drug plant will contain very many specimens and fragments of insects – those who smoke cannabis are probably unaware that they smoke appreciable numbers of insects as well! Although I have been involved in a few cases of this kind, this is not an area in which I have much experience. A celebrated case from New Zealand illustrates how these entomological remains may be used to good effect in police investigations.

Over a period of time the New Zealand Police made a number of seizures of packages of cannabis. Their investigations suggested that three individuals might have been involved in an operation importing cannabis from the area known as the Golden Triangle of Burma, Thailand and Malaysia. In view of this, it was essential to discover whether the cannabis found in the possession of one of the suspects was indeed imported and to determine the place of origin of the drug plant. To do this, forensic scientists and a team of entomologists from all over the world, including many from the Natural History Museum in London, examined insect specimens isolated from the cannabis. Of the species that were identified only one, the rice weevil *Sitophilus oryzae*, a cosmopolitan pest of stored grain, was known to occur in New Zealand. Other insects had more interesting distributions; a wasp, *Tropimerus monodon*, is known only from South-East Asia and a beetle, *Gonocnemis minutus*, lives in termite nests. Another beetle, *Azarelius sculpticollis*, is very rare and is known only from Burma (especially from the Tenasserim region) and Sumatra. A vicious ant species, *Pheidologeton diversus*, is restricted to South-East Asia as are two other beetle species recovered from the cannabis. Of special interest was the wasp, *Parapristina verticellata*, which is a pollinator of a particular species of fig.

The known distributions of these and other insects from the cannabis were delineated on transparent maps, which were laid over one another, revealing the area in which all the recovered species were known to occur together. The evidence pointed to the cannabis having been grown in the Tenasserim region of Burma, within 500 km of the Thai capital, Bangkok. In addition, the entomological investigation revealed that the site from which the cannabis had been harvested was adjacent to a stream or lake, that fig trees and termite mounds were in the vicinity and that ants capable of discouraging human habitation were present in the area.

Dogs have long been used to sniff out drugs. Less well-known is the fact that pigs are also used in this way, especially when seeking buried drugs. Their natural tendency to dig and root out acorns and truffles makes them well suited to this activity.

On a lighter note, some years ago, I assisted the BBC in making a film about the use of animals and plants in the investigation of crime. In one scene I had to appear beside a Vietnamese pot-bellied pig, Primrose by name, while holding its halter. Those who watched the film saw a man calmly explaining the impressive ability of pigs to find concealed drugs; they also saw a pig contentedly munching some food. This scene, I feel bound to say, gave a very misleading impression of what took place before it was filmed. It took more than an hour to cajole Primrose to leave her shelter and an additional half-hour to convince her that I was not her mortal enemy. The piercing squeals and screams that came from this animal brought onlookers from afar to see what was going on. One of the film-making team sought to explain the situation by telling the crowd that we were making a film about murder. I have no doubt that they believed him; the vocal evidence was compelling.

CHAPTER 6

A Medley of Madness

*'Insanity is not a distinct and separate empire; our ordinary life
borders upon it and we cross the frontier in some part of our nature.'*
Hippolyte Taine, *Notes on Paris*

We all have blind spots, attitudes that are not quite rational. As a forensic scientist, I came across many examples of strange and unnatural
behaviour, other than the criminal. People with the strangest ideas and
oddest stories wrote me letters that can only be described as bizarre, to
use a much abused word. Some of these people were harmless cranks;
some were merely trying to do good in a misguided kind of way; but
others were explicitly malicious. It was not unusual for me to receive
letters expressing quite forthright (and unflattering) views of my abilities and character.

'Personally I do not think or believe you are the expert you claim to
be ...', was the opinion of one correspondent. 'You are a disgrace', was
the view of another. Typically, the authors of these letters did not give
the reasons for their beliefs, but they clearly held their views very
strongly. Reading between the lines, it was sometimes possible to conclude that the writer simply objected to my work because of its perceived macabre nature; other people seemed to think that I exploited
criminal acts for my own benefit; if there were no crime, I would not
have been able to practise my profession, so it is clear that I had a
strong interest in increasing the rates of crime. Interestingly, some
people believed that I could not possibly achieve results that were
helpful to the police through the study of insects – that it was simply

not credible that insects could shed light on the circumstances of a crime. Such people considered the whole subject fraudulent and any practitioner of it a charlatan.

Others wrote to me about their views concerning the ways in which bodies should be dealt with after death. Some wrote passionately about aerial burials, in which the dead should be left hanging in the open to decompose completely. These people feel that conventional burial is simply a matter of cultural indoctrination, a complex or 'hang-up' that should be discarded. The intensity with which these views are held is quite remarkable; the authors often give the impression that they are articulating a profound but uncomfortable truth which the rest of humanity is conspiring to suppress.

Some letters were amusing, such as the one that stated confidently that the future of my subject was limited, since there would soon be no dead bodies left for me to examine. 'I think people often prefer to be cremated rather than face a long period of decomposition ...' was this gentleman's considered opinion.

A particularly strange letter was one I received from a woman in Australia on a bleak winter morning, when I was working at Durham University. The letter was sent to the 'Scientific University of Durham'. It ran:

> 'Dear Dr Erzinçlioğlu,
> I have available descents of Durham and other places for sale:
> 1 Uncremated Body, English Lawyer, Female, 1963
> 1 Cremated Male, 1974
> 1 Cremated Female, 1980
> 1 Cremated Male, 1989, with Queen's Birthday Honours, 1973
> Please advise if the above would be of value to you for scientific research. Carefully stored at this time in Collins Bank. I own the rights.'

Beneath the signature were the words 'Durham, 1832'.

It was difficult to know what to do with this letter. In the end I sent a copy of it to the police who looked into the matter. They eventually concluded that the woman was harmless, if deranged.

Apart from letters concerning the writers' views on crime, death and other things relating to forensic matters, I also received many specifically entomological enquiries, both by letter and telephone. Most of these were, of course, quite reasonable, but some were very amusing.

There is a rather unusual but quite interesting book entitled *Why Not Eat Insects?*, written by a Victorian clergyman named Holt and published in 1885. I once received a letter from someone who managed to confuse me with the Reverend Holt. The correspondent said that he needed a copy of my book *Why Not Eat Insects?* urgently; in case I did not know, he told me, the publication date was 1885. He commended me on the good sense that I had demonstrated in writing the book and expressed a hope that the world would listen to my radical ideas on the subject. Apart from the fact that the book was an entomological one, I cannot understand why my correspondent thought I was the author. Neither my name nor title had any connection with those of the true author, not to mention the fact that I was born in a different century! The curious thing was that my correspondent used my correct name on the envelope (clearly that is how the letter reached me), but addressed me as the long deceased Reverend Holt in the letter.

Some of the strangest letters I received had to do with the subject of evolution. I suspect that most biologists receive letters from people with odd views on this subject, since it is seen as impinging on all human thought and understanding. Many people, misunderstanding the ideas of evolutionary theory, feel that it represents a threat to their beliefs, a threat that is totally imaginary. Letters from such people tend to be particularly forceful and, sometimes, quite harsh and vindictive.

I once wrote a letter to the British scientific journal *Nature* in which I expressed disagreement with the widespread usage of a particular scientific term, believing this to be misleading and confusing. Subsequently, a distinguished American scientist wrote to *Nature*, addressing the points I had made and disagreeing, quite properly and amicably, with some of my views. This had a most unexpected result. Some weeks after the professor's article appeared, I received a most virulent, not to say violent, letter from an American army officer in California. Colonel X, as I shall call him, 'congratulated' me on my original article which, he claimed, brought the professor 'out into the open'. The colonel's opinion of the professor and his views on what should happen to him were of a kind that would have brought him (the colonel) into serious trouble had the contents of his letter become public. The man's vindictiveness was extraordinary, even for an extreme religious fanatic, which is what the colonel must have been. A puzzling aspect of the letter was that the articles in *Nature* had nothing to do with evolution as such, but merely an evolutionary term; in other words, my article was of a similar kind to that of the American professor. I should have been equally 'guilty' so far as the colonel was concerned, yet I was congratulated while the professor was attacked. I must assume that the colonel had developed a particular hatred for the professor, whose popular writings are well-known and read throughout the world.

Perhaps the strangest letter – or series of letters – that I have ever received were those that kept arriving on my desk from an individual in the Far East. They are the strangest, not merely because of their content, but because they were written by a man who was a university lecturer and scientific researcher. The subject was evolution and the contents were disturbing, coming as they did from someone in his position.

The first letter, whilst written in a slightly odd style, was quite normal. It was a request to come to England to work on an evolutionary research project with me. I replied, regretting that I did not have the necessary research funds to support him if he came to Cambridge and suggesting others to whom he could write. Unfortunately, I also asked him to let me know the nature of the project he had in mind so that I could copy his letter to other members of staff.

After some weeks, he replied. His project, he said, was concerned with a revolutionary idea of his own devising. He had had the deep insight (his own words) that, in evolutionary history, new species are generated in threes, not in twos, as is usually stated. Dichotomous evolution is false, he said, for do we not speak of 'false dichotomies'? Species, he asserted, are generated by *trichotomous* evolution.

I should, perhaps, explain at this point that it is generally believed that new species come into existence when some members of an existing species are isolated from the rest and start a lineage in a somewhat different environment. Thus, some members of a particular bird species may become isolated on an island where the nuts that form the birds' diet have a harder shell. Individuals with more powerful beaks would be able to cope with the new environment better than those with less powerful beaks. Over a period of time, the descendants of these island birds will all have developed powerful beaks, since those with inadequate beaks will have failed to survive and produce offspring. The birds will also have evolved various other attributes that the original (or 'parent') species did not have. These island birds will have become a separate species, incapable of merging once again with the population from which their ancestors came. Thus, what was once a single species has now split into two.

My Far Eastern correspondent was implacably opposed to this idea, claiming that species always split in three ways. Of course this may happen if individuals from a population are isolated in three, or more than three, different environments at the same time, but the basic premise is that any particular species splits off in the way described above. The letter-writer gave no reason for his opposition to this. His compelling insight that trichotomies were the rule had shaken the roots of civilization. He believed that his idea was so radical and earth-shaking that his university authorities had victimized him as a result and all his attempts to leave the country and come to England had been sabotaged.

But this was not the end of the matter. He believed that everything could be seen or explained in threes. He invoked the Holy Trinity. He pointed out that he had three christian names himself, a fact which he seemed to think clinched the matter. He could speak three languages (and presumably spoke about trichotomies in all three); three nations had occupied his small country in historic times; his country was feared throughout the world because it had three names; he had three children, and so on.

In spite of all this, I kept my promise and showed his letters to some of my colleagues. Understandably, none of them wished to have him as a work colleague. I wrote back and said that no one was in a position to invite him to their laboratory, but the letters continued to come. It was an international conspiracy against him, he wrote. They were all jealous of him. He was about to make a public announcement that would change the world, if only he could come to Cambridge and declaim his new message. His letters would include mysterious mathematical 'formulae', which, he said, supported his conclusions. These so-called formulae were in the following general form:

$$0.000111222333444555666777888999 \times 3 = \text{evolutionary trichotomies.}$$

Presumably, the series of thrice repeated figures was significant. In the end I stopped answering his letters. Some time later, I discovered that somebody at another university had started to receive his missives.

Telephone calls, I find, can be a source of great amusement as well as of irritation. One day I received a call from a man who said that he had found a most extraordinary moth. It was huge, he said, so huge he was convinced it came from the moon. I asked him whether it was a kind of hawkmoth, but the suggestion seemed to offend him. No, no, he said, with some impatience, it was not a hawkmoth; he knew very well what a hawkmoth looked like. As usual in cases of this sort, I asked the man to bring the specimen to me, which he did. It was a hawkmoth; specifically, a poplar hawkmoth (*Laothoe populi*), which, although a large and striking creature, is not by any means the largest hawkmoth to be found in Britain. The man seemed quite disappointed.

This feeling of 'let down' when an insect or any other creature is identified not as a previously unknown organism but as something quite ordinary is very common. A particularly good example of this was that of a man who telephoned with what he said was an urgent message; his cat had brought in a 'flying creature with a man's head'. I asked for further clarification; was it a bat, perhaps? No, said the man, it was most definitely not a bat. Was it alive? I asked. No, it was dead. I asked him to bring it in. He arrived a few minutes later, carrying a box and looking very serious – a man on an important mission. Of course, I could not wait to see what the monstrous creature was. I placed the box on the laboratory bench, opened it and picked up the strange organism with a pair of forceps. It was a dragonfly. In what was, I confess, a very cold tone of voice, I told the man that his flying creature with the head of a man was a specimen of a fairly common dragonfly species. He behaved as if I had short-changed him. Is *that* all? he asked, in a tone that suggested that he might have got a more interesting identification from someone else. I stood up, handed the fellow his box and bade him good day. He left, sulkily.

One of the errors many people make when they telephone to ask for the identification of an insect or other animal is to act as though a cursory description should enable one to identify it. So, one receives telephone calls from people who say things like, 'I found a small black insect walking across the carpet. Can you tell me what it is, please?' Of course, such a description would fit, literally, many thousands of species and it is quite impossible to identify anything on that basis. Often, the description, as far as it went, would turn out to be incorrect, the 'small, black insect' turning out to be quite a large, multi-coloured creature, with some black coloration on its abdomen. So, when I received a call from a very agitated woman, saying that she had found 'a horrible thing with sixteen legs', I was sceptical. I asked her whether she meant that it had quite a few legs, or that it had sixteen legs exactly? She reiterated that it had exactly sixteen legs, which were very long, but the creature itself had a perfectly round body. I could not think what it could be. The perfectly round body meant that it could not be a centipede or a millipede, which are very elongate creatures, even if she had miscounted the legs. (Centipedes and millipedes have considerably more than sixteen legs.) Giving up, I asked her to bring it in but, as she lived in a distant town, she said she would post it.

The parcel arrived a day or two later. I opened it to find a small creature with a round body and a number of what appeared to be legs. I counted them: there were sixteen. The animal was, in fact, a harvestman, a creature similar in appearance to a spider, but with very long legs. Children sometimes call them 'daddy-long-legs', although they are not related to the familiar winged insects of that name. Harvestmen, like spiders, have only eight legs, but the specimen I had been sent had just shed its skin, which had remained attached to the body of the animal. So there were eight actual legs, plus another eight leg 'skins'. The woman had counted them all, believing that they were all functional legs. In that sense, her description was quite accurate.

Some specific insects are the cause of inevitable enquiries during the summer months. Wasps are one such group. During a particular summer when the German Government had been criticized in the British Press for its alleged meddling in the affairs of countries within what was then the European Community, wasps were prevalent in some parts of England and Wales and I received quite a few telephone calls about them. There are several wasp species in Britain, one of which is known as the German wasp (*Vespula germanica*). Several callers, having heard of this creature, telephoned to ask me whether these *German* insects had occurred in Britain before it joined the European Common Market. The implication was that the Germans had introduced these unpleasant insects into Britain for some sinister purpose!

The largest British wasp is the hornet (*Vespa crabro*), a truly formidable insect. It is not surprising that many people who come across one are frightened by it; most people in Britain have never seen one, as it is not a common insect here. Many people who find one are therefore convinced that it is a species previously unknown in this country. Another large wasp-like creature is the wood wasp (*Urocerus gigas*), which has a very long and dangerous-looking spike at the end of its body. Although belonging to the same group of insects as wasps, the wood wasp is a very different creature. The spike is not a sting as so many people quite naturally believe, but an ovipositor, a structure through which the eggs are laid. In spite of its large size and threatening appearance, it is, in fact, a totally harmless insect.

The other insects that never fail to attract attention during the summer months are thrips, better known as 'thunderbugs' because they are associated with warm, humid weather. These are very small insects resembling a short dash made by a pen on a piece of paper. They are usually extremely numerous during July and August and can be a great nuisance, crawling over people's faces and into their hair, getting between the pages of books and behind the glass of framed pictures. They spend most of their time in flowers and, despite the irritation caused by their intrusive behaviour, they are quite harmless. Nonetheless they are often accused of the most serious crimes. During one year when the numbers of thrips were particularly great, I received many telephone calls from journalists and broadcasters, asking me to confirm or refute the rumours that these insects were the carriers of plague and other diseases. One reporter told me that, in one part of the country, people were saying that they expected to be totally wiped out as a result of the unwelcome attentions of these insects. I was interviewed on the radio and by the newspapers and was obliged to emphasize that these creatures were, in fact, completely innocent of disease-carrying habits. Whether this hysteria was encouraged, or even started, by the reporters for the sake of generating a 'story' I do not know, but there did seem to be genuine concern among certain sections of the population!

Stories in the Press sometimes have to be taken with large pinches of salt. The entomological, zoological and other scientific misinformation that is published in the newspapers is so great that it is not possible to give even a brief account of it here and there is certainly no space to go into great detail. I will therefore restrict myself to one remarkable story, published in *The Times* no less, and brought to my attention by my colleague, Roger Northfield. This story claimed that mice had become abundant in Britain in recent years because of the extinction of the lynx and the wild boar in the country! Apparently, lynxes used to prey upon the mice, and boars used to trample them to death. Now that these animals no longer existed in Britain, the article claimed, the mouse population had soared. Setting aside the absurdity of the idea that mice were trampled by wild boars, these animals became extinct in Britain during the sixteenth century. As for the lynx, there is no evidence that it ever existed in Britain during historic times!

While telephone conversations with police officers are not noted for their humorous content, I remember one that was. I had been out of my office for a while and, on my return, I found a message from a particular police force with a request to ring back. I dialled the number given and the telephone was answered by a man with a very suave voice, not unlike the kind one would expect from an old family butler, who asked how he might help me. I said that I was returning a call from the CID of his force. He said he would put me through.

Some seconds later, I heard his voice again, saying that no one in the CID was answering. I asked him to put me through to someone else who might know what the call was about and he tried another number, again with the same result; no one was there to answer the telephone. He tried yet another number, but again failed to find anyone. He tried number after number, including the typists' pool, but with no success whatsoever. Eventually, his voice could be heard again, apologising for his failure. He said, deadpan: 'I'm afraid they're out fighting crime, sir.' 'Are you entirely on your own?', I asked. 'Not quite, sir. There's a cat on the chair beside me.'

I have often been asked whether I found forensic work upsetting. The examination of dead bodies, often mutilated and decomposed; the attendance, during unsociable hours, at scenes where murders had been committed; the ordeal of giving evidence under cross-examination in court; to many people, all these things seem too unpleasant, too dreadful to do at all, let alone routinely, as part of one's working life. Yet these aspects of forensic work are not really difficult to cope with. Examining a dead body is not such a dreadful thing, although, being outside most people's experience these days, it may seem so to many. Visiting murder scenes in the small hours can be inconvenient, but it is no worse than that; and there are worse things than giving evidence in court.

This is not to say that forensic investigation is free of stress. One of the most difficult tasks is carrying out a post-mortem examination of a child's body; here it is not the physical but the mental dimension that creates the problem. As a father of three, I will not pretend that the sight of a murdered child is not upsetting. It is impossible not to think of one's own children at such times. Worst of all is to witness the grief of parents when identifying the body of their child; few things in this life can be more distressing.

Yet it is strange that the emotions of parents under such circum-

stances are not always what one would expect. I remember a case in the
north of England in which the dead body of a young man was found
on the moors after several days of extremely cold, snowy weather. It
was brought into the police station and provisionally identified as the
son of a local farmer. The farmer was notified and duly arrived to identify the body formally. He strode into the room with his shotgun
under his arm, glanced at the body and said: 'Aye, that's 'im. Ah told
'im. Ah told 'im not to go out in t'snow'. Then, uttering a harsh word
of contempt about his son, he turned and stomped out of the room
with the air of one whose valuable time had been wasted by some tom-
foolery.

Sometimes individuals disappear, their murdered bodies being
found some years later. Yet often I have come across cases in which the
parents or relations of the missing person have never expressed any
desire to find them or even appeared to wonder what might have happened to them. These cases did not concern people who were on bad
terms with one another and did not have much contact. They were
quite ordinary people who were greatly distressed when they learnt the
fate of their loved ones.

One of the most disturbing insights one gets from being involved in
the investigation of crime is the realization that the lives of many of the
most underprivileged people are almost wholly without form: one day
is very much like another; this year very much like the last or the one
before. We are accustomed to think of our lives as an unfolding history: we are born, we go to school, we move house, we leave home, we
get our first job, we get married and so forth. Therefore, it is quite jar-
ring to discover that there are people whose lives appear to have no
structure of this kind.

I have watched such people being interviewed. Did the event in
question happen last year? I don't know. Did it happen in winter?
Don't know. Was it cold? I think so; I don't know. Were you wearing
a coat when you went out, or only a shirt? I was wearing a shirt. Were
you wearing a coat *as well as* a shirt? I have a coat, yes. Was it morning
or evening? I think it was morning. Was the sun shining? Were the
lights switched on in the house? I can't remember. This is not a parody,
nor is it a description of a conversation with someone who is not wishing to cooperate. Although such a person may not be very intelligent,
we are not dealing with someone who is clearly mentally retarded,
since they can carry out all the basic functions of life; they may live
quite happily with their family, perform well at their job and so forth.
Yet they will often live in the most squalid conditions. I have known
several cases in which a member of the family or a resident friend died

or was murdered in the house and their body was left there to decompose for days or weeks without any sign that the other residents objected in the least. Often, such people will claim that they had not noticed that the person in question had died; certainly, they will have made no attempt to conceal the fact or remove the body.

I have been in houses in which the floors are covered with rubbish of all kinds so that one has quite literally to wade through it, and the walls too may be covered with dirt. It would be indelicate to describe in too great detail the nature and extent of the squalor in such dwellings. It is often said that the privileged do not know how the underprivileged live but, perhaps, the extent of this lack of knowledge is not fully appreciated.

One of the strangest applications of forensic entomology known to me is the investigation of blackmail. I have not had to deal with many cases of this sort, but they are always interesting. One centred round a wedding reception held by the bride's father at a hotel in Yorkshire. A few days after the reception the father appeared at the hotel and showed the proprietor some photographs that had been taken on the wedding day, with what looked like cockroaches on the walls and tables of the hotel. He demanded that the proprietor should pay him the sum of £3,000 or he would go to the health authorities and show them the photographs. The proprietor, who was no fool, refused to believe that the photographs were genuine and reported the man to the police, saying that he had tried to blackmail him with the use of forged photographs. The accused man countered by saying that he was not blackmailing the hotelier but simply asking for compensation for the ruin of his daughter's wedding reception.

The question, which was quite straightforward, was whether the photographs were forged. If they had not been forged, then the demand for compensation was reasonable enough, but if they *had* been forged, then this was a case of blackmail. The police sent me the photographs, so that I could examine the images of the cockroaches. There were two pairs of photographs, with the second of each pair having been taken very soon after the first, judging by the fact that the people in them did not appear to have moved between the two shots. And yet the second photograph in each pair had insects on the table and wall –

insects that would have had to appear almost instantaneously. Furthermore, cockroaches do not normally emerge in brightly-lit, crowded rooms. It was very suspicious.

I had some of the images enlarged and examined them. They turned out not only not to be cockroaches, but not to be insects at all! They were mites. By comparing the images with other objects in the photographs, they appeared to be several centimetres long; mites measure about 1–1.5 mm in length. It was clear that the images of mites had been fraudulently superimposed on the photographs. When the accused man was presented with this evidence, he protested that the mites could have been inside his camera, either on the film or on the lens. But this would not wash. If they had been on the lens, the light would have gone round them and they would have been invisible. If they had been on the film, the most one could expect to see would be a white dot, not a shape with surface structure and colour. The man was found guilty of blackmail and was sentenced to two years' imprisonment.

The interesting point about this story is not so much that the man was undoubtedly a villain but that, being quite ignorant himself, he clearly believed that everybody else was equally ignorant. Because he could not tell the difference between a mite and a cockroach – presumably, they were all creepy-crawlies to him – he assumed that no one else could. Similarly, his comments about the presence of the mites in the camera were made in the belief that no one else knew anything about such matters.

It hardly needs saying that we are all ignorant of many things. However, most people are aware of this. It is the assumption that because one does not know something no one else does either that is curious. This extraordinary failing is not confined to criminals: I have, on occasion, come across it among people who claim to be forensic scientists. One particular example comes to mind. Some years ago I was involved in the investigation of a case of murder in the north of England. I appeared for the prosecution, but the defence consulted their own entomologist, whose report would have been a cause of mirth had it not been for the fact that the consequences of his evidence being accepted would have been tragic. This man – a maggot farmer by profession – invented names of mythical insects, made statements that were physical impossibilities and revealed his total ignorance of entomology very effectively. Yet it did not seem to occur to him that he could very easily be shown to be ignorant. As it happened, I found myself sitting opposite him at lunch during the midday adjournment of the trial. He was in excellent form and was relating anecdotes about his holiday in South Africa. Apparently, he had stayed at a hotel in which raccoons 'nested' in the roof, being totally unaware that raccoons occur only in North America!

It may be said that in the blackmail case the images of 'cockroaches' were used as a weapon. A peculiar example of insects being used not so much as a weapon but rather as a means of intimidation came to my notice when I was asked to investigate a case involving a woman who had been dismissed from her job. Shortly afterwards her employer was called away for a couple of days and, on his return, was amazed and repelled by the sight of several rotting, maggot-infested kippers lying on the floor just inside the door of his house. He reported the matter to the police and, for various reasons, suspicion fell upon the sacked woman. It was alleged that she had put the kippers and the maggots through the door as an act of malice.

The woman denied putting the maggots through the door, but admitted that she was responsible for the kippers, which, she said, were meant as a gift. She claimed that the maggots must have come from flies that had laid their eggs on the kippers after she had delivered them. I was asked by the police to comment on whether maggots could have grown to that size from eggs laid, at the earliest, two days before the owner of the house found them.

The answer was that the maggots could not have come from eggs laid two days earlier under the prevailing conditions. It was clear that the woman was lying. Moreover, as I told the police, they could have arrived at that conclusion without even consulting me, for the maggots were dyed a deep pink colour like those used by anglers! Since it was obvious that the maggots could not have dyed themselves while in the empty house, the woman (or possibly someone else) must have bought them from an angling shop and put them through the door. As no other suspect could be found and as they did not believe that the kippers were a 'gift', the police concluded that the woman was guilty of that spiteful act.

Insects can be and indeed have been used as murder weapons in a quite literal sense. Many beetle species provide a source of pharmaceutical compounds that can be used as medical drugs or as poisons. The toxicity of a 'poison' often lies more in its dosage than in its chemical composition; consequently a number of beneficial drugs may become poisons when taken in excessive doses. The blister beetle (*Lytta vesica-toria*), which is sometimes confusingly known as the Spanish fly, is a source of compounds known as cantharides which have been used in the treatment of tuberculosis and, in certain medical conditions, as a diuretic (an agent which increases the flow of urine). They have also been employed in murder and suicide – the wing-cases of the beetles have been found intact in the stomachs of victims months after burial – and to cause abortions. Cantharides have also been mistakenly regarded as having aphrodisiac properties.

In Africa and South America, many arrow poisons are used in hunting some of which are derived from beetles. For example, poisons from the pupae of an African beetle, *Diamphidia locusta*, which are very potent and fast-acting, are used by the Kalahari Bushmen to kill their antelope quarry. Although this species is not known to have been used in a murder case, other arrow poisons have, and *Diamphidia* poisons could be used in this way.

Stinging insects, like wasps and bees, have also been used with murderous intent. For example, in a case that took place in Belgium some years ago, a couple described as 'unnatural parents' locked a child in a room full of wasps in order to get rid of it. In another case a nurse placed a bee in a baby's mouth, presumably in order to kill it. In one of my own cases I came across two wasps lying deep in the throat of a murdered man but how they got there remains a mystery. They are very unlikely to have arrived there by accident and it seems probable that they were forcibly introduced. Unfortunately, the cause of death in this case was never established. In this connection, it is interesting to note that, during the Vietnam War, the North Vietnamese fighters used bees as a weapon of warfare and calculated that one hundred bee-stings could kill an American soldier.

Although most people expect flies, wasps, black beetles and other 'nasty' insects to be the 'bread and butter' of forensic entomology, I am sometimes asked whether 'nice' insects like butterflies or the more beautiful moths ever figure in forensic work. Regrettably, the answer is that they hardly ever do, a reply that often fails to satisfy. Indeed, a film crew making a television series about forensic science introduced the subject of forensic entomology with a shot of a beautiful red tropical butterfly, a creature that has never been known to be involved in a forensic case. I am also frequently asked whether I have encountered the dramatically-named death's head hawkmoth *Acherontia atropos* in any of my cases, since the insect's name and the skull-like pattern on its back suggest that it ought to play a central role in many a murder investigation. Unfortunately, I have never come across it in that context.

However, in the film, *The Silence of the Lambs*, the killer would place a death's head hawkmoth in the mouths of his victims, but any dramatic effect this may have had on an entomologist in the audience was destroyed by the fact that the pupa shown in the film was not that of the death's head hawkmoth but that of an American hawkmoth species, the tobacco hornworm *Manduca sexta*!

The nearest that the death's head hawkmoth has come to figuring in a forensic case concerns two specimens of this species preserved in the Museum of Zoology at Cambridge University. They were taken in the room of King George III by his Physician-in-Ordinary, Dr Robert Darling Willis, during the King's third attack of madness in 1801. It is tempting to speculate whether the presence of these large and sinister-looking insects had any effect on the King's state of mind and whether Dr Willis caught and removed them because he was concerned about their possible effect on the King. Unfortunately, there is no evidence to suggest that the King ever saw them.

One day I received a curious telephone call at work.

'Dr Zak?' The man's voice was low and confidential, almost conspiratorial.

'Is that Dr Zak?' I said it was.

'They told me you could help me, Dr Zak ... the people at the Funny Society ... er ... I mean the Forensic Society. My name is Henry Nash.* I'm not well, Dr Zak, but they don't believe me. I ... they told me you could help me ... '

I asked him what his problem was.

'*Lobsters*, Dr Zak. Lobsters in my nose – small lobsters, about half an inch long. Hundreds of them. They crawl in and out of my nose and give me dreadful headaches. My doctor doesn't believe me, and my wife, she doesn't believe me either, but you believe me, don't you, Dr Zak? They told me you know all about the kind of illness I've got.'

Indeed, I did know about this kind of illness – only too well. I asked him cautiously if he had any specimens.

'Oh, yes, Dr Zak, I have some very good samples.' His voice became more confident and cheerful. 'Can I send them to you?' With a heavy heart and knowing what to expect, I concurred.

* Not his real name.

The samples came, parcel after parcel, over a period of several days. One parcel contained no less than twelve jars, each containing whatever Mr Nash could blow out of his nose. Some samples arrived on strips of card and were kept in place with sticky tape; some of these were labelled triumphantly 'This is a particularly good specimen'. I examined all the samples minutely under the microscope. There were large quantities of mucus, bloodstained as a result of the unfortunate man's violent efforts to expel the parasites that plagued him. There were pieces of tissue, there were short lengths of thread, there were fragments of wood (he may have used broken toothpicks to remove the mucus) and there were bits of household fluff. But there were no 'lobsters' nor any insects or other creatures in his samples.

Of course, it was perfectly clear from the outset that this would be the outcome, for I was dealing with a case of what is known as 'delusory parasitosis' – the irrational and mistaken belief that one is infected with large numbers of parasites, a state of mind that goes hand in hand with a feeling of paranoia. We tend to use the word 'hypochondriac' rather lightly in everyday conversation, but a real hypochondriac, as medically defined, is a very unhappy person indeed. Unfortunate people of this sort believe that they are being deliberately persecuted and are extremely difficult to handle. Telling them that they have no infection merely serves to increase their feelings of persecution, confirming their belief that others are wilfully denying what they, the victims, 'know' to be true.

There are two basic kinds of the condition; put simply, they are the usually treatable and the effectively untreatable. The first kind is termed by medics a 'toxic psychosis', in other words an irrational belief resulting from some kind of physical poisoning. Alcoholics, for example, may be subject to such delusions, as may sufferers from pellagra, a vitamin and protein deficiency that causes an inflammation of the skin. In such cases, the successful treatment of the underlying disease often cures the psychological problem as well. However, most cases of delusory parasitosis are purely psychological, in the sense that no physical basis for the condition can be discerned. The sufferers in this category are diagnosed by psychiatrists as being schizophrenics, melancholics or paranoiacs and in the great majority of cases are incurable. Such people see others as their persecutors. Because of their firm belief that they are suffering from a parasitic infection, they frequently scratch the 'affected' parts until they are quite raw. Often such self-inflicted wounds will not heal and may develop bacterial infections as a result, strengthening the hypochondriac's belief that he is, indeed, suffering from a parasitic attack. The newly-developed genuine condition can be treated with antibiotics and the patient may feel that, at last, his complaint is being taken seriously; he will experience an improvement but, unfortunately, after the bacterial infection has been successfully treated, the belief that 'bugs' are infesting the body will continue to persist. Moreover, the patient will feel that his doctors are betraying him once again. People afflicted in this way may be quite rational when discussing matters other than their own imaginary illness. Nevertheless, many become profoundly depressed and may take their own lives. Others may become a danger, not only to themselves but to others. The condition can sometimes be traced to some kind of insect 'shock', such as a genuine infestation of fleas or bedbugs that may have had a traumatic effect. A phobia may then develop, resulting in the delusion of a permanent parasitic infection. Psychotherapy has, on occasion, been successful, but rarely will such people agree to psychiatric treatment in the first place. Indeed, it may be said that if a person accepts the need for psychotherapy he has effectively admitted that the problem is a psychological one and may well be on the road to recovery.

Mr Nash's samples took some time to examine, as one must always entertain the possibility that a genuine parasite may exist, even though the sufferer's description of them – 'lobsters' in this case – may be inaccurate. Having satisfied myself that I was, indeed, dealing with a case of delusion, I decided to take the usual next step which is to contact the doctor in the case. This is not as easy as it sounds, for hypochondriacs of this kind are often on bad terms with their doctors and may become very suspicious if one asks for their name. Fortunately, I had a good reason that I could give Mr Nash for asking him to give me his doctor's name; it is considered unethical in medical circles for a specialist to treat a patient or to produce a report on medical samples from the patient without the knowledge and consent of the patient's G.P. So, one evening, I telephoned Mr Nash.

'Oh, Dr Zak, did you find anything? Did you find the lobsters?' The voice was desperate. I said that my investigations were not yet quite complete, but that I needed his doctor's name, address and telephone number so that I could ask for his formal permission to prepare a report on the samples.

'My doctor? He doesn't believe me. He'll tell you that I'm imagining things. I showed him some of the samples and he still doesn't believe me. He won't be any help at all, Dr Zak, he'll only tell you to ignore me, he'll ... '

I interrupted the hysterical flow of words and said that I could not proceed further without his doctor's permission – it was a case of medical ethics.

'Oh ... well ... I suppose ...'

I telephoned the doctor the next day. He seemed a very patient and kindly man and told me the whole story which was very sad. Nash was married with three children and, at first, the family was very happy. After a time, the delusion began. There seemed to be no obvious cause. But, slowly at first, then much more rapidly, Mr Nash's mental health declined. He lost his job. His wife and children lived under the shadow of the delusion, around which everything in their family life revolved. Every evening, year after year, Mrs Nash and the youngsters would be treated to the latest reports of the lobsters' doings and the family went downhill. Mrs Nash's health suffered and the children lost all the usual zest of youth. No one came to visit. The children and Mrs Nash lost their friends. The children were taunted at school and could not concentrate on their studies. An entire family was wrecked.

The doctor's advice was that I should delay a few days before contacting Mr Nash again and then telephone him with the good news that he was free from any parasitic infection whatsoever. Not that the doctor thought for a moment that this would solve the problem but he felt, rightly, that Mr Nash should be given no encouragement to cling to his delusion. The only possible hope, albeit a very faint one, was to convince him that he was mistaken.

However, Mr Nash telephoned me the following day, sounding rather surprisingly buoyant.

'Dr Zak, I think I know where the lobsters came from!' I asked him to explain.

'You see, doctor, my neighbours used to live in India. When they moved back to this country they brought their furniture with them. I went to visit them a few times after they moved in and I sat on the furniture – big furniture, settees and armchairs – and the lobsters came out of the furniture and went into my nose. They must have come from there, because that was the time when I started getting the headaches. Oh, and something else, Dr Zak. They are going through my body and I have seen them in my stools – I have a very good sample of stools, which I sent you this morning.'

The sample arrived the following day. Fortunately, laboratory fume cupboards allow one to examine such samples with the minimum of discomfort. I examined the contents of the large jar in great detail but again I could find no parasites of any kind.

A few days later I decided to telephone Mr Nash and give him my results. In these situations it is impossible to predict what the reaction will be so I had to proceed cautiously. I rang and said that I had very good news for him.

'Oh, really, Dr Zak? You found the lobsters then?'

I said that my news was even better than that. I told him that I was happy to be able to say that he suffered from no parasitic infection whatsoever and that he could now rest assured that, whatever he might have had in the past, he was now a healthy man.

'Oh ...' I could hear a sob. 'Oh ... Oh, dear ... Oh.'

I said that I hoped he would now be able to relax and look forward to the future, secure in the knowledge that he had no parasitic infection. I spoke in a cheerful tone to raise his spirits; I said that he must now be quite relieved to learn that he need have no more worries as far as this matter was concerned, that no doubt he would be much happier now, that I was sure that he would want to tell his family that all was well ...

But he was not listening. All I could hear was 'Oh, dear ... Oh, dear ... Oh, dear', then the click of the replaced receiver. I telephoned his doctor and told him what happened. He said that he would pay Mr Nash a visit to help him pick up the pieces. He also said that he held out little or no hope of recovery.

I do not know what became of Henry Nash and his family. For his sake and theirs I hope he found peace.

One very hot summer's day I received a letter that began innocuously enough. 'I am not writing to you about *The News of the World*.' I sat back in my chair expecting a humorous if somewhat crankish letter about the correspondent's views on insects, forensic science, universities or any other subject that might have caught his fancy. I receive a steady trickle of such letters so I was not prepared for what followed. The letter was almost incoherent. 'I have been trying for some time now as you can see from the enclosures'. I read the passage again and before reading further looked at the two enclosures. One was a photocopied page of a dictionary with the word 'larva' and its definition highlighted with a felt pen. The other was a copy of a letter from a consultant parasitologist, acknowledging a letter from the correspondent, Mr Thomas Peterson,* and saying that he would be happy to see him if his medical practitioner formally referred him.

---

* Not his real name.

I resumed my reading of Mr Peterson's letter. 'It all started when I felt something in the *left* groin. I had had a biopsy of the bowels but I think we can discard that'. A few garbled and illegible sentences followed, then, 'The worst being the back of my skull at the base. I could feel it inside me, moving like lightning. I then felt a gathering under the left lung area'. He then described his symptoms: diarrhoea, vomiting, sweating, coughing. Next: 'Then in the toilet I saw a small brown case, I put it in an old cup and left it for a while then when I looked again and there was a small white thing which had moved about one inch from the case, then I saw about six or seven black objects about one-eighth of an inch long move slowly across the cup, I had put the cup in a plastic bag and dashed to the G.P. but he wouldn't believe it came from me'.

The letter was very long and very difficult to decipher. It was a detailed account of his symptoms, his dealings with doctors and other people whom he had consulted and his observations on the bizarre things that were happening to him. He said that after one medical test the doctors had 'found BACTERIA' inside him. The contents of his cup apparently became puffed up into 'a clear huge bubble'. He showed this to his neighbour, who opined that he had 'definitely got something dangerous'.

Mr Peterson was convinced that the cause of his illness was a fly and its brood of larvae. His letter ended on an ominous note: 'Until last Sunday when I read about you I had resigned myself to my fate, or consult my priest. My life is in your hands now, there's nothing more to say. All I ask is use your own judgement'. Then followed a postscript: 'If you do recognise the species of Fly and what I say is correct then you must send a senior officer to take me to the right people to clear me, as fast as possible'. This reference to my alleged powers to send senior officers to compel medics to treat him indicates how far detached from reality he had become.

He had included some drawings to help me to identify the fly: a small circle stood for the 'brown case' and a series of dashes were labelled 'from the maggot'. Unfortunately, a day or two later I succumbed to a bout of 'flu and was off work for some days, but I was able to contact the parasitologist, a copy of whose letter was enclosed with Mr Peterson's correspondence. The parasitologist gave me the background; it was the old tragic tale of a man slowly losing his sense of proportion and dragging down those around him. Apparently, Mr Peterson was an elderly man whose elderly wife was being ground down by his obsession and the parasitologist, like the doctor in the case of Mr Nash, believed that there was no prospect of recovery. He said that he thought Mr Peterson was close to committing suicide.

About a week later I received another letter from Mr Peterson. He was angry that I had not replied to his letter immediately and said that I was clearly refusing to help him. He had checked with the Post Office, asking them to confirm that his registered letter had been delivered. He even enclosed a photocopy of their reply, stating that they had, indeed, delivered the letter. Clearly, I had no excuse.

Mr Peterson was very angry because I had not given him the name of the fly that afflicted him: 'If you don't know of such an insect then say so. Crime is suspected now'. This last comment appeared not to be directed at me, but at the various medics who had treated him. One, in particular, he suspected of wanting to murder him. His name, he said, 'spells M.U.R.D.E.R.'. According to Mr Peterson, this man had been transferred to another hospital simply to enable him to escape from his (Peterson's) clutches. But the intrepid Peterson was able to discover his hiding place. He was transferred once again, but Peterson had tracked him down again. Yet again he was transferred, but to no avail, for Peterson managed to run him to earth once more. Having established where he was now, Peterson said that he believed that the culprit 'should be interviewed by murder squad detectives'.

Mr Peterson's belief appeared to be that the hapless medic had tried, deliberately and maliciously, to blind him. Having uncovered the plot and unmasked the villain, Mr Peterson claimed that he was then pursued by the entire medical profession, who, seeking to take their revenge upon him for his exposure of their misdeeds, 'put something inside me to shut me up'. This something was, apparently, the fly in question.

Needless to say, I ignored all this when I wrote to Mr Peterson. I told him that I needed the name of his doctor, so that I could seek his permission to investigate the matter. He responded by telephone. He gave me his doctor's name and telephone number, as well as an interminable account of his illness and its symptoms. I also asked him for some samples.

I received permission from the G.P. to examine any specimens from Mr Peterson When the small packet containing the samples arrived I opened it with some curiosity. There was a short letter and a small folded piece of paper stapled together. The letter was quite reasonable and courteous, thanking me for getting in touch with his doctor and saying that he was feeling bloated and had stiff ankles. He ended his letter, 'I'm very ill Dr Zak'.

I could not wait to see the contents of the little folded piece of paper. I placed it under the microscope and opened it carefully with two pairs of forceps. There was nothing there, except some crystals that were caught in one of the folds. They looked like rock salt. I took the crystals and placed them in a tube with a drop of water – they dissolved immediately and completely. This did not prove that they were necessarily salt crystals, but it showed me that there were no living organisms in the sample, since a detailed microscopical examination of the water revealed nothing.

Before I could write to Mr Peterson, I received an extremely angry letter from him. 'It's apparent to me and my family that you are hellbent on a course of collusion with – and to protect other doctors. You were sent samples from me within the last ten days as you don't or won't reply you must regard me as a liar or a crank ... Too many doctors are getting away with it in this country ... They have no excuse ... I am not afraid of anything ... ' He expressed forcefully his low opinion of me and my professional abilities and by the end his letter had become totally illegible.

I replied to this letter simply saying that I had found nothing in the sample but that I would be willing to examine further samples if he handed them to his doctor first to ensure that they would be preserved correctly. His response was by telephone. No, he said, he was not going to send me any more specimens since I was clearly incompetent. I was, he said, a charlatan and a fraud in the worst tradition of the quack down the ages; I should be 'struck off'; I should be sent to prison for attempted murder ...

He was much more articulate and expressive in speech than he was in the written word.

Whenever I sat in court listening to the evidence in a murder trial, my eyes were always drawn irresistibly to the face of the man in the dock.* Usually there are signs of strong emotion on it; I have seen anger expressed on such faces; in many cases fear is the dominant emotion; occasionally, malice; often remorse and anguish; sometimes even gloating. Yet, while these emotions can be disturbing or moving, according to their nature, none is more disquieting than the total lack of emotion that I have sometimes seen on the faces of accused men.

* I have only very rarely come across a woman in the dock in a murder case.

I remember one case in particular, in which the defendant was a thick-set fellow in his thirties. As I observed him, I could see how unmoved he was by the proceedings in which he was totally uninterested. His world was about to collapse about him yet he seemed to be interested only in the architecture of the court-room ceiling. His face was completely relaxed; occasionally he would look at his finger-nails with an air of sophisticated boredom, but it was clear that he was not pretending or putting on an act. He appeared to be quite genuinely at ease – more so than anyone else in the court-room.

As I watched him, I could not help asking myself, *Is he mad?* Is it possible for someone to be in such a predicament and yet remain wholly detached? Totally innocent people, even saints, brought to trial by unjust and tyrannical persecutors, usually express some kind of emotion; at the very least, they become involved in the proceedings. The defendant in this case conducted himself as though the whole matter was none of his business. He had no cause to have any contempt or disdain for the court, as he might have had if he had been the victim of injustice. The evidence against him was very strong and the crime of which he was accused was the murder of a young woman for no other reason than that she had resisted his advances. He was found guilty and was given a life sentence. Still, he was unmoved. Could such a man as this really understand what was going on? Was he – could he have been – responsible for his actions?

Are criminals bad or mad? What is insanity, and what simply bad or wilful behaviour? These questions are fundamental and the answers to them are of great importance, since they are the basis upon which a judge will pronounce sentence. A jury may find a man guilty, in the sense that he did indeed commit the crime, but the role of the judge is to decide how the guilty man is to be punished. Under English Law, if the perpetrator of a crime *knows* what he is doing and, moreover, knows that what he is doing is *wrong* (that is, illegal or immoral), then he is bad, not mad.* Conversely, if he does not know what he is doing, such as when a crime is committed while sleep-walking, or if he knows what he is doing, but does not know that what he is doing is wrong, he cannot be held responsible for his actions.

All this seems very reasonable and straightforward, but two problems arise. First, the practical one of how we can know whether or not someone *did* know what they were doing and that it was wrong. This is not at all easy to determine. Many people, including people of low intelligence, can be consummate actors.

---

* These guidelines are known as the M'Naghten Rules.

Another problem lies in the fact that the legal definition of insanity given above is very difficult to apply except in the rarest of cases. It is often the case that a criminal clearly knew that what he was doing was wrong (in the sense that he knew it was against the law), yet it is also clear that, under the circumstances in which the crime was committed, he could not be held to be fully responsible for his actions. A man, provoked beyond endurance, may commit a criminal act knowing it to be a criminal act, yet it is something that he would not have done under more normal circumstances. In another situation, someone deemed to be of diminished responsibility due to a general mental retardedness may be given a lighter sentence, even though he would not be regarded as being insane in the way insanity is defined in Law. In these kinds of situation, it is not the man's inability to distinguish right from wrong that is at issue, but his inability to control himself. In the case of a normal person who may well usually be a man of great self-control, the question that needs to be asked is whether anyone else would have lost control in the same way under the circumstances in which the crime was committed. In the case of the person of diminished responsibility, the question is whether such a person could 'help' behaving in the way he did. In practice, insanity is hardly ever invoked as a defence in British courts these days, diminished responsibility being the most commonly used argument in favour of the perpetrator of a crime so far as mental state is concerned.

One condition that decreases the level of self-control is, of course, drunkenness. Interestingly, the Law does not usually regard this as a valid excuse for criminal behaviour, for the very good reason that it is a state which, being self-induced, is also avoidable. The very fact that someone *allowed* themselves to become drunk may be the crime. The obvious example is heavy drinking before driving which may lead to the death of a pedestrian or passenger. Here it is clear that the drunkenness, far from being a mitigating factor, is actually part of the crime.

The problem of what is mad and what is bad is a very complex one. How can one know whether a man could or could not help acting as he did? It seems to me insufficient to say that, because most normal people would have done a certain thing under a certain set of circumstances, then the accused could not have helped doing it. How most people would be expected to behave under certain circumstances has a great deal to do not only with basic human physiology but also with current fashion. It can hardly be disputed that people do things nowadays that would not normally have been done in the past. Moreover, the very desirability of self-control as a manner of conducting oneself has, unaccountably, largely gone out of fashion. Therefore, what is normal or widespread behaviour cannot be used as a basis for deciding whether someone could not help their actions.

It may be argued that the effect of one's culture can be so powerful that it is, in effect, well-nigh impossible for some people to avoid behaving in certain undesirable ways from time to time. This may well be true in many cases, but it is a chicken and egg situation. Teaching people that self-control is undesirable will result in their behaving antisocially. Antisocial behaviour from such people will then be excused on the basis of the current 'normality' of such behaviour. The vicious circle will not only go round and round but will spiral downwards with ever-worsening consequences.

We live in an age in which explanations for human conduct are being put forward by specialists in many fields of psychology, sociology and animal behaviour. None of these ideas are devoid of interest, but we must be very cautious about what we make of them when considering the question of the extent of the control that we have over ourselves and our actions. Professors of Sociology will blame our culture; Professors of Genetics our DNA; Professors of Psychology our upbringing. Many of these theories contradict one another. We must be wary of them all. To be sure, culture, DNA and upbringing do affect our behaviour but in the end, in most cases, we are responsible for our own actions. It is useless to be told that a man, brought up as a child in violent surroundings, had to be violent when he grew up. It is useless, because we know that he knows violence to be wrong, morally and legally. The same applies to genetic tendencies. A man with a naturally short fuse will, if he so wishes, learn to control his temper. We know that he can do it because, while he may shout at his subordinates at work, he miraculously manages to control his temper when talking to his superiors. Therefore cultural and genetic factors, while they may affect us strongly, rarely do so in a manner that deprives us of our ability to do what we know to be right.

The causes of crime, like the causes of disease, war, famine and all the other ills that afflict mankind, must rank high among the greatest concerns of all thoughtful people. For very many years people have questioned the causes of crime or the reason why some people become criminals and others not. These are historical questions, in the sense that they are concerned with discovering early factors in the development of the individual that caused an effect that is observable to us now.

In the nineteenth century, many theories were advanced to try and answer these questions. Most were inadequate and are no longer seriously considered. They included such ideas as the form of the head, the position of the eyes, the shape of the forehead, the shape and degree of protrusion of the teeth, the size of the ears, the general shape of the body and other physical features. It was said, for example, that such features as a thick neck, large ears, protruding jaw and sloping forehead indicated that an individual had criminal tendencies. The possession of five out of eighteen possible 'criminal' features was believed to demonstrate criminality.

This early stage in the search for physical attributes that could be correlated with criminality was soon overtaken by more subtle approaches. Among these, hormonal imbalances and abnormal electrical impulses in the brain came to be seen as indicators of a criminal mind. The link between such factors and proven criminal behaviour was, in fact, rather weak, but that was not the main defect of these scientific researches. Once again we come up against the problem of cause and effect. Do hormonal imbalances and abnormal brain electrical impulses cause crime, or does criminal behaviour cause hormonal imbalances and abnormal brain impulses? This central question was never answered or even addressed in the studies designed to look into a physical basis for criminality. Moreover, the question of the prevalence of such abnormalities in non-criminals was also ignored.

Other physiological states, such as dietary deficiencies and pre-menstrual stress in women, have been invoked as possible causes of crime. Such conditions can indeed affect behaviour, but no link between them and overtly criminal behaviour has been demonstrated.

The next step in the search was to look for basic genetic differences between people which, if shown to be linked to criminal behaviour and because they were present at birth, could only be causes, not effects. Some scientists thought that if a link between certain genes and criminal behaviour could be found, then it could not be argued that the behaviour caused the genes, but rather the genes determined the behaviour.

The first target of genetic criminality research was the sex chromosomes, of which, in human beings, there are two: X and Y. Men possess one X and one Y chromosome (designated XY); women possess two X chromosomes (designated XX). However, some men may have an extra chromosome, either an X or a Y, designated XXY and XYY, respectively; such men are usually very tall.

Studies were carried out on male inmates of mental institutions and it was found that a significant number of them possessed an additional sex chromosome, more commonly a Y than an X. Such individuals were said to be more aggressive than normal. However, further studies suggested that such XYY individuals were less aggressive than normal XY individuals and that they constituted a very small percentage of men institutionalized for antisocial or criminal behaviour; in other words, most criminal men studied had the normal XY complement. Further studies along these lines eventually resulted in the conclusion that there is no demonstrable link between additional sex chromosomes and criminality. Once again, the abundance (or otherwise) of chromosomal abnormalities in the law-abiding population was not examined.

Studies on identical twins, separated at or soon after birth, have also been carried out to see whether such twins behaved similarly, in this investigation criminally, in different environments. If it could be shown that they did, this would be strong evidence that criminal behaviour was heritable. These complex studies are bedevilled with methodological problems. Suffice it to say that the results, when they can be interpreted, suggest that there is little evidence for the inheritance of criminal tendencies.

Next, we can consider adoption studies. In these investigations adopted children whose biological fathers were criminals were compared with adopted children whose biological fathers were not criminals. Although the number of individuals studied was very small, the results showed that a fairly high proportion of children with criminal fathers indulged in criminal activity, suggesting that criminal behaviour can be inherited. However, sources of confusion have crept in. When children are placed for adoption, the prospective parents are selected to correspond with the social background and other features of the biological parents. Moreover, the studies did not take into consideration the fact that an adoptive father need not have committed a crime in order to influence his adopted son to become a criminal.

Recent years have seen the growth of a new school of genetic criminology. Its exponents differ from the earlier investigators in that they have set themselves the goal of establishing that crime is heritable. It is a 'party line'; studies are conducted specifically in order to make this point. Also, the proponents of this new discipline have stepped so far outside the limits of science as to propose that action should be taken on the basis of their theories. They advocate that genetic counselling should be given to parents whose expected child may, according to them, be genetically predisposed to commit criminal acts. The ultimate purpose of such advice would be to abort the foetus. Thus, in time, a superior, non-criminal race of people would come into existence.

Not so long ago, a symposium organized by this group of scientists was held in London. The meeting was to last for several days and various people were invited to attend most of its sessions, but the last day was a closed meeting, to be attended only by those who accepted the dogma – a course of action almost without precedent in scientific meetings. I was invited to the open part of the meeting but declined to attend. When asked by journalists why I refused to take part, I said that the symposium was irresponsible and mischievous. This admittedly harsh response puzzled many members of the Press and I was obliged to explain my objections in some detail. As I believe that this matter is of very great legal and social importance, I will set down my arguments against this new fashion of genetic predeterminism, which is a great threat to freedom and human dignity.

One of the most fundamental problems with the notion of genetically-determined criminality lies in the difficulty of defining the concept of crime scientifically. When the assertion is made that crime is genetically determined, one has to ask whether all crime, or only certain types of crime, are determined in this way. Are murder and the theft of a pencil from one's employer both crimes? More seriously, is the embezzlement of funds controlled by the same genes as those that control grievous bodily harm? The fundamental problem is that crime is either a legally- or a morally-defined concept, or both, but it is not and cannot be *biologically* or *scientifically* defined. Certain kinds of behaviour are criminal because they are against the law or because they offend against a moral code. In other words, it is quite impossible to arrive at a scientific definition of crime. Any so-called 'scientific' conclusion about a particular person's criminality would be based on the scientist's own moral convictions and legal knowledge and not on any objective scientific criterion. The most a scientist can do is to describe the behaviour of an individual, but he cannot, *as a scientist*, conclude whether such behaviour is criminal or not.

Crime is not a biological or scientific concept; the very question is beyond the remit of scientific inquiry. This point can be made very clearly by the following hypothetical example. Let us say that a law is passed, making it a crime to eat meat. Overnight the bulk of the population would become criminals, but it would have been impossible to deduce their criminality by a prior genetic study. All that a scientist can do is to explain why, in physiological terms, human beings in general like to eat meat. While these points may seem too obvious to be worth making, they seem not to have been grasped by genetic determinists.

Another problem with the approach of genetic determinists is their hidden assumption, although this is never made explicit, that 'crime' consists of overt and unsubtle acts such as murder or burglary. White collar crime does not fit into this picture. Their concerns seem to be more with the methodology of crime rather than with the criminal tendency itself. Subtle or sophisticated criminal – or at least immoral – acts such as plagiarism, lying, emotional blackmail or verbal intimidation are not included among the crimes that interest genetic determinists and one must ask why this should be so. It is impossible to avoid the conclusion that, to those who seek to explain criminality by invoking genetics, crime is that kind of antisocial behaviour that is committed by the underprivileged classes in society.

Scientists who believe that the genetic make-up of an individual can tell us whether he is, or will become, a criminal defend their position by saying that, since an aggressive disposition may be heritable (and this is by no means proven), it is possible to tell whether a person is genetically predetermined to become a criminal. This argument is fallacious. Assuming for the sake of argument that an aggressive temperament is, indeed, heritable, it does not follow that aggressive individuals are necessarily criminally inclined, yet this is the link that is being explicitly made. There is, however, no correlation between the possession of an aggressive temperament and the possession of criminal tendencies. It is well known that aggressive individuals can be a great force for good and that many brutal criminals were known to be of a mild disposition. Reports from the United States suggest that, if the gene for aggression could be found, the parents of an unborn child would be given eugenic advice so that they might have the option to abort the foetus. Such advice, if given and acted upon, would result in a great deal of human misery, not to mention the loss to humanity of many able people.

Further evidence against what may be termed the genetic theory of crime comes from two other sources. First, crime statistics. These show very clearly that crime has increased dramatically in Western Europe and North America during the past twenty years or so. If criminality is, indeed, a genetically controlled condition, then one must further hypothesize that a fundamental change in the genetic make-up of the populations of Europe and North America took place during the second half of the twentieth century, which is simply not a credible proposition, nor is there any evidence of any kind to support it.

Secondly, the notion of inheritance itself. Biological traits are, of course, heritable; the offspring of blond, blue-eyed parents will have blond hair and blue-eyes, while those of dark parents will have dark hair and brown eyes. As evidence in support of their theory, the apologists of the genetic theory of crime often quote the fact that criminality often runs in families in a similar way; a criminal father begets criminal children and they, in turn, beget similar children. One cannot nor would one wish to deny that this does indeed often happen. The conclusion to be drawn from this kind of study is that criminality may well be inherited but there is no reason to suspect that it is genetically inherited. One may inherit great wealth, a treasured possession of one's parents, or even a particular political outlook, religion or philosophy, but it does not follow that these things are in any sense genetically acquired. Good or bad habits learned in childhood are likely to be transmitted to one's own children but this has nothing to do with genetics.

When a biologist states that a particular trait is genetically determined, it is often considered inevitable that it will be expressed. This is not true. I could say that I am genetically determined to speak Spanish or Chinese, in the sense that my brain and vocal cords are adequately equipped for the purpose, and yet I cannot speak either of these languages. However, were I to find myself surrounded solely by Spanish or Chinese speakers for a period of a year or so, my genetic predisposition would be expressed and I would find myself being able to speak the relevant language. Similarly, I could say I was genetically determined to die of asphyxia: if I were to be placed in a room devoid of oxygen I would die in a very short time. In both these cases it would have been my genes that brought about the result, but these results were in no sense inevitable. I doubt if I will ever learn Chinese and I hope not to die of oxygen deficiency!

To take a more directly relevant example: cat-burglars are usually persons of small stature and slender build. It is not possible for a tall, broadly-built man to succeed in this occupation. Therefore those who are genetically of slight build are more likely to become cat burglars than those who are born with a heavy build but this cannot be said to be genetically-predetermined. They could equally well become jockeys or take up a profession that is unrelated to their build; their choice of career will depend mainly on other factors, such as their moral code, their other abilities or pure chance. Being endowed with the ability to do something does not mean that one has to do it. Nevertheless, this is the fatal step that genetic predeterminists take. After all, most of us have sufficient physical strength and mental ability to commit murder, but this does not mean that we are born cut-throats.

Consider another example: most criminals are men. Women rarely commit serious crimes; in fact, only about ten per cent of criminals are women. It follows that a child born with a Y chromosome is genetically far more likely to become a criminal than someone who does not have a Y chromosome. There is no doubt about this statement; it is incontrovertibly true. But I suspect that not even the most extreme genetic determinist would advocate that the male foetus should have been aborted or that male babies should be put to death at birth.

There is no doubt that genetics play a *part* in determining certain personality traits. One individual may be taciturn, another garrulous; one may be extrovert, another introvert and so on. It may, indeed, be the case that some are born aggressive and others meek and mild, but there is no link between any of these traits and criminality. Human behaviour is the product of the interaction between nature and nurture and is effectively impossible to predict. An interesting cooking analogy has been used to illustrate this point. One can compare the development of the character of a human being to the baking of a cake, rather than to the making of muesli. In muesli the various ingredients are still quite recognizable after mixing and can be separated from one another with ease. The raw flour, eggs and butter that go into a cake, if consumed uncooked and on their own, will taste nothing like the cake. However, in the baking, the ingredients (nature) become transformed by the cooking process (nurture), just as in the development of a human personality the ingredients of nature (the genes) and nurture (diet, environment, experience, etc.) become changed and change one another to such an extent that they are no longer separable or identifiable.

I trust that the danger from the theories of the genetic predeterminists is now apparent, but it is worth looking at the possible consequences to humanity if such ideas are not firmly quashed Most people would agree that the Holocaust was a crime against humanity and that the Nazis who committed this deed were criminals. The perpetrators were motivated by a racist (genetic) theory and justified their crimes by invoking that theory. In our own day we have witnessed ethnically-based genocide in Bosnia-Herzegovina and Rwanda by individuals who, implicitly or explicitly, hold similar genetic views to those to which the Nazis subscribed. The adherents of the genetic theory of criminality would, presumably, argue that these horrific crimes were the acts of people who were genetically-predetermined to commit them. If one accepts these theories, one will find oneself in the position of invoking one genetic theory in order to excuse the deeds of those who committed their atrocities in the name of very similar genetic theories. In short, if crime is genetically-determined, like the colour of one's eyes or the length of one's nose, then it cannot be helped. One is no longer responsible for one's actions. Right and wrong disappear.

We already know to our cost how deadly genetic theories can be when they fall into the hands of tyrannical régimes: genocide has been the result. But we must not forget that other consequences, less horrific but nonetheless evil may follow. If all behaviour, not only criminal behaviour, is genetically-determined as some claim, there is nothing to stop a ruthless government from declaring that this or that piece of behaviour, deemed to be a threat to the régime, is the consequence of a genetic condition. Whoever behaves in such a manner would be considered sick and, possibly, in need of treatment. Such people would not end up in prison as criminals, but in hospital as patients. The despotic régime could present itself as enlightened and humane. Prison allows a person to change his ways; a genetic disease does not. There would be no release from the hospital, which would kindly and beneficently care for the 'patient' for the rest of his life.

It may be considered that I exaggerate a little; that this nightmare prediction is far-fetched; or perhaps that I shout to make myself heard. I think not. There are already reports that American courts may soon accept the plea of genetic-predeterminism as a valid defence in murder trials. DNA is already being invoked as a plea for the defence. In Britain, newspaper articles with headlines like 'It wasn't me, m'lord, it was my DNA', have begun to appear. No British court has yet accepted such a defence, I hasten to add. If they do, we will have come full circle.

So, while I do not believe that most criminals are unable to help committing their crimes, my experience is that most criminals are of below average intelligence or, more accurately, the ones I have come across have struck me as being so. I have yet to meet a criminal of the Professor Moriarty sort. Should one conclude that only stupid people become criminals? I think this would be most unwise since our observations could equally well lead to the conclusion that it is only stupid criminals who are caught which, in my opinion, is most likely to be so since, although some very clever criminals are caught, it is usually almost by accident.

For example, there was once an old lady who was in hospital. Every week her devoted husband would send her a cake. She always ate this cake on her own and looked forward to receiving it every Friday. One Friday, the old lady felt rather unwell. Knowing the cake had arrived but feeling too ill to eat it, she gave it to her nurse. Later that day, the old lady died. The staff were sorry that their elderly patient had gone but, as she was a *very* old lady and had been unwell for a long time, going steadily downhill for some months, her death came as no surprise. That evening the nurse took the cake home and ate a slice. The next day she did not feel at all well and went to her doctor who asked her whether she had eaten anything that might have caused her to feel sick. She remembered the cake which was taken for chemical analysis and found to contain arsenic. Subsequent tests on the old lady's hair revealed large amounts of arsenic – a poison that accumulates in the hair and finger-nails. It was clear that she had been receiving sublethal doses for a long time and that her death was the result of slow, long-term poisoning. Of course the cakes from her husband, who stood to inherit all her money, were the source of the poison. He was arrested, put on trial and eventually sent to prison, but the crime would never have been found out if the lady herself had eaten the cake and died afterwards. Her death was not, initially, treated as suspicious. It was only because the cake was subsequently eaten by the nurse that the crime was discovered. A very clever criminal almost got away with his crime.

If it is difficult, on occasion, to distinguish between what is mad and what is bad; it is also often very difficult to distinguish between what is mad and what is stupid, or simply eccentric. When the notorious 1930s murderer, Dr Buck Ruxton, was being pursued by the police, he went into hiding in a certain hotel. A woman staying at the hotel thought little of his hiding place. She could, she said, have told him of a much better one, 'if he'd nobbut asked'.

Cases of Identity

I cannot tell what the dickens his name is.
Shakespeare, *Merry Wives of Windsor* Act III, Scene 2

The crab and the prawn met on the ocean floor; they merged together, lost their distinctive shapes and identities, re-formed and became a sea anemone. The tentacles of the sea anemone grew longer and longer and fewer and fewer, until it was not a sea anemone any more, but an octopus, whose legs increased in number and became a coral reef, upon which crabs and prawns met and merged ... My temperature was 105° F. and showed no sign of dropping. My delirious dream of marine life was doubtless the result of my having assisted my colleagues at some practical classes at Cambridge University a few days earlier. Now, the animals had come into my feverish dreams, swirling in a hot sea, appearing and disappearing ... In the middle of this delirium I heard my wife's voice. Professor Bernard Knight was on the telephone and would like to speak to me about a suspected murder case in Cardiff – did I feel well enough to talk to him? I took the receiver but remember little of the conversation, apart from the fact that a skeleton had been discovered buried in a garden and that the police would like to know whether I could assist them. I said I would do what I could and Professor Knight told me that a Detective Constable James from Cardiff would come to see me the following day.

I was feeling much better when D.C. James arrived, bringing several large specimen bags of samples with him. Over a cup of tea, he told me about the macabre discovery at Number 29, Fitzhamon Embankment in Cardiff. The street consisted of a row of terraced houses on one side with the River Taff flowing past it on the other. Number 29 had been neglected for some years and workmen had been engaged in some restoration works. They had dug a trench in the garden to instal a sewer pipe but found that it was too shallow. As they dug deeper, one of the workmen's pickaxes struck a soft object lying in the soil at the bottom of the trench. Pulling it out of the moist soil and scraping off the mud with their hands, the workmen were astonished to find that the object was a rolled-up carpet, bound with a strong cord. Undoing the cord and unrolling the carpet, they discovered a complete human skeleton.

Whose skeleton was it? When did the person die? Why and how were they killed? There were many questions to answer but, as yet, there were very few clues to help the police to answer any of them. However there were some: around the skull was a mass of long blonde hair and a pair of ear-rings; taken together with the small size of the skeleton, it seemed that the remains might have been those of a young woman, but this evidence was not conclusive. The South Wales Police, in the person of D.C. James, were asking me to determine an approximate time of death so that they could concentrate their enquiries on people who were known to have gone missing before and up to the date of the victim's demise.

I set to work on the samples from the soil and the carpet later the same day. There was a considerable amount of insect and plant material to examine but, even so, I felt that I needed further samples if I were to arrive at a useful conclusion about time of death. These duly arrived and I was, at last, able to offer an opinion. In my report to Detective Superintendent Neale Evans, who was supervising the investigation, I said that there was no doubt in my mind that death had occurred at least five years earlier, and quite probably several years before that. I also concluded that the body had been left exposed for about a day before being buried. From the point of view of the police investigation, the important point was that people who had gone missing during the last five years could definitely be eliminated from the enquiry.

Meanwhile, Professor Knight had been active. Having examined the skeleton, he concluded that it belonged to a teenaged girl, five feet four inches in height. The police then took the skull to Dr David Whittaker, a forensic dentist, who examined the stage of development of the teeth and concluded that the girl had been about fifteen and a half years old when she died. Further study of the skull by anthropologists Dr Christopher Stringer and Dr Theya Molleson at the Natural History Museum in London suggested that the skull belonged to a white girl, though possibly not of purely British extraction. The investigation inched slowly forwards but there was still no hint as to who the murdered girl might have been. Hundreds of people were interviewed by the police, including many former residents of Number 29 and neighbouring houses but, astonishingly, no one could remember a young girl with blonde hair. The police were no closer to an identification. Detective Chief Superintendent John Williams, in overall charge of the investigation, is reported to have said, 'It would be a tragedy if this young girl were to be buried without a name'. Indeed it would, but D.C.S. Williams need not have worried because a very dramatic forensic breakthrough was about to take place.

Mr Richard Neave of Manchester University is a medical artist, specializing in the reconstruction of the faces of long-dead individuals from the study of their skulls. He has had many successes in the identification of people in historical as well as police investigations, having reconstructed the faces of King Midas and of Philip of Macedon, father of Alexander the Great. One member of the police investigation team, Sergeant Ron Ashby, remembered having read an article about Neave and his work and decided to consult him. It was the most felicitous decision of the investigation.

The skull was first taken to Professor Ian Isherwood, Professor of Diagnostic Radiology at Manchester University, who X-rayed it to see whether there were any abnormalities. There were none. The skull was then handed over to Richard Neave who made a replica cast of it, gradually building up the face of the deceased to reconstruct the musculature. After two long days, when this reconstruction was complete, D.C.S. Williams held a press conference and exhibited photographs of it which were shown on television and published in local and national newspapers, together with a request for anyone who recognized the face to come forward with a name. Very soon afterwards, a social worker telephoned the police and said that the face belonged to a girl named Karen Price, who had run away from a children's home eight years earlier. Some time later, another social worker contacted the police, saying that Karen Price had been in the care of the establishment for which she worked; she was also able to produce a photograph of the girl. The photograph matched Neave's reconstruction remarkably. Interestingly, it turned out that she was of mixed British, American, Spanish and Greek extraction, a fact that bore out the conclusions of the scientists at the Natural History Museum. Other people also contacted the police suggesting the names of other girls, but they were all later traced. Karen Price, however, could not be found.

This was a great step forward, but there was still some uncertainty about the skeleton's identity. The dental records of Karen Price were obtained and handed to Dr Whittaker, who found that they matched the teeth in the skull. Dr Peter Vanezis, then Senior Lecturer at the London Hospital, used video techniques to superimpose images of the photograph and the skull. The match was exact.

One afternoon, Superintendent Evans telephoned me to thank me for my report and to bring me up to date with the progress of the investigation. In spite of the many successes so far, he was still anxious about the identification. He said that some people were not convinced by the evidence presented in favour of the deceased being Karen Price and that there were those who were casting doubt on the validity of Neave's reconstruction. He told me that he had hoped to carry out DNA 'fingerprinting' on the remains and to compare the results with DNA fingerprints from Karen Price's parents, but that he had been advised that this would be impossible in view of the age of the remains.

At that time, I happened to be studying some fossil insect fragments found among the bones of mammoths and I was aware that other scientists involved in the project on the mammoths were trying to extract DNA from the bones. I also knew that DNA had been extracted from Egyptian mummies and other very old human and animal remains. It is not so their much age that matters, as far as the state of preservation of DNA is concerned, but the physical properties of the surroundings in which they have been lying. An eight-year-old skeleton should, in principle, offer the distinct possibility of finding some DNA for analysis. I told Superintendent Evans all this and he asked me to recommend someone who could undertake the task of extracting DNA from the remains for 'fingerprinting'. At my suggestion he contacted Dr Erika Hagelberg, then at the John Radcliffe Hospital in Oxford, who was one of the leading authorities on 'ancient' DNA. She extracted a DNA sample which was 'amplified', using a technique known as the polymerase chain reaction or 'PCR'. This technique generates sufficient DNA material for analysis. The work on the DNA fingerprinting was carried out by Professor (now Sir) Alec Jeffreys, its inventor. The results were entirely consistent with the skeleton being the child of Karen Price's parents. It was the first time that bone DNA analysis had been used successfully to identify an individual. The validity of Neave's reconstruction was demonstrated. The investigation, as far as the matter of identification was concerned, was complete. As yet, however, there was no clue as to who had killed Karen Price and why; the police investigation appeared to have arrived at a dead end. But at least D.C.S. Williams had achieved his aim of burying the girl with a name.

As the police investigation progressed, BBC Television made a film about the case. When this was broadcast, a member of the public contacted the police and gave them information that led to the apprehension of one Idris Ali, a small-time criminal. Ali was questioned by the police for two days, before breaking down and confessing that he had been present at the murder of Karen Price. He had been to the same school as Karen and, much later, had prevailed upon her to work for him as a prostitute. He had also involved another man, Alan Charlton, in the prostitution racket and, during an argument at Number 29, Fitzhamon Embankment, when Karen refused to pose for nude photographs, Charlton and Ali had beaten and strangled her and buried her body in the garden. Charlton had gone to live in England, where he was arrested by the police after Ali's confession.

After I had given evidence at the trial of Charlton and Ali, I stayed in court to listen to that of the others. I was particularly interested in the DNA evidence given by Dr Hagelberg and Professor Jeffreys as it was an historic occasion, being the first time that PCR-related evidence had been accepted by a British court. A teenaged girl friend of Karen's also gave evidence, saying that she had witnessed the killing. The evidence was overwhelming; Charlton and Ali were both convicted, Charlton being sentenced to life imprisonment and Ali, because he was under age at the time of the murder, was detained at Her Majesty's Pleasure. Both men appealed against their sentences; at his re-trial, Ali pleaded guilty to manslaughter and was released, having already served enough time for his offence. Charlton's appeal was thrown out and his life sentence was confirmed.

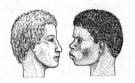

The forensic evidence from this case made it a classic of police detection. In particular, the facial reconstruction and the DNA work showed how even the totally unknown remains of a human being can, with skill and patience, be identified. Since that investigation took place, the Karen Price case has been used as a model by other police enquiries in cases involving unknown human remains, but there was a time when such an investigation could not have taken place at all and the identity of the victim would have had to be determined by very different means.

One evening, in the days before Alec Jeffreys had invented his DNA fingerprinting technique, I received a telephone call from Professor

Alan Usher, then Professor of Forensic Pathology at Sheffield University. He told me that dismembered human skeletal remains had been found at a house in Wakefield in West Yorkshire. There was insect activity on many of the remains and he wondered whether I would like to look into the case. Of course I agreed and he said he would ask the police to send the samples to Cambridge the next day.

The background to this case is unique in my experience, the accused, like myself, being a university-based scientist. His name was Anthony Samson Perera and he was a Lecturer at Leeds University's Dental School, specializing in Oral Biology, the science concerned with the structure and function of the mouth, teeth and jaws. He was married with two small sons and had an adopted thirteen-year-old daughter, Nilanthi. The family, including Nilanthi, hailed from Sri Lanka. Nilanthi appeared to be well liked in the neighbourhood, but there came a time when neighbours slowly realized that they had not seen her for some time. At first they were concerned about the child, but over the months their concern turned to alarm when, even at the height of the hot summer, Nilanthi still did not appear. Thinking that the girl might have left and gone elsewhere, some of the neighbours asked the parents where she was, but the answers they received suggested that Nilanthi was still residing in the house. In desperation, the residents of the street wrote a letter to the Social Services Department expressing their concerns.

A few days after the social workers received the letter they contacted the police. Detective Inspector Tom Hodgson, a very determined and tenacious officer, took charge of the case and immediately paid a visit to the Perera household. The first thing he observed was that Dr Perera was an insufferably arrogant man. His manner towards Hodgson and his colleagues was one of condescension, bordering on the ill-mannered. He seemed to believe that, as a scientist, he was superior to other men. He certainly did not seem worried that the police were interested in his activities and he behaved as though nothing and nobody could touch him. He was eventually to be disabused of this notion.

When Inspector Hodgson asked Dr Perera about Nilanthi's whereabouts he was told that the girl was an orphan whom they had adopted and brought to England to be educated, but that she could not settle down to life in England and had eventually been sent back to Sri Lanka, where she was now living with Dr Perera's mother, Mrs Winifred Perera. Nilanthi, said Dr Perera, was really only a simple 'jungle girl' – why was such a fuss being made over her? Inspector Hodgson wanted to know how Nilanthi had returned to Sri Lanka. Dr

Perera said that he had taken her by air to Sicily, where his brother was living, and had asked his brother to take her back to Sri Lanka. He added that he hoped to bring Nilanthi to England again when she was older.

Inspector Hodgson was still suspicious. He made enquiries with the airline company, but found no evidence to confirm that Nilanthi had left England. It was possible, however, that if she had travelled as a minor with Dr Perera as her father, her name might have been omitted from the passenger list. Hodgson asked the airline company's representative in Sri Lanka to check whether Nilanthi was, in fact, living with Dr Perera's mother, but the company were unable to carry out the enquiry. Interpol were then contacted and, through them, a request was made for the enquiry to be undertaken by the Sri Lankan Police. The results of the enquiry eventually came through; Mrs Winifred Perera had not seen Nilanthi since she left for England over three years earlier. Once again, Inspector Hodgson called at Dr Perera's house. He confronted him with the results of his investigations and asked him for an explanation. Quite unperturbed, Perera insisted that he had taken Nilanthi to Sicily and handed her over to his brother, but that he had illegally overstayed his permitted period of residence in Italy and had had to leave. Perera said that he did not know where his brother was now and had written to his parents to ask for his address. Dr Perera was not going to budge an inch, but his overbearing self-confidence proved his undoing.

The breakthrough that Inspector Hodgson was waiting for came totally unexpectedly and was the direct result of Perera's contempt for the thoughts and feelings of others. One day, Frank Ayton, Perera's colleague at the university, contacted Inspector Hodgson and told him that he had found some bones lying in enamel dishes and glass jars in the laboratory they shared. Apparently, Perera had brought these items to the laboratory, his arrogance being such that it never occurred to him that Ayton might be suspicious. That same day Inspector Hodgson visited Ayton at Leeds University. At last he had the evidence he needed. Ayton showed him a coffee jar containing what appeared to be human bones, as well as a five-litre beaker with similar contents in a green fluid. A further search of the laboratory revealed a stainless steel tray with human bones lying in decalcifying fluid. All these finds were removed for further examination.

The next time Inspector Hodgson arrived at Dr Perera's house he was armed with a search warrant which he used to good effect. Examination of the house revealed human remains (mainly vertebral bones and rotting flesh) inside three indoor plant pots. Further investigation resulted in the discovery of human bones beneath the living room floorboards. A search of the garden revealed a recently-disturbed burial spot behind the garage; it contained human bones and quantities of long black hair. There was no shortage of incriminating evidence.

One might have thought that these discoveries would have confounded Dr Perera but his self-confidence remained unshakeable. When asked to explain why he had human bones under the floorboards of his house, he said that they were biological samples from his scientific work and that he had nowhere else to put them and that, in any case, concealing them under the floorboards would avoid any 'misunderstandings' when visitors came to the house. Why did he have *long* bones, when he was an *oral* biologist? He had broad interests in biology; he was not a narrow-minded academic. Why were there vertebrae and rotting flesh in the plant pots? They were pork chops, placed there as fertilizer. But the remains were definitely human; how did he account for that? He had obtained a cadaver from Peradeniya University in Sri Lanka for scientific study, but when it began to deteriorate he placed parts of it in the plant pots and the garden because their nutritive properties would benefit the plants. Did he attempt to remove some of the buried material from the garden before the police came? Of course not, why should he? Were all the remains from one cadaver? Probably not, since he had bones from various individuals for scientific study. How did he explain the fact that the Italian authorities had no record of Nilanthi's arrival in Sicily? They were clearly incompetent at keeping proper records. He was brazen and unrepentant to the last. In view of the discoveries in the house and the laboratory, Dr and Mrs Perera were put under arrest.

D.Cs King and Jaworski duly arrived at my laboratory in Cambridge a few days after my conversation with Professor Usher, armed with several bags of samples and a number of questions. Had any of the remains that had been found under the floorboards been removed from the garden? Was there anything to link all the remains – those in the plant pots, those under the floorboards, as well as those in the garden and the laboratory – to one another? D.C. King began to unpack the samples and handed me a specimen bag containing some of the remains found beneath the floor. I held it up to the light and the first question was answered instantly. Yes, Dr Perera had removed some of the remains that had been buried in the garden or, at least, in a garden, for swarming inside the transparent plastic bag were hundreds of tiny mites belonging to species that are predatory upon other small invertebrate animals in the soil. Of course, a microscopic examination would be necessary to confirm this, but it seemed that here was strong evidence that Dr Perera had lied. The remains under the floorboards had been lying on a concrete base some eighteen inches below. There was no soil there and yet there were hundreds of mites. What had they been feeding on? What were they doing on a concrete base that could not have supplied them with their invertebrate prey? The answer must be that they had been brought there with the remains that were exhumed from the garden. My subsequent microscopic examination confirmed the identity of the mites.

There was a great deal of other evidence to examine. Various fly larvae were found among all the remains from house, garden and laboratory; these provided evidence of a link between the samples. Among the species involved were insects associated with human dwellings that are extremely unlikely to occur naturally in a laboratory environment. This suggested that the remains in the laboratory had been moved there from the house. Moreover, there were larvae belonging to a species that starts breeding in the spring, the time of year in which Nilanthi went missing and when Dr Perera had said he had taken her to Sicily.

I needed further samples to complete this work and went up to Yorkshire to collect them from the house and garden. I also wanted to examine the area beneath the floorboards to satisfy myself that the mites could not have been living there. It was a cold and desolate winter's day when I arrived at the railway station and was met by D.Cs King and Jaworski who drove me to the house. It was of fairly modern construction and had clearly been recently decorated. There was an unpleasant, pervasive smell. I went out into the garden with King and Jaworski to seek the further soil samples I needed – three men digging in a Yorkshire garden on a grey wintry day, searching for evidence to explain the death or disappearance of an innocent thirteen-year-old girl. I have searched many murder scenes for clues and have been involved in the investigation of many a brutal crime, but I cannot remember examining a scene with such a bleak feeling of the wickedness of mankind as I had in that garden that day. Perhaps my knowledge of Dr Perera's contempt for his so-called 'jungle girl' and his total lack of remorse fostered this mood. Perhaps the cold, grey weather contributed. I noticed that the two normally ebullient constables also looked subdued.

When we finished our search outside we entered the house and I examined the space beneath the floorboards. The base was, indeed, made of solid concrete and no part of it could have provided a breeding place for mites. I collected more samples, including some strands of very long, jet-black hair. Eventually, I finished what I had come to do and was glad to be out of the house.

On my return to Cambridge I completed my examination of the new evidence which amply confirmed my earlier conclusions. I wrote my report and sent it to Inspector Hodgson who came for a visit to discuss my findings. Though most improbable, it was still *possible* that Dr Perera was telling the truth and that the remains might not have been those of Nilanthi. Inspector Hodgson told me that he was going to Sri Lanka to make some further investigations since Nilanthi was not, in fact, an orphan and might indeed be alive and well and living with her parents. These confirmed what had always been suspected. Nilanthi's parents were contacted but they had not seen her since Dr Perera had taken her to England. It was Hodgson's unhappy duty to tell them what had become of their daughter. The records at Peradeniya University revealed that no human cadavers had been made available to Dr Perera for scientific research. Nilanthi was nowhere to be found. She was not in Sri Lanka, she was not in England, she was not in Sicily.

But the crucial question of whether the remains were those of Nilanthi still had to be answered. It was therefore necessary to establish their age, sex and race. A number of other specialists had joined Professor Usher in examining the bones. Dr Geoffrey Craig, a dental scientist, concluded that the teeth might have been those of an early teenaged girl but could not exclude the possibility that they were the teeth of a slightly older boy. He also tentatively concluded that the teeth might have belonged to someone of Asian origin but again he could not be absolutely certain. All the pathological, anatomical and anthropological investigations suggested that the remains could have been those of a thirteen-year-old girl of Asian origin, but these conclusions were a matter of general probability, no more.

Inspector Hodgson continued to try to persuade Dr Perera to admit his guilt. He accused Perera of murdering Nilanthi in the garage and then locking up her body in the boot of his car. Predictably, Perera denied this. Hodgson pointed out that the carpet lining the boot had disappeared, probably because it had been blood-stained. Came Perera's defiant reply: 'If the carpet is missing, so is your evidence'. Hodgson told him that he was going to be tried for murder. Again, the answer came with cool confidence: 'You prepare your case, Inspector, and I will prepare mine'.

At the trial, Dr Perera observed the proceedings with an expression of barely-concealed contempt. Professor Usher, Dr Craig and I gave evidence, as did a number of other forensic witnesses, but it was impossible for science to prove beyond all doubt that the remains were those of Nilanthi. Nevertheless, the entomological evidence weighed heavily against Dr Perera and the evidence as a whole proved the case against him beyond reasonable doubt. For if Dr Perera, her guardian and father by adoption, did not know where Nilanthi was and if she was in none of the three countries in which she could reasonably be expected to be found, she must be dead. In that case, to whom did the bones in Dr Perera's house, garden and laboratory belong? There was nothing in the bones to suggest that they could not have been Nilanthi's. There was no doubt in the mind of the jury. She was dead, murdered by a man who thought of her as nothing but a 'jungle girl'. The verdict was 'Guilty', and Dr Anthony Samson Perera was sentenced to prison for life.

In court Mrs Perera, on the other hand, struck me as an innocent woman, devastated by what had happened. By all accounts, she had been devoted to Nilanthi and was unaware of her domineering husband's horrific deed. She was given a suspended sentence and released from custody.

One question remained unanswered; what led Dr Perera to murder Nilanthi? On this question discretion must prevail. Certainly, no motive was ever proven, but many people puzzled over why Dr Perera, the self-important scientist, should stoop to murdering a defenceless girl. She meant nothing to him; as far as he was concerned she was little better than an animal. He was an arrogant man, whose word was law in his own house. He expected to be given what he wanted and would not be crossed ...

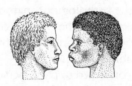

Dr Perera's trial ended just as Alec Jeffreys was preparing to announce his DNA fingerprinting technique to the world. It had not yet entered the armoury of forensic science and so could not be used in the attempts to identify Nilanthi's putative remains. In contrast, as a result of Jeffreys' technique and Neave's facial reconstruction, the investigation into the murder of Karen Price had been a great success and the identity of the victim established well beyond reasonable doubt despite the remains, when found, belonging to a person then totally unknown. In the Perera case, there was always a very good idea who the victim might have been, yet it was not possible to establish her identity with the same certainty as in the Karen Price case.

With the techniques now at the disposal of the Criminal Justice System, the identification of human remains has become much easier. This is not to say that the establishment of identity is an easy matter. In spite of its great power and sensitivity as a technique, DNA fingerprinting cannot help when there is no idea who a dead person might be. It was successful in the Karen Price case only after Neave's facial reconstruction suggested an identity for the remains. The DNA from the skeleton could then be compared with that of Karen's parents. Although this technology can be used to determine certain attributes, such as the sex of the deceased, a DNA fingerprint, on its own, can tell us nothing. One must be able to compare two such 'fingerprints' in order to arrive at a conclusion.

I was once involved in the investigation of a case of murder in which an unknown body was discovered lying shallowly buried in a field in Hampshire. A farmer unearthed the body when he was working his land in Little Abshot Farm; as he drove, he felt something slowing his tractor down, so he stopped to investigate. To his horror, he found a human arm and shoulder-blade caught in the machinery. Going over the ground he had covered, he found some way back the body of a man lying, now only half-concealed, and realized that he had partly pulled the body out of its 'grave' and wrenched off the arm. He immediately called the police.

The body had been buried inside a sleeping bag, but despite this it was still to some extent maggot-infested. The police wanted to know when the man had died; when he had been buried and above all, who he was. Here was a case in which DNA, at that stage at least, would not have been able to establish identity, so it was necessary to determine what kind of person he was: his race, stature, medical history and so forth.

The first person to examine the body was the pathologist, Dr Roger Ainsworth, who concluded that the victim was of either East European or Asian origin. The body was uncircumcized, so the man was probably not an orthodox Muslim or Jew. His stomach contents were examined and it was discovered that his last meal had been of wheat, tomatoes and beans and that it had been consumed only a few hours before he died. Damage to the back of the skull revealed the cause of death to be blows to the head with a blunt instrument.

The possible racial identification of the remains was particularly interesting, because the company that managed the farm where the body was found was in the habit of employing as many as 200 itinerant labourers, many from Eastern Europe and the Indian sub-continent. Other curious finds followed. An Indian scarf, known as a *chunni*, was found on the body, although it is a garment usually worn by women. This seemed to suggest that the man was Asian, but it could also have suggested that an Indian woman might have been involved, either in the role of murderess or girlfriend. It might even indicate that the man was homosexual. The body was measured and found to be 5 feet 4½ inches tall. He took size 5 in shoes and there was a stud in his left ear.

My role was to determine the time and place of death. The body was infested with two kinds of maggots: those of the common bluebottle and much smaller ones belonging to scuttle flies. The mere presence of the bluebottle maggots suggested that the body must have lain unburied or, at least, exposed to fly activity, for some time before burial. Studying the extent of development of the maggots, I was able to conclude that the latest time at which the victim could have been killed was two weeks prior to discovery.

There had apparently been a heap of gravel above the spot where the body had been lying, but this had been removed some time before the remains came to light. The burial place was examined by archaeologists, Dr Margaret Cox and Mr Robert Edwards. They could find no gravel inside the grave, so concluded that burial had occurred after the removal of the heap, which had taken place three days after my minimum estimated time of death. Dr Peter Bull, a soil scientist, examined the soil inside the sleeping bag and found that it was not the same as that in the field. Clearly, the body had been moved from another, temporary burial spot.

It was the skull that was to supply the most important clues. It was taken to Dr David Whittaker, a forensic odontologist. He sectioned some of the teeth to study the proportion of living tissue in them. Since the ratio of living to non-living tissue changes with age (the living tissue steadily decreases), such a study should give an estimate of the victim's age at the time of his death. Dr Whittaker concluded that the man had been between 39 and 42 years old when he died. He also made other discoveries. The man's two top front teeth were not in the middle. This feature was so odd that Dr Whittaker said that even a casual acquaintance would have noticed that there was 'something funny about his teeth'. He also found that, although the teeth showed little decay, they were excessively worn down, which could have been caused by sand in a diet of vegetables. Thus the person could have lived in a sandy region. The metal crown on the lower left molar was made of gold that had probably been melted from jewellery, suggesting dental work carried out in Eastern Europe or Asia. The odontological conclusion agreed with the other evidence.

Finally, enter Richard Neave, the medical artist. He was sent the skull which was in several pieces, as it had suffered some damage when it was unearthed. With the help of colleagues at Manchester University, he reconstructed the skull and made an exact plaster of Paris replica of it. Using this and working with potter's clay, Neave built up the face by degrees. After three days, he had a model of the unknown man's head. The face appeared slightly lopsided, with prominent, rounded cheeks.

So, what did all this forensic activity reveal? That the victim was probably either Asian or Eastern European and about forty years old; that he was not a Muslim nor Jewish; that his face and teeth were peculiarly lopsided; that he had distinctive, rounded cheeks; that he wore a stud in his left ear; that he was short and had very small feet; that he had fed on an abrasive diet; that he had lain exposed for some time before being buried; that his body had been moved from one place of concealment to another; that he had been dead for at least two weeks before his body was discovered; that a woman was probably involved in the case; and that he had been killed by a series of blows to the back of the head with a blunt instrument.

The police released a photograph of Neave's reconstruction and the other forensic evidence at a press conference. These were then published in the newspapers and shown on television. Before long, people came forward who recognized Neave's rebuilt face. The victim was identified as one Harjit Singh, an Indian who lived in London and who had disappeared.

There remained one last thing for the police to do. They tracked down Singh's dental records and took them to Dr Whittaker, who examined them and found that they matched the victim's teeth exactly. The investigation as to the man's identity was now complete.

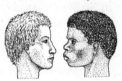

The stories of Karen Price, Nilanthi Perera and Harjit Singh show how difficult it can be to establish the identity of the dead. Naturally, the problems become much greater when the remains of long-dead individuals are examined. One of the main sources of error in such matters comes from once-fashionable death masks. I have seen many images and reproductions of these and I remain quite unconvinced of their authenticity in most cases. I have looked at the alleged death masks of Bonnie Prince Charlie, Sir Isaac Newton, Admiral Nelson and the poet

Keats, among others, but can only say that the faces do not look like those of dead men. To be more specific, the lips are usually full and often protruding, the cheeks appear to be rounded and the whole expression is that of one who is 'holding still', as the photographers say; in other words, there is a tension in the face, however serene and calm the expression may look. A dead man's face is sunken, the lips are fallen in, the cheeks collapsed and the 'expression' is one of complete relaxation. The death mask of Oliver Cromwell is among the few that I have seen that seems to me to be genuine.

There seem to me to be three possible explanations for these so-called death masks. They may be masks made before the death of the individual, straightforward forgeries, or – and I feel the most likely explanation – they are made from moulds that were taken after death and then modified to produce a more pleasant or flattering effect, or at least an effect that reflects the person's appearance in life. The purpose of taking a death mask at all was so that relations and friends might remember the living appearance of the departed one. It seems highly unlikely that the moulds would have been made shortly before death, since this would clearly be a dreadful thing to do to someone dying. One cannot now determine how many are forgeries, but some proba-bly are and they would more likely have been made some time after the person's death since the motive could only have been financial gain.

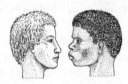

Although there are great difficulties in establishing identity when con-fronted with actual human remains from historic times, nevertheless, this does not mean that one cannot arrive at some very reasonable con-clusions. The following event from English history is a good illustra-tion of what can be achieved under such circumstances.

'Nor among the English was any worse deed ever done than this, since they first sought the land of Britain', wrote the anonymous author of the Anglo-Saxon Chronicles for the year A.D. 978. The event he was describing was so awful that during that year 'a bloody cloud was seen many times, in the likeness of fire, most often manifested at midnight'. The terrible deed to which the chronicler was referring was the murder of King Edward, henceforth to become known as Edward the Martyr, son of the revered King Edgar the Peaceable.

Edward was born in or about the year A.D. 963, but his mother,

Queen Æthelflæd, died shortly after his birth. Two years later, his father King Edgar married again and the new Queen, Ælfryth, bore him another son, Æthelred. When Edgar died in 975, Edward became king – the first English king to succeed in his minority. Ælfryth resented the new king, desiring her own son to sit on the Throne. However, there was little that she could do to bring this about until one day fate played into her hands.

William of Malmesbury, a most meticulous and scholarly Benedictine monk, recorded that the sixteen-year old King Edward was out hunting in the West Country, when he found himself in the vicinity of Corfe Castle. Tiring of the chase and wishing to see his half-brother Æthelred, he approached the Castle, where he was greeted by Queen Ælfryth. Affecting pleasure at seeing him, the Queen offered him a drink while he was still seated upon his horse. Then, as he drank, one of her retainers stabbed him with a dagger. Trying to save himself, the young King spurred his horse, but he slipped from the saddle and, with one foot caught in the stirrup and leaving a trail of blood on the ground, was dragged a long way before he died. Wrote the Anglo-Saxon chronicler: 'King Edward was killed in the evening at the gap of Corfe on March 18th; he was buried at Wareham, with no kingly honours'. Yet even this dishonourable burial was almost denied him, for the vindictive Queen sent her retainers to throw Edward's body into a bog so that no one could find it. Miraculously, a pillar of light illuminated the spot and the body was recovered and removed to Wareham. In A.D. 980, Dunstan (later St Dunstan), Archbishop of Canterbury, disinterred the bones and buried them at Shaftesbury Abbey.

The years passed. In the sixteenth century, following the Dissolution of the Monasteries, the Abbey of Shaftesbury fell into ruins. The land upon which it stood eventually passed to the family of Mr John Claridge. In 1931, Mr Claridge unearthed some bones from the ruins, however, it was not until 1962 that the bones were subjected to forensic examination. A distinguished pathologist, Dr Thomas Stowell, conducted an investigation, the aim of which was to determine the age, sex, stature and race, and the cause of death. The bones were without doubt those of a young man, between 5ft 5in and 5ft 8in in height. The age at death, deduced from the degree of maturation of the bones, was estimated at being between seventeen and twenty-one years. Although it is believed that Edward was sixteen when he died, we cannot be certain. Dr Stowell concluded that the most probable age was at the lower end of this range. Examination of the skull showed it to be of the 'long-headed' type, typical of Saxons, not 'round-headed', typical of Celts. Edward was, of course, a Saxon.

The injuries sustained by the skeleton were the most revealing finds of the investigation. The left arm was broken in several places, suggesting that it had been violently twisted behind the back. The left thigh bone had sustained fractures of a kind that would be expected if someone had fallen backwards from the saddle and then been dragged by the foot along the ground. The evidence from the Shaftesbury bones seems reasonably strong and supports the premise that the remains did, indeed, belong to Edward the Martyr.

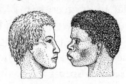

So often it is not the passage of time that makes identification difficult; rather it is the nature of the evidence available and the exact question being asked. The true identity of the perpetrator of the murder that took place at Deadman's Hill, Buckinghamshire, in August, 1961 – a case that became famous as the A6 murder – has yet to be determined. This is the much-discussed case of James Hanratty.

Late on 22nd August, Michael Gregsten was sitting with his girl-friend, Valerie Storie, in his parked car when suddenly an armed man entered and sat in the back. Ordering Gregsten out, he shot him dead on the spot, then raped Valerie and shot her. She survived but was crippled for life.

Police investigations resulted in the discovery of two empty cartridge cases in a hotel room occupied by James Hanratty. The cartridges were shown to be from the murder weapon. However, this same hotel room had been occupied the previous night by a man named Peter Alphon. Both men were arrested.

Interviewed by police, Valerie Storie said that her assailant had deep-set brown eyes. From her general description of him the police produced an 'Identikit' picture. Evidence from other witnesses who had seen a man driving Gregsten's car later in the day was used to produce a second Identikit picture. The two pictures did not resemble one another and neither looked like Hanratty. Then, a curious thing happened. Valerie Storie changed her mind about her assailant's eyes. From being deep-set and brown, they now became saucer-like and ice-blue — the real colour of Hanratty's eyes. Storie failed to pick out Alphon from an identity parade, but she did pick out Hanratty. At his trial, Hanratty said that he had been in Liverpool at the time of the murder, but he later changed his story and said that he had been in

Rhyl with friends. He did not name them and none came forward to support his story. He was found guilty and sentenced to death.

After the trial, a number of witnesses did come forward to say that they had seen Hanratty in Rhyl at the time of the murder. In another most extraordinary development, Alphon began boasting that he had been hired by an interested party to break up the romance between Michael Gregsten and Valerie Storie. Consequently, great doubt was cast on the safety of the conviction. Nevertheless, James Hanratty was hanged at Bedford Prison in April, 1962. The argument continues and, at the time of writing, further evidence is being sought to establish the identity of the guilty party.

It is a strange irony that while we can be reasonably sure that the bones that lay in the grounds of Shaftesbury Abbey for 1,000 years are those of King Edward the Martyr, we remain uncertain of the identity of the perpetrator of a crime committed less than forty years ago.

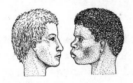

Astonishingly, it is sometimes difficult to recognize a dead body as *being* a dead body. I have been involved in a number of police cases in which those who discovered a corpse were, initially at least, unable to recognize it as such. The first example I can give of this kind of mistake concerns the rather horrific experience of two elderly people. Their son was in the habit of visiting them every Sunday for lunch, but one Sunday he did not appear. When several days had passed and the parents had still not heard from him, they went to his flat and entered it, using a key that their son had given them. They found the place in a mess and began to tidy it up. As they went about the flat, they stepped over a large object on the floor several times. This object, they said later, looked like a dummy or a gorilla suit. It took them three-quarters of an hour to realize that it was, in fact, the body of their murdered son. It is true that the body had begun to decompose and the skin to blacken, but it was wearing their son's clothes. It was also maggot-infested and the smell must have been overpowering. Yet they suspected nothing until they decided to tidy the object away. The experience of these unfortunate people was a very traumatic one and it may be that their minds simply refused to acknowledge the truth until it could no longer be avoided.

Other cases support the belief that recognition of a dead body as such is often strongly resisted. In one case I investigated, the courtyard of a block of flats had become flooded. The cause was a blocked drain and a plumber had been called in to unblock it. He had some difficulty, but was eventually able to extract the object causing the blockage. It was, in fact, the dead body of a woman, but the plumber identified it as a clothes-shop dummy. It was some time before he could be convinced that it was not.

The identification of living people can even present difficulties. Witnesses who are asked to pick out a particular individual during a police identity parade frequently make mistakes and, incredibly, such errors are sometimes made by people who know the individual very well.

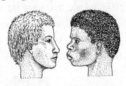

One of the first recorded cases of forensic identification was carried out with the help of a fly. The story is recorded in a thirteenth-century Chinese manuscript entitled *The Washing Away of Wrongs*, which is probably the earliest known manual on forensic science. One day, a farmer was found dead in a paddy-field, having been struck down with a sickle; the wounds could not be interpreted any other way. The investigating officer asked all the local farmers to stand in a row, each placing his sickle on the ground before him. It was a hot day and flies, attracted by the smell of blood and other body fluids that still emanated from it, arrived and settled upon one particular sickle. Its owner was arrested and, presumably, dealt with in a suitable manner.

CHAPTER 8

Past Times

O, call back yesterday, bid time return.
Shakespeare, *Richard II* Act III, Scene 2

The small, golden-brown objects under the microscope each measured less than one millimetre in length. They were clearly the pupal cases of some very small flies, but their highly distinctive appearance suggested that they belonged to one particular species, which, under the circumstances, was baffling. I examined them as closely as I could, though there was only one possible identification, improbable though it was, in view of where they had been found. The fly in question rejoices in the name of *Thoracochaeta zosterae*, which does not easily roll off the tongue. The specimens I was examining had been recovered from a Viking chamber that was being excavated during the archaeological diggings at the Coppergate in York. The puzzling thing was that these little insects breed in the rotting seaweed so often found lying on the beach and which is not known to occur far inland. How, then, did pupal cases of this insect come to be found in a subterranean chamber so far from the sea?

I took the results of my work on these and other insect specimens from the archaeological dig to Mr Harry Kenward, who was directing the study of the faunal and floral remains recovered from the York excavations. I told him what I thought these pupal cases were and that I was quite puzzled by the whole business in view of the insect's known habits and distribution. To my surprise, he did not find this at all odd; indeed, what I had told him about the insect made perfect sense to him in the context of the excavation.

He told me that when the Danes settled in England over one thousand years ago they were relative newcomers to agriculture. Settlement changed them from marauding pirates into more gentle farmers; nevertheless, they maintained a special relationship with the sea. The Danes would collect great quantities of decaying seaweed for use as manure and transport it inland to their farms, where they stored it in special chambers. Clearly, the larvae and puparia of the fly came with the seaweed, to be examined more than a millennium later by a very puzzled entomologist!

I have examined remains from York, St Kilda and Hadrian's Wall; from the crypts of London churches; from Egyptian mummies; and from North American Indian burial sites. Observations on the fragmented remains of flies and their progeny can often lead to a better understanding of history. In this example of the seaweed fly, evidence was provided supporting the idea that the chamber in question was used for a particular purpose, but the general conclusion to be drawn from the remains of flies in archaeological deposits is that conditions in and around many – indeed perhaps most – human dwellings in those far off days must have been extremely unhygienic. This may not seem surprising to many people, but the extent of the squalor and the consequent fly nuisance may not be fully appreciated. I once examined puparial samples from a trench, many yards in length and several feet deep, in Viking York. The trench was solid with puparia – there was nothing else in it – all of which belonged to one species, *Musca domestica*, the housefly. From this and other evidence, it was concluded that the trench was the run-off from a latrine. It is easy to imagine the numbers of flies that must have been buzzing about at the time, making life and every day activities extremely irksome, to say the least. Today, it is still customary to think of the housefly as a common insect but, in fact, it is not all that common in Britain any more. Higher standards of hygiene and more efficient sanitary and sewage systems have resulted in a dramatic drop in its numbers. The flies most commonly seen in British houses these days are not true houseflies but other species. In other countries, houseflies are still common enough, but even in some tropical countries they have been greatly reduced in number, or even eradicated. For instance, in Singapore it was made a legal offence to have houseflies in one's home and within a few years no houseflies remained.

A visit to the tropics, or indeed to the cold parts of northern Canada, will reveal the real extent of fly nuisance. Large parts of Canada remain uninhabited, not only because of the prevalence of biting flies, such as mosquitoes and horseflies, but because of the superabundance of swarms of non-biting, 'nuisance' flies. A single, persistent fly on a hot summer's day can be irritating enough, but is as nothing to the enervating and debilitating effect that millions of such creatures can have on the human mind. The entomological evidence from Hadrian's Wall suggests that the lives of the Roman legionaries in that remote frontier of the Empire must have been extremely uncomfortable during the summer months.

The transmission of disease by flies was another serious problem in the past and remains so in many parts of the world. Flies can transmit bacteria to food simply by walking over it, having recently walked on faeces or other decomposing matter. The way flies feed, by 'spitting' on their food to soften and partly 'digest' it before sucking it up, is another source of bacterial contamination. Medical entomologists have long argued about the true role of the mechanical transmission of disease by flies, but it now seems clear that, whatever its extent, it is considerable.

Worldwide, flies are undoubtedly responsible for very many deaths annually, but the exact, or even approximate, numbers can only be guessed at. One can, however, get some kind of idea of the magnitude of the problem when one considers that, with the decline of horse-drawn vehicles during the first half of the twentieth century, the incidence of deaths from summer diarrhoea in Britain decreased. It seems clear that the reduction in the amount of manure on the roads reduced the number of flies that could contaminate food.

In regions of the world where large numbers of fly breeding-sites are still common, the medical problem continues to be appreciable. But, if flies were removed, say by chemical insecticides, without first addressing the problem of the breeding-sites, the decomposing matter would generate truly unimaginable amounts of bacteria which would infect everything. Flies, although transmitting bacteria, nevertheless keep the situation under control, for their progeny consume the prime source of the germs and remove it entirely from the environment. So, it is no use removing the flies and leaving the source of infection, for it would make the problem much worse. Seen in this light, the fly is not the cause of the problem, but its natural ameliorator.

As my work on the lives of maggots has taken me into the worlds of forensic science and archaeology, I am sometimes asked whether I have ever been able to combine both fields of inquiry and solve a crime committed hundreds or even thousands of years ago. I must confess that I have often thought that it would be wonderful if the opportunity to investigate such a case presented itself. The idea of discovering the murder of a Pharaoh of Ancient Egypt for example has an irresistible attraction, but alas such an opportunity has yet to present itself.

It is often possible to determine how soon after death a body has been buried by studying the insect remains associated with it. For example, I have been impressed by the fact that bodies in church crypts seem almost always to have been buried very soon after death. As might be expected, the insect fauna of buried bodies is very different from that of exposed bodies. Underground, bodies decompose at a much slower rate and far fewer species are involved. Bluebottles and greenbottles, which form such a dominant component of the corpse fauna above ground, are generally absent. It is interesting that, although they will not lay eggs on the soil above a carcass they cannot reach, blowflies clearly can detect the presence of such bodies. Experiments have shown that bluebottles and greenbottles are even attracted to the carcasses of white mice buried under soil in plastic containers; they will arrive in some numbers and walk over the soil, but will not lay their eggs. However, if any bodily exudate such as blood is present on the surface, these flies will lay their eggs, the resulting maggots eventually burrowing their way through the soil to the body. This has been demonstrated both in laboratory experiments and in observations in nature. Moreover, even without the presence of any exudate, a number of other flies can accomplish the amazing feat of reaching buried bodies. For example, if their antennae can detect the presence of a body underground, the so-called false stable flies of the genus *Muscina* will lay their eggs on the surface of the soil, the hatching larvae burrowing into the soil and invading the corpse.

The small, enigmatic scuttle flies, mentioned in an earlier chapter, are of special importance. A number of scuttle fly species have the uncanny ability to find buried corpses, though how they do this is not fully understood. There is also a great deal of evidence to show that they can pass their entire life-cycle underground and, indeed, go through a number of generations deep in the soil. Many years ago, an entomologist named Charles Colyer buried the body of his dog in his garden. Eighteen months after the burial he saw swarms of scuttle flies over the burial place. He decided to exhume the body and found that it was heavily infested with larval scuttle flies and that there was a one-way traffic of adult flies from the dog to the surface.

Dr Henry Disney, an authority on scuttle flies, conducted an interesting experiment by burying the carcasses of white mice in his vegetable garden in Cambridge. I was with him when he dug up the carcasses some weeks later. Although the topsoil was loose and crumbly, as one would expect in a vegetable garden, the lower levels in which the mice were buried were composed of a heavy clay. When we cracked open the clods of clay to extract the remains of the carcasses, large numbers of scuttle flies swarmed out. It is difficult to see how these minute flies could have gone about their business in the heavy, sticky clay without getting their legs and wings clogged up, but clearly they were able to come and go freely, presumably through pores and cracks in the clay.

Information from forensic cases and experimental work has shown that scuttle flies can find corpses lying up to six feet beneath the surface of the soil. All buried corpses that I have examined have had scuttle flies, or their larvae and pupae, associated with them and it seems fair to say that they are the underground equivalent of blowflies. Although the rate of development of scuttle fly larvae can, in principle, be used as a measure of time since death, our knowledge of the development of most species is very limited. Their real forensic significance lies in further long-term interpretations. For example, bodies are sometimes exhumed from illicit burial sites and exposed above ground; the presence of a typically subterranean fauna on such bodies will often reveal the fact that the body had previously been buried.

One particular species of scuttle fly, *Conicera tibialis*, has acquired the common name of 'coffin fly', because it is frequently found on buried bodies and in coffins. In many cases it was clear that several generations had developed, lived and died within the coffin, the flies leading a completely subterranean existence. This association of small flies with coffins has been known for a long time. For example, an article in *The Monthly Magazine* of December 1805, described the following event:

'In preparing for the foundation of the New Church at Lewes, it became necessary to disturb the mouldering bones of the long defunct, and in the prosecution of that unavoidable business a leaden coffin was taken up, which, on being opened, exhibited a complete skeleton of a body that had been interred about sixty years, whose leg and thigh bones, to the utter astonishment of all present, were covered with myriads of flies (of a species, perhaps, totally unknown to the naturalist) as active and strong on the wing as gnats flying in the air, on the finest evening in summer. The wings of this non-descript are white, and for distinction's

sake, the spectators gave it the name of the coffin-fly. The lead
was perfectly sound, and presented not the least chink or crevice
for the admission of air. The moisture of the flesh had not yet left
the bones, and the fallen beard lay on the under jaw.'

The bodies of most scuttle flies, including *Conicera tibialis*, are black or
dark brown in colour and the wings are the usual semi-transparent
membranes of flies. The author of the article did not give the colour of
the flies' bodies, only the wings, but it is possible that he commented
on the whiteness of the latter because they contrasted so strongly with
the colour of the bodies. In any case, it is not easy to see what they could
have been if not scuttle flies.

Another historical event is somewhat more curious. In 1285, during the
War of the Sicilian Vespers, the French army took the Spanish town of
Gerona in the territory of King Pedro of Aragon. It is said that, on
their arrival, a great swarm of white flies emanated from the body of St
Narcis in the church of St Phelin. These flies then proceeded to sting
the French troops, causing such mortality that the invaders were forced
to evacuate the city and return home defeated. The 100,000-strong
army was decimated and the King of the French, Philip III, died on his
way home. Here, we have two puzzles: first, what were the flies; and secondly, did they really bite the French soldiers, causing so many deaths?

As we have seen, scuttle flies are typically very dark-coloured insects,
yet the insects from the saint's body were described as being white. I
cannot think of any corpse-breeding fly of any size that can be
described as white, yet I can offer a tentative explanation of the description. When a fly emerges from its puparium, it is usually very pale in
colour, the full pigmentation taking place during the ensuing hours or
days. However, during the early stages after emergence the flies are not
able to fly because their wings take some time to expand and become
functional. Nevertheless, in many species the wings do expand fully
before the complete pigmentation of the body is attained and the
insects may be able to fly while still pale in colour. Alternatively, it is
possible that those who reported the incident embellished and altered
the truth; the flies became white, because white is a more spiritual
colour, better befitting a saint. Of course, I am only guessing.

The flies seen emerging from the saint's body may have been credited with the miracle that brought ruin upon the French but it is almost certain that these flies, whatever they were, could not have bitten the French soldiers and killed them in large numbers. There is no fly known whose larvae breed in dead bodies and whose adults bite human beings or animals. What, then, assaulted the French troops with such devastating the results? The attack upon Gerona took place during a particularly hot summer. The plains of Gerona were known to be malarial and it seems reasonable to conclude that the deaths among the French, including that of their king, were due to the bites of mosquitoes carrying the terrible disease. Certainly, King Philip was described as sickening with a 'fever' as he fled, 'disgracing the lilies', as Dante scornfully observed.

Another event experienced by a French army may also help to explain what happened at Gerona. In 1249, during the crusade of King Louis IX (Saint Louis) against Egypt, the French soldiers suffered great hardship from the intense heat and from 'the great plenty of flies and the great large fleas'. Clearly, the army was attacked by at least two different kinds of insects, one non-biting, the other biting. The observer in this case recognized this, but it may also have been the case that, in Gerona, two or more insect species were attacking the soldiers.

Other flies, notably the large, grey-chequered fleshflies belonging to the genus *Sarcophaga*, instead of eggs lay active maggots that have hatched within the fly's 'womb'. Often the fly will drop these maggots on to a suitable medium, even though it cannot reach it. The great French entomologist, Jean Henri Fabre, conducted some classic experiments to determine the lengths to which the female fly would go in this regard. He placed some meat at the bottom of a container, covered over with a mesh that would not allow the fly to enter, but would allow the larvae to pass through. The flies would arrive and drop their larvae on to the meat. By degrees, he increased the height of the container until there came a point when, although the fly could clearly still detect the meat, she would not drop the maggots. Fabre interpreted this as motherly love, which prevented the fly from dropping her 'babies' from too great a height!

Prehistoric and ancient burial sites can yield interesting insect evidence. This is sometimes initially confusing, since insect damage to bodies after death has occasionally been misinterpreted as an indication that the deceased person might have been suffering from disease while alive. Fly puparia have also been found associated with Egyptian mummies, which suggests that the ancient art of embalming was not as perfect as it is widely believed to have been!

The excavation of a prehistoric burial site in Canada provides a useful example of the way in which entomological evidence can contribute to the reconstruction of events. When the 2,000-2,500 year old graves in the Augustine Mound in New Brunswick were excavated, very large numbers of puparia were found associated with the remains. Of these, almost 600 belonged to blowfly species that are known to attack bodies above ground, while only 28 specimens belonged to fly species that are known to be able to invade buried bodies. The conclusion reached by the entomologist, Dr Herb Teskey, and his colleagues was that the bodies must have lain exposed above ground for a considerable time before interment, but that enough flesh remained on the body after burial to attract other species.

Another insect, associated with man since the earliest times, has managed to leave tell-tale signs of its unwelcome association in many ancient graves; it is the head louse, an insect that continues to afflict schoolchildren, even in affluent countries, to this day. The clue that the louse leaves behind is the nit – the empty casing of its egg. Nits have been found on the hair of Egyptian and Peruvian mummies and even on combs found in some of the caves in which the Dead Sea Scrolls were discovered.

The effect of insects on human affairs and human history has been and still is profound. Much has been written about this subject so I will restrict myself to discussing some little-known aspects, especially those with which I have been involved in my own work.

It is often said that many myths and legends contain at least a grain of truth. This is certainly true, but it is also the case that many stories that seem to be legendary are almost entirely factual or, at least, very likely to have happened. Discussing the plagues of Egypt, recounted in the Old Testament, Professor Bernard Greenberg assessed the probability of these events. He arrived at the conclusion that the plagues made perfect ecological sense. Although I agree with his general conclusion, I will add a few of my own, based on a reading of both the Authorised (King James's) Version and the New English Bible Version. The two translations are somewhat different and, although the earlier version has a greater literary power, the newer version is more accurate philologically and reveals information of greater interest in this particular context.

The first plague that concerns us is that of frogs. The relevant passage (*Exodus* 8: 3-4) in the King James's Bible reads:

'And the river shall bring forth frogs abundantly, which shall go up and come into thine house, and into thy bedchamber, and upon thy bed, and into the house of thy servants, and upon thy people, and into thine ovens, and into thy kneadingtroughs: And the frogs shall come up both on thee, and upon thy people, and upon all thy servants.'

The account in the New English Bible is essentially the same.

The next plague (*Exodus* 8: 16-18) according to the Authorised Version, reads:

'And the Lord said unto Moses, Say unto Aaron, Stretch out thy rod, and smite the dust of the land, that it may become lice throughout the land of Egypt. And they did so; for Aaron stretched out his hand with his rod, and smote the dust of the earth, and it became lice in man, and in beast; all the dust of the land became lice throughout all the land of Egypt. And the magicians did so with their enchantments to bring forth lice, but they could not: so there were lice upon man and beast.'

The New English Bible presents the same verses as:

'The Lord then told Moses to say to Aaron, "Stretch out your staff and strike the dust on the ground, and it will turn into maggots throughout the land of Egypt", and they obeyed. Aaron stretched out his staff and struck the dust, and it turned into maggots on man and beast. All the dust turned into maggots throughout the land of Egypt. The magicians tried to produce maggots in the same way by their spells, but they failed. The maggots were everywhere, on man and beast.'

The third plague, that of flies (*Exodus* 8: 21, 24) according to the Authorised Version reads:

'Else if thou wilt not let my people go, behold, I will send swarms of flies upon thee, and upon thy servants, and upon thy people, and into thy houses: and the houses of the Egyptians shall be full of swarms of flies, and also the ground whereon they are. And the Lord did so; and there came a grievous swarm of flies into the house of Pharaoh, and into his servants' houses, and into all the land of Egypt: the land was corrupted by reason of the swarm of flies.'

The New English Bible's account is essentially the same.

The final plague in this series (*Exodus* 9: 3, 6) in the words of the Authorised Version, is as follows:

'Behold, the hand of the Lord is upon the cattle which is in the field, upon the horses, upon the asses, upon the camels, upon the oxen, and upon the sheep: there shall be a very grievous murrain. And the Lord did that thing on the morrow, and all the cattle of Egypt died: but the cattle of the children of Israel not one.'

Again, the New English Bible agrees with this account in all essentials.

The sequence of plagues was, therefore: frogs; maggots (not lice); flies; and a disease of livestock. Greenberg points out that a mass outbreak of frogs would be followed by the death of these creatures, the accumulated heaps of whose bodies would not dry out quickly (unlike the case with individual frogs), thus providing the ideal breeding ground for flies. However, basing his argument on the Authorised Version alone, Professor Greenberg made no reference to the plague of 'lice' and argued that the plague of flies would have been the natural consequence of the deaths of so many frogs. However, the fact that the plague that followed that of the frogs was of maggots provides further evidence in support of Greenberg's argument; the missing link, so to speak, between the frogs and the flies. Finally, having had a plague of flies, it is perfectly reasonable to expect a murrain to follow.

It is important to remember that this sequence of events was described by people who did not necessarily understand the biological link between them. Their given order seems to indicate that they actually took place and were recorded faithfully. I would add one last point: a plague of frogs does not strike me as being so terrible. If I wanted to make up a fictitious catalogue of horrors, I could think of far worse things to be plagued by than frogs. To my mind, the plague of frogs gives credibility to the whole account since it is unlikely to have been mentioned unless it actually happened.

The plagues of Egypt raise another entomological point of interest. We have seen that the Authorised Version referred to 'lice' attacking men and beasts, whereas the New English Bible corrected this to 'maggots'. The word lice was probably used in the earlier version, because these insects were familiar and known to be closely associated with humans. But what about the 'beasts'? The human louse does not normally attack animals, being very closely dependent upon people. Maggots, however, are far less discriminating.

This raises another matter. So far in this book, we have mentioned maggots only in the context of dead bodies. Less well-known is their association with the living, for the maggots of many flies will, under certain circumstances, lay their eggs on live animals and people; the maggots that eventually hatch feed parasitically upon the living tissues, causing a disease known as myiasis (from the Greek *myia* = a fly).

I believe that the account in *The Book of Exodus* represents the earliest known record of myiasis. Other biblical accounts also mention the disease. Consider Job's heartfelt comment on his suffering (*Job* 7: 5):

'My flesh is clothed with maggots and clods of dusts,
My skin rotted and fouled afresh.'

The Seleucid King of Syria, Antiochus IV Epiphanes, antagonized the Jews by his attempts to impose Greek customs upon them, a policy that resulted in the revolt of the Maccabees. For his arrogance and insolence, he was struck down by a terrible disease that caused him great pain. Maggots issued from his body, even from his eyes, and his flesh rotted and fell from his body, causing so great a stench that his own soldiers could not bear to come near him. The whole story is recounted in *The Second Book of Maccabees* in the Apocrypha.

In A.D. 44, Herod Agrippa, King of Judaea, was similarly punished for ungodliness. According to *The Acts of the Apostles* (12: 23): 'And immediately the angel of the Lord smote him, because he gave not God the glory: and he was eaten of worms, and gave up the ghost.'

Robert Graves, in his book, *Claudius the God*, uses this incident dramatically, by making Herod Agrippa write a last letter to his friend, the Emperor Claudius. Herod writes: 'My last letter: I am dying. My body is full of maggots. Forgive your old friend ... '

Interestingly, although Flavius Josephus, a Jewish historian of the

first century A.D., mentions the death of Herod Agrippa, he does not
tell us the manner of it, saying only that he died in Cæsarea. Josephus
does, however, tell us about the death of an earlier Herod – Herod the
Great, who died in 4 B.C., although curiously, the Bible does not. Josephus wrote: 'But now Herod's distemper greatly increased upon him
after a severe manner, and this by God's judgement upon him for his
sins: for a fire glowed in him slowly … His entrails were also exulcer-
ated, and the chief violence of his pain lay on his colon … Nay, further,
his privy-member was putrified, and produced worms.'

Other early, non-biblical, texts refer to myiasis. Herodotus gives an
account of the Persian expedition against the Libyans, a campaign conducted at the behest of Pheretima, the mother of Arcesilaus, Greek
King of Cyrene. The people of the city of Barca had murdered the King
to avenge injustices done to them, and Pheretima, in grief and rage,
determined to take her revenge on the Barcæans. Seeking the help of
the Persians in Egypt, she assaulted Barca, rounding up all those she
believed guilty of the crime. The men were crucified on the walls of the
city and the women's breasts were cut off and similarly fastened to the
walls. For her wickedness in inflicting such unjust punishment, Pheretima did not end her days happily. According to Herodotus, she was
judged by the gods and punished: 'For on her return to Egypt from
Libya, directly after taking vengeance on the people of Barca, she was
overtaken by a most horrid death. Her body swarmed with maggots,
which ate her flesh while she was still alive. Thus do men, by over-
harsh punishments, draw upon themselves the anger of the gods.'*

There is some evidence that the cause of myiasis was well-known
and fully exploited as an instrument of torture in mediæval times. In
1153, when Reginald de Chatillon, Prince of Antioch in the Crusader
states of Outremer, was preparing a military expedition against the
island of Cyprus, he asked Aimery, Latin Patriarch of the city, for funds
to aid his campaign. The Patriarch refused, whereupon Reginald threw
him in prison, had him flogged, then bound to the roof of the citadel.
Honey was rubbed into his wound to attract flies more strongly. This
brutal treatment succeeded as far as Reginald was concerned, for the
Patriarch eventually agreed to finance the expedition.

I do not mention these early records simply as anecdotes or historical curiosities. It is very clear that the peoples of the Eastern Mediterranean were familiar with the infestation of living tissues by maggots
from the earliest times. This fact is not only interesting in itself, but,
when taken together with the known habits of flies, it suggests some-

* Herodotus uses the Greek word for 'men' in the generic sense, to include women. He
is referring to Pheretima, not the Barcæans.

thing about the evolution of this strange parasitic habit and of the age-old association between flies and men.

Consider what we know about fly biology in this regard. Some blowfly species are obligate parasites, that is to say, they have to breed in living tissues and cannot breed in dead carcasses. Such species occur mainly in the tropical parts of the world. Other species, including many of those that occur in temperate regions, are able to breed both in living tissues and in dead bodies; these are the so-called facultative parasites.

The common bluebottle and greenbottle, species associated with man that occur in Britain and Europe, are known to cause facultative myiasis in both people and domestic animals, but are only very rarely found to parasitize wild animals *in the wild* although they are often found to parasitize them in captivity. None of the other four British species of bluebottle are known to attack living animals, wild or domestic. A common obligate parasitic species, *Chrysomya bezziana*, known in the vernacular as the Old World screw-worm fly, is likewise a cause of virulent disease in domestic animals wherever it occurs but, as far as I have been able to ascertain, there is only a single record of its attacking a wild animal in nature – an antelope in Africa. In spite of its abundance in Africa, decades of research there on this fly and other parasites that attack wild mammals have consistently failed to find evidence that the screw-worm carries out such attacks, although many other highly-specialized fly (but not blowfly) species do.

Several endemic species of bluebottle in Australia, that is those species that occurred there before the arrival of European colonists, are known to cause myiasis in sheep in that country. Curiously, in spite of the fact that Australian mammals and their diseases are among the most intensively studied in the world, none of these flies has ever been recorded as a parasite of the indigenous mammals – marsupials, bats or dingoes – so it is possible that these species have evolved the parasitic habit in association with man. How else can the habits of Australian blowflies which solely parasitize sheep be explained? No sheep existed in Australia before the arrival of the Europeans and the blowflies must have bred exclusively in decomposing carcasses.

This may be an example of unwitting, human-directed evolution. Archaeological evidence indicates that early human communities were often plagued with flies. In the Eastern Mediterranean, the crucible of civilization, settled communities, with their cattle and sheep kept in large numbers, often in small enclosures, must have attracted hosts of flies and still do so today. Domestic animals very often exist in unhygienic conditions, surrounded by manure and refuse of all sorts, their own bodies often stained with faecal matter and urine in a manner one does not normally see among wild animals. Sheep kept in such conditions are among the most malodorous and soiled of domestic animals and are particularly prone to myiasis.

There are relatively few fossil flies known, compared with the fossils of some other groups of insects. Unfortunately, flies have very fragile bodies and, unlike such insects as beetles, which have hard exoskeletons, they are rarely preserved after death. Of these fossil flies, most are small, easily-trapped species, related to the modern-day gnats and similar so-called 'primitive' flies. Very few fossil 'higher flies'* like bluebottles and houseflies have been discovered and most are individuals that have been preserved in amber.

In contrast, the puparia of flies are quite durable structures and do tend to be preserved. During the 1930s, a 70 million-year-old piece of ironstone from the Cretaceous rocks of Alberta, Canada, was found to have what appeared to be fossil fragments attached to it. However, it was not scientifically studied until 1970, when Dr Frank McAlpine of the Biosystematics Research Institute in Ottawa published a paper about it. He concluded that the small structures attached to the rock were the fossilized puparia of flies. He was so convinced of their identity that he gave the remains a scientific name: *Cretaphormia fowleri*. *Phormia* is a genus of common Canadian blowflies and the prefix '*Creta*' referred to the Cretaceous origin of the fossils; the specific name was in honour of the discoverer. Many people believed that McAlpine had gone too far in identifying the remains as fly puparia and in taking the formal step of giving them a scientific name. Some scientists did not hide their belief that he had made a serious error and that the fossilized remains were in reality, something quite different. In a letter to me some years after the publication of his paper, McAlpine wrote that some of his colleagues still teased him about describing fossilized 'mouse-droppings' as entomological remains.

I was very intrigued by all this and was eager to see this enigmatic

---

* In order to avoid using the cumbersome term 'higher flies', I will refer to these insects simply as flies for the rest of this chapter. Gnats, mosquitoes, 'daddy-long-legs' and other insects classified by scientists as flies, are excluded from the definition for the purposes of this discussion.

piece of rock. I wrote to Dr McAlpine asking him whether he would be willing to send me the rock on loan so that I could study it and arrive at my own conclusions, although I did not believe that he would allow such a valuable specimen to leave Canada, albeit for a short while. To my surprise and delight, and to Dr McAlpine's everlasting credit, the rock arrived by return of post, with a letter wishing me luck in my examination of the stone.

McAlpine's identification was based on a light microscope examination of the rock. The general shape of the remains, as well as various structural features, convinced him of their identity. My purpose was to examine the fossils under the scanning electron microscope in order to be able to see the surface structure of the 'puparia' in greater detail. Unfortunately, the specimen was too large to fit into the electron microscope's vacuum chamber. Cutting the part of the stone that contained the fossils would have overcome this problem, but the terms of the loan expressly forbade me from doing this. Disappointing though this was I decided to conduct a light microscope examination with the best instrument and lighting I could get. I took photographs of the specimens under the microscope and produced large prints and picture slides for ease of examination. I went through all the points made by McAlpine in support of his conclusion that the remains were evidence that flies existed in the world when dinosaurs were still roaming the Earth. It was all very exciting but, alas, it did not last. I could see none of the structural features described by Dr McAlpine, or rather I could see some of them, but could not convince myself that they represented the structures known to occur on fly puparia. One of the fossils in particular was a flattened structure quite unlike a puparium. I concluded that McAlpine was mistaken and put the matter out of my mind for the time being.

Afterwards, it occurred to me that there might be another way of tackling the problem. Some time before I received the fossils, I had been developing ways of identifying the puparia of different fly species by means of calculations that would describe the shapes of these structures mathematically. I am ashamed to admit that it did not occur to me initially to subject the fossil specimens to this treatment, but the technique was still new and I had not yet acquired the habit of applying it routinely! I therefore re-examined the specimens and took as many measurements as I could. The best preserved – the one that looked most complete and most like a real puparium – gave a result that was typical of most puparia. The dimensions were right and the shape was right. This was encouraging, but I was still puzzled by the flattened object, which did not look like a puparium. All of a sudden, the thought came to me that what it did strongly resemble was the *abdomen* of a fly.

I took large numbers of flies from laboratory colonies and set to work measuring their abdomens. I compared their dimensions and the shape measurements with those of the flattened fossil. They were effectively indistinguishable; the object stuck to the rock was identical in shape and size to the abdomen of one of the commonest living bluebottle species, *Calliphora vicina*. Clearly, caution dictates that one should not leap to conclusions; however, it seems reasonable to hazard that flies may well have existed at the time of the dinosaurs, albeit when those giants were disappearing from the Earth.

Once, when lecturing on the evolution of flies, I made mention of McAlpine's fossil and said that, since almost every palaeontologist seemed to have a theory to explain why dinosaurs became extinct, I would like to make my own contribution to the debate: they fell victim to myiasis. Of course, I was only joking!

The Tertiary Geological Period, which began roughly after the departure of the dinosaurs, saw the rise of mammals and flowering plants. If our reading of the fossil record is correct, and whether or not *Cretaphormia fowleri* was really a fly, the insects popularly called flies are so closely associated with them that they must have blossomed and evolved in parallel with those two groups of organisms. In the absence of much hard evidence about their evolution in the Tertiary, one can only speculate about the way this association could have developed. The only fossils that I have seen from this period date from the very end of the Tertiary – about one and a half million years ago. These, again, were puparia, from the Transvaal, South Africa, and were of particular interest, since they were associated with the remains of the early humanoid, *Australopithecus*. Unfortunately, I was not able to see the best preserved specimens as these could not be allowed out of the country but, from the remains that I was able to see, it would appear that flies of some kind were associated with these early people. It is not possible to draw very confident conclusions, but there seems to be a case for believing that the human/fly association began an extremely long time ago.

Closer to our time, the Pleistocene Epoch – the Ice Age – has yielded much more information about the association of flies with mammals. Undoubted fly puparia have been found among the remains of the bones of Pleistocene animals and I myself have seen such puparia associated with the woolly rhinoceros, the musk-ox and, above all, the mammoth.

Dr Adrian Lister, an authority on mammoths and elephants, once observed that we know more about mammoths than we do about any other extinct prehistoric animal. Moreover, we know more about their ecology than we do about that of many living mammals. In addition to their bones, hair, tissues, stomach contents and even dung have been preserved. Early man left a record of them in cave paintings. Consequently, insect finds associated with these animals not only enable us to interpret their natural history, but our knowledge of mammoths can help us to understand the significance of such associated remains.

Of the various insect remains associated with mammoths and other Pleistocene animals that I have examined, the most interesting were those found among mammoth remains discovered in the English Midlands. One day, a woman walking her dog by a gravel pit near Condover (a name that was soon to become celebrated in the annals of palaeontology) saw the driver of a bulldozer lift up a large ribbed structure. Originally thought to be part of an ancient boat, closer examination revealed them to be mammoth bones.

Dr Lister and Professor Russell Coope jointly took charge of the investigation. The bones turned out to belong to at least four, probably five, mammoths – one of which was an adult, the others juveniles. They dated to between 12,700 and 12,300 years ago and provided the first evidence that mammoths had existed in Britain after the ice began to retreat. The geological evidence revealed that the animals had fallen into a muddy water-filled crater and had become mired in the sediment. On examination of the skulls, Dr Lister discovered hundreds of fly puparia inside the sinuses of one skull and on two of the mandibles belonging to two or three of the juvenile individuals. He asked me to examine these puparia and report upon them. An approximate identification was not difficult to determine. The specimens were remarkably well preserved and were clearly the puparia of blowflies, having the distinguishing morphological characteristics of a particular group of which only three species are known. I and other workers had come across such puparia from Pleistocene mammals before, but it had not been possible to assign them to any particular species with confidence. On the basis of probability these other remains had been tentatively identified as *Phormia terraenovae*, often referred to as the black blowfly, since this species is by far the most widespread of the three.

However, prior to the discovery of the Condover mammoths, I had embarked on a special study of this group of flies, all of which favour cold climates being found in the northern parts of Europe, Asia and America, and on mountain tops. With my new-found knowledge of the structure of their puparia, I felt that I should be able to establish with a considerable degree of certainty which of the three species was present among the bones. Having dissected and studied the fly remains under the electron microscope, I was satisfied that they did, indeed, belong to *Phormia terraenovae*. But there was another surprise in store. During my search through the specimens I found three unopened puparia. All the others were open, the adult flies having emerged.

Male flies are usually much easier than females to identify because they possess genital armature – a structure of hard, jointed plates and rods – at the tips of their abdomens. These structures have a highly distinctive 'architecture' which is unique to each species. It occurred to me that, even if the adult or developing fly within these closed puparia had decomposed, the hard genital armature might have remained intact. I decided to dissect them and find out. To my delight, one of the three puparia revealed part of the genital armature. It was not complete, but the cerci – a pair of rod-like appendages – were intact. There was no longer any doubt; the flies in question were definitely *Phormia terraenovae*.

Some aspects of the behaviour of this fly might shed light on the mammoth remains. Whereas the maggots of most blowfly species migrate some distance away from the carcass and pupate in the soil after they have finished feeding, presumably in order to avoid being eaten by scavengers feeding on it,* those of the black blowfly pupate on or in the remains of the carcass, a habit that may have something to do with temperature regulation. Lying together inside a carcass may keep their temperature at a higher level and lying on top of the body would make use of the sun's rays, especially in a species whose puparia are very much darker than those of most flies; the nearly black colour will absorb and retain more of the sun's energy.

As an insect adapted to cold conditions, the black blowfly is capable of depressing its freezing point in response to low temperature stress by synthesizing glycerol. This allows it to survive the cold much more easily than many other fly species. Nevertheless, the fly needs a temperature of at least 10°c to enable it to fly actively and lay eggs.

What did this tell us about the life and death of the mammoths? First, one can conclude that at about the time the mammoths died the

* Carrion crows are often seen feeding upon the maggots in carcasses, rather than on the flesh of the carcass.

ambient temperature was likely to have been above 10°C. Temperatures at the time when the mammoths lived are believed to have fluctuated between –3° and +16°C. Egg-laying under normal circumstances would have occurred within the first few days after death, since the carcasses would have ceased to be attractive to the flies thereafter. Secondly, the carcasses (or at least the heads, where the puparia were found) could not have become submerged until about two weeks after death, since the maggots would not have been able to complete their development, which they clearly did since most of the puparia were open. However, a thin covering of soil would not have prevented their development and the emergence of the flies.

It is quite conceivable that the mammoths may have died under freezing conditions and themselves have become frozen after death, only to thaw out later under warmer conditions. If this had happened, the flies would still have been able to lay their eggs on the carcasses after the thaw since freezing would have preserved the tissues in a state acceptable to the flies upon thawing. Laboratory cultures of black blowflies have been maintained for several years by providing the flies with defrosted mouse carcasses (that had been frozen months earlier) for egg-laying. Another possibility is that the maggots may have been parasitizing the mammoths while the latter were still alive. The animals, mired in the mud, could easily have fallen victim to the parasitic behaviour of this fly, which is known to cause a virulent myiasis in weakened animals.

The pattern of infestation in the remains raises two further questions. First, why were puparia found in only two or three of the four mammoths, the mandibles of the adult containing no trace of puparia. Secondly, why was this infestation restricted to their heads? The answer to the first question depends on whether or not the mammoths all died at the same time. If they had died at different times, it is easy to imagine that those which did so during the season of fly activity became infested, whereas the animal that died in a colder season, when the flies were not active, would not have become infested. Even if this latter specimen had been frozen at death and later thawed, it might still have remained uninfested if it had been below water or buried beneath a thick sediment before it thawed. Alternatively, if all the animals died together, the uninfested one might, for some reason, have been inaccessible to the flies. It might, for example, have been immediately buried in the sediment whilst the other three remained exposed. It is also quite possible that the other animal was infested, but the puparia did not get into the mandibles.

A possible answer to the second question is that the heads were infested first (the head being the preferred site of egg laying), and that the bodies of the animals subsequently became buried, giving little time for the flies to attack them. Another possibility is that the flies were at low density (due to a seasonal fall in temperature) and that the numbers of larvae were consequently small and had no need to invade parts of the body other than the head, where they had obtained adequate nourishment to complete their development. In such a case, the flies would not have attacked the body when the temperature rose at a later season, since the carcass would then have been unattractive to them, having lain decomposing for a period at higher temperatures. The third possibility is that the entire bodies of the animals may have been infested, but that the puparia were preserved only in the head. The skull and mandibles have spaces in which the puparia are protected; puparia in other parts of the body would lie externally on rather than inside the skeletal elements, there being normally no point of entry into them. If, for example, the carcasses decayed under water, any maggots in the bodies would have been killed and either washed away or become decomposed, giving the impression that the bodies had never been infested. Yet another possibility is suggested by the work of Dr Malcolm Coe in the Tsavo (East) National Park in Kenya, where flies are abundant. Coe studied the decomposition of elephant carcasses and found that fly larvae of two species, *Chrysomya albiceps* and *Chrysomya marginalis*, consumed only 3–5 per cent of the available soft tissues (the remaining 95–97 per cent being consumed by microorganisms). Moreover, Coe found larvae in all parts of the carcasses.

Science progresses step by step and which one of these various scenarios might eventually prove to be the true one will depend on the completion of the study of all the remains associated with the find.

'The maggots will not turn into flies within you.' This strange inscription, written on a piece of papyrus found inside the mouth of an Egyptian mummy, is the earliest indication that people knew, from the earliest times, that maggots were the begetters of flies. It may seem that no such indication is really necessary. Surely the association between maggots and flies is so obvious, particularly to people living under relatively primitive conditions, that no proof of that knowledge is needed. Indeed, one would have thought so, but it remains true that only very few people seemed to know this simple fact. Since the time of the Egyptians, there have been many instances of men, even learned naturalists, who have had very confused ideas about the natural history of flies and insects in general. Knowledge of such things grew erratically until relatively recent times.

A very early reference to the association between maggots and flies – and to myiasis – is to be found in Homer's *Iliad*. It is believed that the poem dates from around 1,000 B.C., although the first authenticated text, that of Aristarchus of Samothrace, dates only from 150 B.C. If the following passage was not a more recent addition to the epic poem, then it would seem that, for most of antiquity, warriors at least were familiar with some of the facts of fly biology: 'I much fear, lest with blows of flies, his brass-inflicted wounds are fil'd.'

The Egyptian papyrus showed that flies developed from maggots; Homer revealed that maggots, or at least eggs, were produced by flies, the passage suggesting that soldiers wounded in battle might frequently have contracted myiasis, the wording expressing not so much a factual observation but a fear of what might happen to a wounded man.

Disappointingly, Aristotle, writing in the fourth century B.C., made no mention of the breeding habits of flies, although he did record some curious notions about them. For example, in his *De Partibus Animalium*, he asserted that they suffered from poor eyesight because their eyes were made of a hard substance. According to Aristotle, this poor vision explained why flies constantly passed their front legs over their eyes, clearing them of any obstruction.

Pliny the Elder, too, made little mention of flies in his encyclopædic *Natural History*, written during the first century A.D.. He did, however, make one very interesting remark, stating that the maggots that infest rotting wood are produced by the decaying sap of the wood itself; an early example of belief in spontaneous generation. This comment shows that it was not yet known that maggots are the offspring of flies. This is particularly revealing, coming as it does from a man like Pliny who, for all the limitations of his *Natural History*, was devoted to the study of the natural world – a devotion that led directly to his death when he insisted on observing the eruption of Vesuvius at close quarters.

It is often said that because a fact or an observation is recorded in an old document it does not follow that it was common knowledge but more likely represented the knowledge of the learned few. This is probably correct, but it seems to me that there may be an alternative view. That Pliny, a learned man, did not know that maggots were the offspring of flies does not necessarily mean that the simple and unlearned were also ignorant of the fact. I suspect that a great deal of sound knowledge of natural history resided among those who lived close to nature.

In several of his plays, William Shakespeare showed that he was fully conversant with the details of the life-cycle of blowflies. In *Love's Labour's Lost* (Act V, Scene 2), he wrote:

'These summer flies have blowne me full of maggot ostentation';

again, in *The Tempest* (Act III, Scene 1):

'to suffer the flesh-fly blow my mouth';

and in *Antony and Cleopatra* (Act III, Scene 1):

'Rather on Nilus mud,
'Lay me stark naked and let the water flies
    Blow me into abhorring.'

The use of the word 'blow' and its derivatives is interesting. The noun 'blow' refers to a mass of fly eggs. The verb 'to blow' means to lay eggs and anything that is 'fly-blown' has fly eggs on it. Hence, the name 'blowfly'. The names bluebottle and greenbottle are thought to have arisen from the word 'bot' which means 'maggot', as in bot-fly, which is itself derived from the Gaelic word 'boiteag', also meaning maggot. A 'bottle' is, therefore, a small maggot (small, that is, when compared with those of bot-flies). So, a bluebottle fly is a blue fly that produces small maggots. According to the *Oxford English Dictionary*, the earliest appearance in print of the word 'blow' was in *Love's Labour's Lost*, first published in the quarto edition in 1598, although its first performance had taken place earlier still in about 1594–95. I suspect it had been in spoken use much earlier still. *The Tempest* was first performed around 1611–12 and *Antony and Cleopatra* in 1606–07. All of this suggests that the words 'blow' and, possibly, 'blowfly' were in widespread use much earlier than the 1590s, as it is unlikely that a word first used only four years before appearing in print would have had sufficiently wide currency to be spoken in a play that was clearly intended to be comprehensible to the majority of the audience.

The point of interest here is that the existence and apparent widespread use of the word 'blow' in the sixteenth century indicates that most people in England were probably aware of the link between maggot and fly and that the one was the offspring of the other. By the middle of the seventeenth century this knowledge must have been well established, since Samuel Purchas, in his book *A Theater of Politicall Insects* (1657), states that: '... the blotes of the flies are nurished by the flesh wherein they are blowne ... '. Later, in 1692, Thomas Wagstaffe the elder, in his *Vindication of King Charles the Martyr*, wrote: ' ... it is the Nature of Flies to be ever buzzing, and blowing upon any thing that is raw ... '.

These pieces of documentary evidence would suggest that by the end of the seventeenth century all men of learning in western Europe were well acquainted with the facts of fly propagation. This, however, was not the case. In the second half of the century, Father Athanasius Kircher, a German Jesuit, compiled his monumental *Book of the Subterranean World*, in the twelfth volume of which he gave the following account of fly development:

'The dead flies should be besprinkled and soaked with honey-water, and then placed on a copper-plate exposed to the tepid heat of ashes; afterwards, very minute worms, only visible through the microscope, will appear, which little by little grow wings on the back and assume the shape of very small flies, that slowly attain perfect size'. These were the observations of a man who had spent most of his life studying natural history and natural objects. In many ways he reminds one of Pliny who amassed such a vast amount of information uncritically. Like Pliny, Kircher was interested in the volcanic activity of Vesuvius and had himself lowered into its crater after an eruption in order to make observations. Unlike Pliny, however, he survived the experience.

In 1668, there appeared an Italian book entitled *Esperienze intorno alla Generazione degli Insetti* (Experiments on the Generation of Insects) by Francesco Redi. Redi was the Duke of Tuscany's physician, but his real interest lay in scientific research. He became interested in the origin of maggots and conducted a series of experiments designed to establish beyond doubt where these creatures came from. Redi killed some snakes and placed them in jars, some of which he sealed; the others he left open. He noted that flies arrived on the snake carcasses in the open jars and placed their 'droppings' (eggs) on them. He made observations on the maggots that emerged and saw that each 'worm' (maggot) eventually became encased inside an 'egg' (puparium), from which a fly would, in due course, 'hatch'. In none of the closed jars did any maggots appear. Redi concluded: ' ... I began to believe that all the worms found in the meat were derived from the droppings of the flies, and not from the putrefaction of the meat, and I was still more confirmed in this belief by having observed that, before the meat grew wormy, flies had hovered over it, of the same kind that later bred in it.'

Thus he laid to rest the notion that maggots were spontaneously generated from extraneous matter. And yet this is perhaps not wholly true, for Francesco Redi continued to believe that the larvae in plant galls were generated by the plant itself, because in many galls there was no obvious hole through which the insect could have laid its egg. Nevertheless, it was through his own legacy that he was proved wrong on this point, as it was one of his students, Vallisnieri, who eventually demonstrated the true origin of plant gall larvae.

CHAPTER 9

Maggots and Medicine

The physician heals, Nature makes well.
Aristotle

Returning from their trading voyages to the West Indies and Mexico during the early days of Spanish colonization, merchants of Tudor England reported that swarms of 'mesquitoes' often accompanied fever epidemics in the New World. Sadly, this pertinent observation like so many others in the history of science was unappreciated at the time and, with the passing of the years, it was forgotten.

For centuries it was known that malaria, or the ague as it was called in England, was a disease of swamps and marshes. It was believed that it was caused by the noxious fumes – the *miasma*, as learned men called it – that emanated from the malodorous mud and decomposing vegetation of such regions. It is this belief that gave rise to the name of the disease; *mal aria* – bad air. The knowledge that malaria was, in fact, caused by micro-organisms and transmitted by mosquitoes did not come until the second half of the nineteenth century.

After the great bacteriological discoveries of Louis Pasteur, medical men began to consider the possibility that malaria might be a bacterial disease. A bacterium isolated from swamp mud was identified as the probable cause. The theory that this organism, *Bacillus malariae* by name, was the causative agent of malaria had powerful adherents in the medical world, especially in Germany and, in the excitable atmosphere of the early days of bacteriology, it was not a theory to be readily abandoned. The first clue to the real cause of the disease came in 1880 when

Alphonse Laveran, a French doctor working in Algeria, conducted a microscopical examination of the blood of a soldier suffering from malaria. Under the microscope he saw small 'flagellated bodies' (i.e. cells each having a whip-like flagellum at one end) writhing in the blood samples. He concluded that a single-celled parasite was the true cause of the disease. Unhappily, his conclusions were opposed by the medical establishment; Laveran was an unknown military physician working in a backwater and too much had been invested in the bacteriological theory. It was not until 1907 that Laveran was finally recognized for his seminal discovery and awarded the Nobel Prize.

Patrick Manson – a doctor working in China who later, as Sir Patrick Manson, deservedly became known as the Father of Tropical Medicine – made the discovery that the small nematode worms that caused the disease known as filariasis were transmitted by a mosquito. He persuaded an Indian Army doctor, Ronald Ross, that malaria too might be transmitted by a mosquito. A great deal of work was carried out as a result of Manson's influence, not only by Ross but by other, notably Italian and Canadian, researchers. All were looking for Laveran's now accepted flagellated bodies and, in 1897, Ross observed them developing in *Anopheles* mosquitoes. Ross was knighted, and in 1902 he received the Nobel Prize. Unfortunately, the progress of science is not always accompanied by great ability or a nobility of spirit. Ross was not in fact a very able scientist, frequently taking his lead from others: after receiving his Nobel Prize, he spent much of the rest of his life denying that others had made a significant contribution to the great discovery.

The fact that insects have long played an important role in the dissemination of human disease is familiar to most people. It is well known that mosquitoes transmit malaria, yellow fever and a host of other diseases and that tsetse flies transmit sleeping sickness. Many will have heard that blackflies transmit the worms that cause the dreaded disease of river blindness in Africa – a disease now mercifully under control. The list of insect-borne diseases is endless and the science and history of medical entomology are vast subjects which I will not explore in detail here. Nevertheless, there are two points that I would like to raise. First, I wonder whether people are aware of the full extent of the role of insects in disease. The World Health Organisation has a list of six diseases – or more accurately groups of diseases – that are the main scourges of mankind. They are: malaria; trypanosomiasis (sleeping sickness and related diseases); leishmaniasis (a disease caused by various species of Leishmania, which are protozoan parasites transmitted by phlebotomine sandflies); filariasis (diseases caused by nematode worms); leprosy; and schistosomiasis (a disease caused by blood flukes). Every year, malaria alone kills three million people and more than 300 million will contract it. Of the six listed diseases, the first four are all insect-borne – they cannot continue to exist without their insect vectors. The bacterial disease, leprosy, is transmitted in a number of ways, one of which is mechanical transmission by a variety of insects in much the same way that flies transmit bacteria on to our food. Only schistosomiasis has no entomological component.

This summary does not include the huge number of other diseases transmitted by insects and ticks that, collectively, take a considerable toll of human lives. Take one such group of diseases: those caused by the large collection of viruses known as 'arboviruses' (i.e. *ar*thropod-*borne viruses*). These include yellow fever, dengue (or break-bone fever), Chikungunya, O'nyong-nyong, Sindbis, encephalitis (of various kinds), West Nile virus, Bwamba, California virus, haemorrhagic fever – all dreadful and often very painful diseases. Apart from the arboviruses, there are many other insect-borne diseases that afflict mankind – it is no exaggeration to say that their names would fill a small dictionary.

Clearly, the adverse effect of insects on human health and human history cannot be overstated. And yet there is a correspondingly positive side, which brings me to my second point. As so often happens in nature, a disease is a disease only in the context in which it expresses itself. Certainly, most people suffering from malaria are diseased, but matters may not always be as simple as this.

During the 1880s, an Austrian neurologist and psychiatrist, Julius Wagner (whose title was Ritter [i.e. Knight]) von Jauregg (later known as Julius Wagner-Jauregg), became interested in the condition known as syphilitic meningoencephalitis, a disease of the nervous system. Working at the University of Vienna, he noticed that the condition of some of his patients improved after contracting a fever. It occurred to him that he could treat the disease by deliberately inducing fever in the sufferers of this terrible and, at the time, fatal disease. However, it was not until he became Professor of Psychiatry and Neurology at the University of Graz in 1889 that he conducted his first trial. He took extracts from the tubercle bacillus and injected them into his patients. Unfortunately, while there was some improvement in a few of them, the experiment was not a success.

Later, he returned to the University of Vienna and took charge of the university hospital where, in 1917, he decided to infect some of his patients with malaria. The trials were dramatically successful; the high temperatures caused by the malarial parasite killed the spirochaetes (the causative organisms of syphilis), thus curing the disease. A previously incurable disease was at last brought under medical control. Although the patient had now acquired a new disease, malaria, this could be kept under control by drugs such as quinine, and the patient was able to lead a more or less normal life.* In 1927, ten years after his discovery, Wagner-Jauregg was awarded the Nobel Prize. Thus, even the dreaded malaria has had some beneficial effect on humanity.

More recently, Lieutenant-Colonel Dr George Watt, working in Thailand, discovered that Aids patients who were also suffering from scrub typhus, a disease caused by *Rickettsia tsutsugamushi* and transmitted by chigger mites of the genus *Trombicula*, showed lower levels of the HIV virus in their blood compared with other Aids patients. Interestingly, when Aids patients contract diseases other than scrub typhus, the HIV load tends to rise, sometimes by up to 800 per cent. Scrub typhus can be a serious disease, often causing heart damage and circulatory failure. It also causes fever, which *may* be the reason why it suppresses the Aids virus, although the true mechanism has not yet been established. The apparent effect of the *Rickettsia* on the Aids virus was announced only as this book was going to press; it will be interesting to see whether these findings assist in the search for a vaccine.

They say that it is an ill wind that blows nobody any good, but can we find some good, some silver lining in the vast, black cloud of biting, disease-bearing insects that plague the world? It is often said, quite correctly, that history would have taken a very different course had it not been for these pestilential creatures. It is not only the disease but also fear of the disease that can affect human behaviour and human fortunes. Biting flies – not only mosquitoes, but tsetse flies, horseflies and other insects – have determined the movement of African tribes year after year, in much the same way that biting flies have controlled the migration of caribou in North America. People and animals have fled annually to avoid their attentions and have returned when their active season has passed. Even today, the Canadian North is largely uninhabited because of the great abundance of biting and non-biting nuisance flies. I remember a conversation I had many years ago in Ottawa with

* Today syphilis and related diseases are treated with antibiotics, to which spirochaetes respond.

an entomologist, the late Guy Shewell. I commented that the great swarms of mosquitoes, blackflies, horseflies and all manner of other flies had impeded progress in Canada. Imagine if these insects could be eradicated! Surely I said, Canada would then be able to develop to its full capacity. But my host was not impressed. He said, yes, if the insects went, man would move in but then there would no longer be a wilderness. The great Canadian North, one of the last huge tracts of unspoiled nature, would be gone. For his part, he hoped that the flies and mosquitoes would never be eradicated.

It is difficult to disagree with this. The mental picture of the Canadian North as a region of huge cities and towering skyscrapers is unappealing. If outsiders like the Arabs, Portuguese, Chinese, Dutch, Turks, English and French had not been kept out of all but the coastal periphery of Africa by disease-bearing flies for most of history, what would the interior of Africa be like now? One can never know the answers to such questions, but it is not difficult to imagine that the continent would have been devastated long before at least a large part of it could have been saved as a result of conservation policies and the responsible use of renewable resources.

A fundamental scientific discovery might never have been made had it not been for the intervention of a bloodsucking insect. For the last forty years of his life Charles Darwin was a chronically sick man. He rarely left his house in Kent and never left England after his return from his voyage around the world on board *The Beagle*. He suffered from weakness and lethargy, he experienced heart palpitations and stomach pains, he often felt sick and shaky and had difficulty in sleeping. Various physicians attended him, but none could diagnose his illness and the consensus of opinion was that he was a hypochondriac. Since his death and up to the present day people have continued to offer explanations for Darwin's mysterious illness. Most such diagnoses have been of the psychoanalytical type, claiming that Darwin's illness was psychosomatic or that he was simply a malingerer who feigned illness in order to escape from the storm of controversy raised when his *Origin of Species* was published. None of these ideas is supported by any hard evidence.

The only explanation that is 'based upon the use of reasoning' as Sir

Peter Medawar put it, is the theory propounded by Professor Saul Adler of the Hebrew University of Jerusalem. During the night of 25th/26th March 1835, when Darwin was sleeping in the village of Luxan in the Argentinian province of Mendoza, he was attacked and bitten by a bloodsucking bug, the Benchuca. This insect, *Triatoma infestans*, which has many other names including the Chindass, the Giant Bug of the Pampas, the Great Black Bug of the Pampas, was and is greatly feared in South America. It belongs to a group of bugs, the Reduviidae, with the dreadfully appropriate name of 'Assassin Bugs'. Darwin's diary entry for that fateful day reads as follows:

> 'At night I experienced an attack (for it deserves no less a name) of the Benchuca, a species of Reduvius, the great black bug of the Pampas. It is most disgusting to feel soft wingless insects, about an inch long, crawling over one's body. Before sucking they are quite thin, but afterwards they become round and bloated with blood, and in this state are easily crushed. One which I caught at Iquique (for they are found in Chile and Peru,) was very empty. When placed on a table, and though surrounded by people, if a finger was presented, the bold insect would immediately pro-trude its sucker, make a charge, and if allowed, draw blood. No pain was caused by the wound. It was curious to watch its body during the act of sucking, as in less than ten minutes it changed from being as flat as a wafer to a globular form. This one feast, for which the benchuca was indebted to one of the officers, kept it fat during four whole months; but, after the first fortnight, it was quite ready to have another suck.'

What was not known until twenty seven years after Darwin's death is that a pathogenic trypanosome known as *Trypanosoma cruzi* (a single-celled animal or protozoan, belonging to the same Phylum as *Amoeba* and the malarial parasite) is transmitted by the bite of the Benchuca. The disease caused by this pathogen is called Chagas' disease after Carlo Chagas Sr, the Brazilian pioneer who first defined and described it. Its symptoms are remarkably similar to those of Darwin – palpita-tions, stomach pains, lethargy and weakness. It would seem that the mystery of Darwin's illness is best explained by the bite of the dreaded Benchuca. An interesting additional point is that even today Chagas' disease is sometimes misdiagnosed as hypochondria or neurotic illness.

What if Darwin had never been bitten, if he had never fallen victim to Chagas' disease? It is tempting to speculate whether the energetic and fun-loving young Charles Darwin would have stayed at his home and never left it after his return from his voyage on *The Beagle* if he had not been too unwell to travel. As it was, he remained in his house, working only a few hours each day, studying, experimenting, writing. Would the theory of evolution by means of natural selection have been conceived and developed had Darwin not had the peace and time to reflect? It is of course possible, since Alfred Russel Wallace had had the same idea while travelling in the Tropics, but Wallace did not have the time and leisure to amass the formidable amount of evidence marshalled by Darwin. Perhaps, but for the Benchuca, natural selection might have remained simply an interesting idea for many more years.

Myiasis, that loathsome invasion of the living body by maggots, never fails to engender revulsion in those who hear about it for the first time. Seen in real life, on the body of another human being, it is disgusting. As for those who are actually suffering from the condition, their self-loathing and low self-esteem can become psychological problems in themselves. Nevertheless some good *can* be salvaged from this vile affliction for we now know that maggots can be therapeutic. Because they normally feed not on the living healthy tissues but on the diseased and dying tissues in the wound, and also devour the bacteria which they destroy in their guts, they can actually heal wounds and aid recovery. Moreover, maggots secrete antibacterial substances – antibiotics – which help to kill or halt the growth of the bacilli in the wound.

After the Battle of Saint Quentin during the war between the French and the Spaniards in 1557, the great surgeon Ambroise Paré noticed that some wounded soldiers, who had been neglected, suffered from maggot infestation of their wounds. He wrote that they were: '... greatly stinking and full of maggots with Gangreene and putrefaction ... To correct and stay the putrefaction and to kill the maggots which were entered into their wounds; I washed them with *Egyptiacum* dissolved in wine and *Aqua vitae* ... '

Of course there was nothing new about such an infestation but Paré made a further observation. He treated a patient who had an infected wound beneath a skull bone from which a large number of maggots eventually emerged. A large bone was lost, but the patient recovered 'beyond all men's expectations', to quote Paré's astonished comment, although he had no idea why. He certainly did not attribute the patient's recovery to the maggots.

Yet it was an interesting observation, the validity of which was only made clear 250 years later as a consequence of the ambitions and activities of no less a figure than Napoleon. On 29th June 1798, a great French fleet arrived off the coast of Alexandria in Egypt. On board the ships was a 40,000-strong military force under Napoleon's command. The purpose of the expedition was not only the conquest of the land and the consequent acquisition of a geopolitical advantage over the English, but also the systematic, scientific study of all aspects of the country. Napoleon took with him some 200 scholars, representing all branches of knowledge; they included some of the finest French minds of the age, many of whom were members of the Institut de France. Among them were astonomers and botanists; mathematicians and geologists; chemists and zoologists; engineers and archaeologists. Their combined researches eventually resulted in the publication of that monumental and most wonderful nine-volume work, *Description de l'Égypte* – The Description of Egypt.

One of the men who accompanied Napoleon on his heroic expedition to Egypt was a young surgeon by the name of Dominique Jean Larrey. Dr Larrey was destined to become the most distinguished of Napoleon's medical staff and later in life the Emperor rewarded him by creating him a Baron. Although he made many important contributions to medicine and surgery, his name is surprisingly little known outside France. It is no exaggeration to say that through his fortitude and surgical skill Baron Larrey was able, to a quite considerable extent, to ameliorate the sufferings caused by the Napoleonic Wars. Apart from his great skill as a surgeon, his invention of a light, swift, horse-drawn ambulance alone saved many lives.

After consolidating his hold on Egypt, Napoleon and his army, accompanied by Dr Larrey, launched an expedition to fight the Turks in Syria. The army began its march in February 1799, reaching El Arish on the Mediterranean coast of the Sinai Desert later in the month. There a sharp engagement ended with the French occupation of the town. When Larrey arrived to treat the wounded, he found them lying in appalling conditions. It was clear that many were suffering from plague and malignant fevers but Larrey also noticed something else, possibly for the first time. He wrote: 'I first sought out the sick and wounded whom the defenders had left behind and discovered some fifty of these in subterranean apartments lacking both light and air and lying on dirty rotting mats, without bedding and covered with vermin. These unfortunates had received no medical help at all and, in almost every case, their wounds were undressed, gangrenous and full of maggots.' Thus we have the typical fate of warriors in the Middle East, recorded since the time of Homer and the authors of *Exodus*: they fell victim, almost immediately, to myiasis.

The army moved on eastwards and northwards, eventually reaching Acre late in March. The city was besieged by Napoleon's troops and bombarded mercilessly but Acre did not fall. Casualties on both sides were very heavy but, towards the end of May, Napoleon began his retreat – a minor rehearsal of the dramatic retreat from Moscow that still lay in the future.

Larrey was busy with his surgical duties and once again he found that the wounds of the soldiers were filled with maggots. He wrote:

> 'There remains an unusual matter which we do not believe ought to be passed without mention; it concerns that which we have had occasion to observe in Syria, during the Egyptian expedition, among the majority of our wounded. While their sores were sup-purating, these wounds were bothered by worms or larvae of the blue fly, common in this climate. These insects formed in a few hours, developing with such rapidity that, from one day to the next, they were the size of a small quill which frightened our sol-diers very much, despite all we could do to reassure them in this regard: there had been the experience to convince them that, far from being harmful to their wounds, these insects, by accelerat-ing cicatrization, shortened the work of nature, and also by less-ening the cellular eschars which they devoured. These larvae, in effect, have an avidity only for the putrefying matter, always spar-ing the living parts; also, I have never seen, in these circum-stances, evidence of haemorrhage, the insects are carried only to that depth which is the extent of the wound.'

This was the first recorded observation that maggots in wounds could actually hasten recovery; myiasis was not necessarily a disease. Baron Larrey laid the foundations of what was to become known as maggot-therapy, although he himself never used maggots in this way. How-ever, in spite of his conclusions and because of the frightening and repellent effect on the soldiers, Dr Larrey, being a humane man, tried to remove the maggots from the wounds by using a concoction of rue and small sage to destroy them, as he felt that by so doing he would help the morale of the wounded men. As a child, I myself remember being told by my grandfather that, after the battles between the British and the Turks in Syria and Palestine during the First World War, a per-fusion of fenugreek was used to treat those afflicted with myiasis.

Baron Larrey was that rarest of men, loved and respected by friend and foe alike. During the Battle of Waterloo, he was often near the front line. On one such occasion he was seen by the Duke of Wellington, who asked: 'Who is that bold fellow over there?'. On being told that it was Baron Larrey, the Duke said: 'Tell them not to fire at him. Give the brave fellow time to pick up his wounded'. So saying, he raised his hat. 'Whom are you saluting?' asked the Duke of Cambridge. 'The honour and loyalty you see yonder', Wellington replied.

Larrey's humanity was such that it almost led to his death after the Battle of Waterloo, where he once again came upon cases of myiasis among the wounded. It was his habit, given the opportunity, to tend both the French and enemy casualties after a battle. After Waterloo, he became separated from what remained of the French Army and, with some medical colleagues, he wandered about on the field, tending wounded men wherever he could find them. The sun set, but Larrey was still on the field of battle although Prussian soldiers were roaming about. During the hours of darkness he at last tried to make an escape but was suddenly cut off by a group of Prussian lancers. He tried to gallop away from danger, but a shot brought down his horse and several Prussians pounced on him, striking him on the head and shoulder with their sabres. He was left for dead.

Larrey did however recover consciousness and continued to make his way back to his own lines, but was intercepted by another detachment of Prussians. This time he was forced to surrender. He was treated atrociously: his weapons, his money, his ring, his watch, even most of his clothes were taken and he himself was brought before the Prussian General commanding the advance guard. The General decided that his captive must be Napoleon himself, but another, higher-ranking officer realized the mistake and, in a fit of rage, ordered Larrey to be shot. Fortunately, just as the sentence was about to be carried out, a regimental surgeon recognized him and pleaded with the Prussian not to have him executed. Somewhat grudgingly, the officer agreed and sent Larrey, half-naked, bloody and with his arms bound behind his back, to the Grand Provost of the Allied Armies, General von Bülow. Bülow, who had met Larrey in Berlin, ordered him to be released from his bonds and sent to the Commander of the Prussian Army, Field Marshal von Blücher. Larrey had saved the life of Blücher's son during the Austrian campaign and Blücher, remembering him, treated him very well.

In his final days on St Helena, Napoleon sat writing his will. He was a man who had known so many people – including 'most of those who mattered', to quote the words of Henry Dible. He understood human nature very well and could assess the characters of men with surpassing shrewdness. As he wrote, the ink, like his life, was running out. 'The ink, Montholon', he said to his companion. More ink was brought to him. The pen scratched on along the paper. He remembered everyone, the great and the small. A legacy here, a legacy there. Then: 'I leave my surgeon-in-chief, Larrey, a hundred thousand francs. He is the most virtuous man I have ever known.'

Later in the nineteenth century, The American Civil War again brought the activities of maggots to the attention of doctors. A medical officer in the Confederate Army, Dr Joseph Jones, noticing that wounded soldiers often contracted myiasis and presumably unaware of Baron Larrey's observations, wrote: 'I have frequently seen neglected wounds filled with maggots ... As far as my experience extends, these worms only destroy dead tissues, and do not specifically injure the well parts.' But it was left to another Confederate officer, J. F. Zacharias, to take the pioneering step of deliberately using maggots to heal wounds. These are his own, now classic, words: 'During my service in the hospital at Danville, Virginia, I first used maggots to remove the decayed tissue in hospital gangrene and with eminent satisfaction. In a single day, they would clean a wound much better than any agents we had at our command. I used them afterwards at various places. I am sure I saved many lives by their use, escaped septicaemia, and had rapid recoveries.'

The years passed and, in 1914, the horrors of the Great War began. In all theatres of this conflict, from France to Mesopotamia, flies and maggots took their toll of the living as well as the dead. Fly numbers increased, as they always do at such times. The works and writings of Larrey, Jones and Zacharias were all but forgotten. Wounded men, lying in trenches or exposed in no-man's land between the warring armies, were afflicted by the loathsome, noisome horror of myiasis. This extract from the diary of a young subaltern in the 5th Inniskillings, wounded on a beach in Gallipoli in 1916, gives some idea of how such men felt:

'With my free hand I took off my puttees at my leisure and bound them round my head. Next came the ampoule of iodine, which I broke and poured into my shoulder through the torn shirt. It seemed to attract the flies, who came, green- and blue-bottles, in dozens to the feast. I began to stink horribly in the sun ... I heard a little rustle in the bush behind me. It was the water carrier. A real boy with real water came and knelt beside me, giving me drink and talking to me ... After a while I sent him off because I was stinking so vilely, telling him to let someone know where I was in case the wounded could be moved that night. My shoulder was by this time full of maggots ... Though there was no other wounded man in sight, the whole valley was resounding with that ghastly cry, 'Stretcher-bearers! Stretcher-bearers!' and awful curses ... No stretcher-bearers came ... I turned over and lay on my face in the sand.'

With a note of desperation, he added: ' ... the stench of wounds and the swarms of flies [were] quite undescribable ... There was no shade – nothing but flies and stretchers.'

In spite of such horrific experiences, the Great War was to provide the stimulus that finally raised maggot-therapy to the level of a respectable medical technique. In 1917, William Baer, an orthopædic surgeon seconded to the American forces in France, recorded that two wounded soldiers had been overlooked on the field of battle where they had lain for a week. They had compound fractures and abdominal wounds and all swarmed with maggots. Dr Baer noticed that the soldiers, far from being in as bad a state as might have been expected from their ordeal, were actually recovering. The maggot-infested wounds had, in fact, begun to heal – to granulate, as the medics would say. Furthermore, there was no indication of sepsis. In those days, injury from wounds of this sort would normally have resulted in death in about 75 per cent of cases. Around the same time two other surgeons, George Crile and Edward Martin, were discussing the benefits of maggot therapy at a meeting of the Clinical Congress of surgeons of North America. By the 1920s and '30s, maggot-therapy had become a more or less established surgical technique.

But maggot-therapy did not remain unchallenged for long. During and after the Second World War, antibiotics made their appearance. Medical practitioners now felt they had a simpler, more effective and – most importantly – a much less offensive method of dealing with wounds. The days of what many believed to be a somewhat barbaric technique appeared to be over. Antibiotics have certainly been extremely beneficial in the treatment of disease, but their story is not one of unqualified success. In many cases, medics found that infected wounds did not respond to their use. In severe cases antibiotics cannot reach the infected parts of the wound because there is no effective blood supply to carry the agent to the bacteria. Moreover, antibiotics also kill beneficial bacteria whose natural role is in wound-healing. Thus in many cases antibiotics not only have no effect, they may actually hinder recovery, with the result that since the 1980s there has been a renewed interest in maggot-therapy. In the United States, several cases of leg ulcers and skin tumours have been treated in this way. Entomological laboratories in that country now supply hospitals with maggots reared under special sterile conditions. An 'old-fashioned remedy' has, once again, been found to be the most efficacious!

One day in the early 1990s, I received a letter from Mr John Church, a retired orthopædic surgeon. He said that, with his life-long interest in wound-healing, he had become interested in the possibility of promoting maggot-therapy, especially in African countries where he had spent a large part of his professional career, as well as in other developing countries. He wrote that he would like to visit me, as one who studied maggots, in order to discuss the matter. I replied that I would be delighted to meet him and talk about this interesting idea. Some time later, John Church came to visit and I thereby acquired both a useful working knowledge of wound care and a good friend.

John Church's extensive experience in Africa had shown him that many serious injuries often went untreated for want of antibiotics and expensive medical equipment. It occurred to him that maggot-therapy might well be the solution in many such cases and he determined to explore this possibility to the full. We talked for a long time during this and subsequent visits, and he sought the opinions of many others – entomologists, surgeons, medical practitioners and specialists in wound-healing. He travelled the world, from Africa to China to the United States, giving a lecture here, organizing a conference there, and generally exciting great interest in his ideas. Many people applauded his endeavours and it seemed that he would get all the support he needed. But, as often happens with innovative ideas, there appeared an obstacle – one that was not entirely unexpected. On one of his visits, John Church told me about the proceedings of an international meeting on wound-healing at which he had delivered a lecture on maggot-therapy. After he concluded his lecture, he asked the audience what they thought of his proposal to establish a centre in an African country that would supply sterile maggots cheaply and speedily to any part of the continent where such treatment was needed. Almost everyone thought it was an excellent idea, but when he asked them whether they would use such a facility, the majority replied that they would not.

The problem was not a medical but a social one. It was felt that people in developing countries might consider that they were being offered second-rate treatment – antibiotics for the rich and maggots for the poor. Clearly, maggot-therapy was not being proposed as a 'second best' remedy but as a very important technique in the armoury of surgeons. Nevertheless, this negative perception had to be addressed if the idea was to come to fruition.

It is easy to see that it requires some measure of confidence in the efficacy of the treatment for a patient to accept the idea of having maggots deliberately introduced into his wound. When asked whether the term 'maggot-therapy' repelled patients, Dr William Baer's curt response was: 'The treatment by any other name would smell as sweet'. I am not convinced that he was right, for much depends on how an idea is presented, especially to a sick person. If there is the added complication of a sense of being offered an inferior remedy, the resistance can be very great. Despite the fact that the need was much greater in Africa, John Church felt that the initial trials should take place in Britain, to establish its use in a developed country first. Eventually, the idea was taken up by Dr Steve Thomas of the General Hospital in Bridgend in Wales, where there is now a thriving maggot-therapy clinic providing therapeutic maggots to hospitals nationally and internationally.

It is often said that there is nothing new under the sun. This certainly seems to be true about maggot-therapy. Despite its unacceptability in Africa, it is interesting to note that, during the Second World War, medical servicemen in northern Burma came across its use by the isolated hill people of the region. Maggot-therapy is also practised in parts of China, and the Australian aborigine tribe of the Ngemba use maggots for therapeutic purposes, as did the Mayan healers of Central America. With hindsight, one feels rather astonished that so many comparatively primitive peoples had discovered the medical use of maggots, but that it remained unknown and unthought of in the civilizations of Europe and the Mediterranean until relatively recent times.

Maggots undoubtedly do engender revulsion in most people. Even those who study them and know a great deal about them sometimes find them a little off-putting. Dr Lewis Davies, who studied blowflies for many years, used to rear his maggots on liver. One evening, when he returned home after a long day of working with them, he asked his wife, Alice, what was for dinner. The reply was 'liver'. I remember Dr Davies telling me that he did not have much of an appetite for dinner that evening!

Sheep-strike, a condition long known to European farmers, is a virulent form of myiasis in sheep. Interestingly, it is not a form of wound myiasis, but a condition caused by flies laying eggs on unwounded tissue. The maggots feed actively upon the living tissues of the sheep, seriously weakening and eventually killing the animal. The disease has caused great economic loss to sheep farmers in Britain, Australia and South Africa, although various treatments, such as sheep 'dipping', have considerably reduced the incidence of the disease in Britain during recent years. Unfortunately, the organo-phosphates used for dipping were found to have unpleasant medical effects on farmers and new methods of dealing with the disease are being explored, including direct attempts to reduce the fly population itself.

The flies that most commonly cause sheep-strike are the same species as those that are most commonly used in maggot-therapy. It is not yet understood why the maggots of these flies, so virulently pathogenic in sheep, are so benign and therapeutic in man; nor why these flies sometimes cause a malignant myiasis in human beings outside the controlled conditions of the hospital and the laboratory; nor what makes them change their behaviour so fundamentally. There appear to be no simple answers to these important questions.

Factors such as odours, humidity and temperature, which affect the behaviour of flies, interact in such a complex way that it is very difficult to determine which combination causes the flies to lay eggs. Moreover, the conditions of the tissues must play a part in determining whether the maggots will cause a benign myiasis (feeding only on the dead tissues), or a malignant one (feeding on living tissues).

As regards this behaviour, the odours and other factors that attract flies to a body, living or dead, are not necessarily the same as those that induce them to lay eggs. The dry, clean fleece of a sheep certainly attracts flies, but they will not lay eggs on it, unless other conditions are fulfilled. Sheep whose wool is soiled by urine or faeces or contaminated with specific bacteria or certain mite species are, as might be expected, much more susceptible to 'strike' than are sheep with clean fleeces.

In human beings, too, myiasis can be a deadly disease. In Britain, human myiasis is rare, but it does occur. In all medical cases in which I have been involved, the patients were elderly, neglected, had wounds that were undressed or not properly dressed, and suffered from hypothermia. In such people, myiasis can be a truly virulent condition. Hypothermia, in particular, seems to render people as well as animals susceptible to the disease, and unwounded animals (not only sheep) that are afflicted with myiasis are often hypothermic.

While we do not understand fully the precise reasons why maggots are benign in some cases and malignant in others, it is clear that the general medical condition of the victim plays a part in determining which way the condition will develop. There is also evidence that the same fly species cause a benign myiasis in some parts of their range, but a malignant form in other parts.

We have already come across the Old World screw-worm fly, an obligate parasite of domestic animals. The New World has its own equivalent of this insect, known as the New World screw-worm fly, *Cochliomyia hominivorax*. Its specific name, meaning man-eater, is well chosen and describes the viciousness of it habits. For many years, this fly invaded the southern United States from Mexico and afflicted domestic and wild animals alike. Cattle were particularly susceptible. In 1935, 1,200,000 livestock cases were reported, as well as fifty-five human cases, although the true figure for humans was thought to be about three times that number. The fly has now been controlled by a technique called 'sterile male release', an ingenious method that exploits a simple biological characteristic of this fly: the female mates only once in its life time. Researchers hit upon the idea that if a sterilized male mated with a female the resulting eggs would be infertile. Huge numbers of captive-bred male flies were therefore gamma-irradiated and then released into the wild to mate with the naturally-occurring females, thus solving the screw-worm fly problem in the United States.

We live, of course, in an age in which intercontinental travel is easy, rapid and very frequent. A natural consequence is that insects can be inadvertently introduced into areas that lie far outside their natural range. If the insect concerned is a medical or agricultural pest, the consequences can be serious. One such disturbing introduction took place in the late 1980s. One day I received a telephone call from Dr William Beesley of the Liverpool School of Tropical Medicine. He told me that some camels in Libya had been found to have myiasis and that on examining a sample of the maggots it had been found that the fly in question was the New World screw-worm. This was seriously worrying news. Never before had this American fly been found in Africa, or anywhere else in the Old World. The fact that maggots, not adult flies, were discovered indicated that the fly had already established itself and was breeding in the country. How it had been introduced was a mystery; it could not have arrived as maggots, because they do not breed in dead tissues, such as meat. Moreover, no livestock is imported into Libya from the Americas and so the fly could not have arrived as maggots parasitizing the animals. The only possibility was that the flies arrived as adults that had entered a ship or an aeroplane.

As we have seen, *C. hominivorax* is a parasite of wild as well as domestic animals. It is very strongly attracted to wounds, even minute ones such as tick-bites. Clearly the introduction of this fly into Africa presented a threat not only to domestic livestock but to the incomparable wildlife of that continent. Libya, of course, is a largely desert country and is far to the north of the African plains where the great herds of antelope, zebra, wildebeeste and other susceptible hoofed animals occur, but the fly could still reach those parts without much difficulty. Although the Sahara desert is a formidable barrier, camel caravans still regularly cross it from the Mediterranean coast to central Africa, and any parasitized animals could introduce the fly into the heart of the continent. Another route by which the fly could have invaded the tropical parts of the continent would have been along the Mediterranean coast to Egypt and thence along the Nile valley into the Sudan and beyond. If this had happened, both the economic and cultural loss to Africa would have been very great but mercifully it did not.

Dr Beesley asked me whether I would assist in monitoring the extent to which the fly had established itself in Libya by carrying out routine examinations of samples of maggots from veterinary cases to determine whether or not *C. hominivorax* was involved; human cases had also been recorded. I was happy to do it, in view of the likely outcome if the problem were left unaddressed. I also informed people studying African wildlife of the danger, since most of them were unlikely to have heard of this alien parasite.

An international team arrived in Libya and the American policy of sterile male release was applied to good effect. Thanks to hard work, good luck and the desert barrier, the fly was eradicated – a happy ending to a story which, if the fly had not been noticed at an early stage, could easily have become a tragedy.

It is, of course, all too easy to relax one's guard, with unpredictable results. I remember receiving some insect specimens from some friends who had been on holiday to Iceland. One of these insects was a species of greenbottle not previously found there and which was known to cause myiasis. Since Iceland is a sheep-breeding country, I notified the Icelandic authorities of this find. They replied that they would keep an eye on the situation to make sure that the fly did not establish itself. In view of the long, cold Icelandic winters the chance of this happening was small, but the fly, or its maggots or pupae, could conceivably have overwintered beside the great fissures from which warm gases emanate all year round. In the event, the fly did not establish itself.

In 1996, I visited the forensic science laboratories of the French Gendarmerie at Rosny-sous-Bois, near Paris, to confer with colleagues in the area of forensic entomology and to write a report on the laboratories for the British Home Office. While there I learned that a tropical and sub-tropical fly, *Chrysomya albiceps*, had extended its range to the north of France. The reason for concern about the advance of this fly was that it is known to cause a malignant myiasis in domestic animals. I was already aware that it had moved northwards as far as southern France and Switzerland, but did not know that it had reached the Channel coast. My French colleagues told me that the fly had been found in no less than ten forensic cases north of Paris. Clearly, it was well established. Equally clearly, it could cross the Channel at any time and invade England. As a frequent traveller by ferry between England and France, I was only too aware that flies come aboard ship in larger numbers than the paying human passengers. There was no reason why *Chrysomya albiceps* would not avail itself of a free ride in the same way!

Although it is unlikely for various reasons that this fly would become a serious pest in Britain, it is not possible to predict how a newly introduced insect could affect the ecology of these islands. I had carried out research on its maggots and had once written a short paper with Dr Robert Whitcombe on its role as a myiasis agent in Arabia, so I was aware that it was a possible source of economic loss. On my return to England, I wrote my report to the Home Office and I mentioned the arrival of this potential pest at the French coast. I also wrote to the Ministry of Agriculture several times, urging them to watch out for the arrival of the fly at the Channel ports. My letters were never acknowledged and no action was taken.

Since maggots can invade the body before death, one cannot be sure that the estimated age of the maggot will give an accurate minimum time of death. However, the incidence of human myiasis in Britain is so rare, being essentially restricted to very sick people, that this problem is more theoretical than real. Nevertheless, one can imagine situations in which confusion could arise. For example, a person might be attacked with a knife and be left mortally wounded in some out-of-the-way place in the country. The victim might be attacked by flies and begin to suffer from wound myiasis, dying a few days later. Under such circumstances, any subsequent time of death estimation based on the age of the maggots would be faulty.

This hypothetical situation is not entirely imaginary, for I am basing it on a true event that was related to me by John Church. A man had been driving along a remote country road when he crashed into a ditch and was badly injured. Several days later he was discovered alive but with maggots in his wounds. He was successfully treated and recovered. This story is an example of how maggots can aid recovery, but if he had not been found at a reasonably early stage, he might have died. It is clear that, if a time of death estimate had then been carried out, it would have been incorrect.

Although this is a very rare scenario, it is one that ought to be kept constantly in mind. In other countries, such as the United States where forensic entomology is routinely applied, the danger of error is much more real, since human myiasis is considerably commoner there than it is in Britain and northern Europe.

Peter Costello, in his book, *The Real World of Sherlock Holmes*, observed that a particular kind of horror attaches to murderous medical men.

Men like Dr Crippen, who murdered his wife and cut up her body, and Dr Knox, who was widely believed (perhaps unjustly) to have colluded with the notorious murderers Burke and Hare, arouse a special kind of revulsion.

In my own forensic career, the nearest I came to a case involving a murderous medical man was Dr Antony Samson Perera, whose crime was described in an earlier chapter. Yet it is interesting to record that the first time forensic entomology was applied to a police investigation in Britain, the murderer was a medical man – the notorious Dr Buck Ruxton, whose story has now entered the folklore of crime detection.

Near Moffat, along the main Edinburgh-Carlisle road in Dumfriesshire, Scotland, there is a ravine known as the Devil's Beef Tub, through which runs Gardenholme Linn, a narrow tributary of the River Annan. In the eighteenth century, cattle thieves used to take their stolen livestock there to slaughter them, hence the name. It was a macabre name for a place that was to acquire an even more sinister reputation in the twentieth century.

On 29th September 1935, a woman walking over the bridge that spanned the ravine happened to look over the edge into the gully beneath. To her horror, she saw a human arm lying on the bank of the stream. Later that day the police collected seventy pieces of human remains, including two heads and a trunk. It was clear from the outset that the remains came from at least two bodies but probably not more. In the initial stages of the inquiry, it was thought that one body was female and the other male, since one of the heads had certain male characteristics, whereas the trunk was undoubtedly female. Later medical examination showed that the head of uncertain sex fitted the undoubtedly female trunk, making it certain that both bodies were female. Further finds included three female breasts and internal sexual organs, proving beyond doubt that two women were involved.

The remains were horribly mutilated, almost certainly to prevent identification. The nose, lips, ears and eyes had been cut away from the two heads and the internal and external sexual organs had been removed from the trunk. It was clear that the butchery was the work of one who had accurate anatomical knowledge. Yet the grisly task had been botched, for the murderer left many clues behind. The very fact that certain areas of skin were removed from the bodies drew attention to those parts, which were subsequently shown to have borne identifying marks of the victims. Also, some of the remains were wrapped in identifiable items of clothing, such as a blouse, a child's woollen rompers and a pillow-slip. Even more foolishly, the murderer had wrapped some of the remains in newspapers, one of which – a copy of

The Sunday Graphic dated 15th September – showed part of a photo-graph of a girl wearing a crown. Another fragment of the newspaper bore the headline: '-----AMBE'S CARNIVAL QUEEN -ROWNED'. Police investigations revealed their source to be a special 'slip edition' of the newspaper, distributed only in the Morecambe/Lancaster area of Lancashire.

Clearly, the remains could not have been placed in the ravine before 15th September, the date on the newspaper. Nor could they have been deposited after 19th September when the river had last been in flood. Some of the remains had been washed several hundred yards down-stream by the water. The rest were lying where they had been dropped on the bank on which the stream overflowed, not in the stream itself. This suggested to the police that the perpetrator was not a local man and probably performed his deed in the dark. Many of the remains were infested with maggots and their ages indicated that the macabre parcels of human flesh had been deposited in the gully ten or eleven days before they were discovered.

On 9th October, a Scottish newspaper reported that Mary Jane Rogerson, a maid in the employ of a Dr Buck Ruxton of Lancaster, had disappeared three weeks previously. Inquiries revealed that Mary Rogerson and Dr Ruxton's wife had both left the doctor's house at that time. Mrs Ruxton had last been seen alive on 14th September on a visit to Blackpool to see the lights. She drove home in her motorcar at 11.30 that evening and was never seen again. All the evidence – the maggots, the newspapers, her own known movements – pointed to the conclu-sion that she had died that evening.

Dr Ruxton's name was not, in fact, Ruxton at all but Bukhtiyar Hakim, an Indian doctor who had studied medicine in Bombay and London and who eventually set up in private practice in Lancaster. He lived with a woman named Isabella Ruxton who was not his wife but who became known as 'Mrs Ruxton'. He himself came to be known as 'Dr Ruxton'. He was a violent man; he often beat Isabella and several times threatened to kill her. More than once the police had been called to his house as a result of his violence. He was an excitable, melodra-matic man – characteristics that brought about his downfall.

After her disappearance, Dr Ruxton put it about that Isabella had gone to Edinburgh, although he varied his story several times. He then started to behave very oddly. Another woman named Mrs Smalley had been murdered and Ruxton, totally unnecessarily, went to the police to object to the fact that some of his servants had been questioned about this murder. He said that he had had nothing to do with it, an accusa-tion no-one had made. Astonishingly, he invited the police to search his house. The following day he told Mary Rogerson's stepmother that the girl had become pregnant and that his wife had taken her to Scotland to deal with the matter.

On 4th October, Ruxton again went to the police station to protest about the Smalley investigations and said that his wife and maid had gone to Edinburgh on 15th September and that he had not heard from them since. On 9th October, he went to Edinburgh to see Mrs Ruxton's sister, demanding to know whether she was hiding his wife. As if all this bizarre behaviour was not enough to arouse suspicion, on 10th October Dr Ruxton asked a Mrs Hampshire to come to his house. She and her husband had been employed by him to scrub the staircase at his home the day after Mrs Ruxton and Mary Rogerson had disappeared. Incredibly, he now gave Mrs Hampshire some carpets and clothes that were blood-stained. He later arrived at Mrs Hampshire's house in a state of great agitation and told her to burn the clothes and one of the carpets. On leaving her house, he went to the police station and complained that the rumours that the remains in Dumfriesshire were said to be those of his wife and maid were ruining his practice. Ominously, the police response was to ask for a description and a photograph of his wife, which he supplied.

Soon after this, Mrs Hampshire handed over the blood-stained items to the police. The police were now hot on the scent. The blouse used to wrap some of the remains was shown to Mary Rogerson's stepmother, who identified it as one she had bought for Mary from a jumble sale; she had mended it, putting a patch under one arm, and recognized her needlework. The woollen rompers were identified by another woman, Mrs Holme, who had given them to Mary for one of the Ruxtons' children.

On 12th October, Ruxton was charged with the murder of Mary Rogerson. Some time later, he was also charged with the murder of his wife.

The trial began on 2nd March 1936. It was not a complicated affair and, although ably defended by the legendary Norman Birkett, K.C., Dr Buck Ruxton was found guilty of murder and hanged. He was put on trial for the murder of his wife only, not for that of Mary Rogerson. There is a certain irony in this. It became clear that Ruxton killed his wife by manual strangulation in a fit of rage, having discovered that she was having a liaison with another man. In the opinion of Sir Sydney Smith, one of the pathologists on the case, Ruxton probably did not mean to kill her. Mary Rogerson was probably killed because she discovered the murder and had to be silenced; the medical evidence suggested that Ruxton probably cut her throat. In the event Dr Buck

Ruxton was hanged not for the cold-blooded murder of his maid, but for a *crime passionel*.

Many years ago, I wrote an article in which I discussed some aspects of the Ruxton case. A woman living in Scotland read it and wrote to me about her recollections of the event. As a child she had lived in Dumfriesshire, not far from where the gruseome remains were found. She told me that one of the songs that she and her little friends sang in those days ran as follows:

Doctor Buck Ruxton ye murdered yer wife;
Ye murdered yer wife and her maid as well.
Ye cut them up both with yer murderin' knife;
Och, Doctor Buck Ruxton ye'll end up in Hell!

There is another small matter of natural history interest in this tale of maggots and medics, for among the remains found near Moffat there was an eye of a Cyclops. In Greek legend the Cyclops was a man-eating, one-eyed giant who was killed by Odysseus, as Homer recounts in his *Odyssey*. The remarkably well-preserved cyclopean eye found in the Devil's Beef Tub was not that of a giant; it was the eye of an abnormal newly-born but was not human. Deformations of this kind sometimes occur among sheep and goats but rarely among humans. All such babies die at, or shortly after, birth.

One can only guess how this strange object came to be in the ravine and why it was lying, so conspicuously fresh and undecayed, among the rotting remains. It has been suggested that it was an interesting specimen preserved by Dr Ruxton in a jar of fluid as a medical curiosity. Perhaps at some point Ruxton tried to empty the preservative over the remains and inadvertently lost the eye in the process.

Be that as it may, the finding of an eye of a Cyclops at the scene is most uncanny for back in the early nineteenth century, Thomas de Quincey, in his essay, *The Vision of Sudden Death*, commenting on his monstrous one-eyed coachman, had presciently written, while under the influence of laudanum: 'But what was Cyclops doing here? Had the medical men recommended northern air, or how? I collected, from such explanations as he volunteered, that he had an interest at stake in some suit-at-law now pending in Lancaster.'

CHAPTER 10

The Ends and the Means

When money speaks, the truth is silent.
Russian Proverb

Mr Bumble, the Beadle in Charles Dickens' *Oliver Twist*, famously remarked that 'the law is a ass, a idiot'. I suspect that most people at one time or another and for one reason or another have found themselves in agreement with that pithy assessment. Yet, in truth, I have not found it so. While some laws are, indeed, asinine and idiotic, the Law in general has always struck me as being very reasonable.* This is not to say that all is well with the administration of justice; alas, far from it. The problems reside, not in the Law itself, but in the conduct of many of those who are entrusted with the enforcement of the Law and the administration of justice in the courts.

So many people, through their experiences, have become bitterly disillusioned with the machinery of justice. The great American lawyer, Clarence Darrow, who defended John Scopes at the infamous 'Monkey Trial' in Tennessee in 1925, once remarked that there is no such thing as justice, in or out of court. Such a harsh judgement is easy to understand when one has seen injustice perpetrated close at hand and by those from whom one would have expected justice. Indeed, I have often emerged from a court-room with a very similar feeling. But let us not confuse the singer with the song. The song seems to me to be sweet enough, albeit capable of further improvement and refinement, though

* In the context of this discussion, my comments refer to the situation in Britain and the West generally. I am not arguing that the Law in *all* countries is equally reasonable.

the voices of many of the singers can be very harsh and discordant.

Miscarriages of justice are much commoner than most people real-ize. In one year no fewer than forty-eight alleged miscarriages of jus-tice came to my notice. I am often asked why they happen and how they can be allowed to happen. To answer these questions it is impor-tant to understand the way in which crimes are investigated. There are two processes involved in dealing with a suspected criminal and both of them are fallible – the police investigation and the trial. I am neither a police officer nor a lawyer but as one who has been involved with the administration of the Criminal Law for twenty-five years I have wit-nessed these procedures at first hand.

In my experience, most police officers are decent, honest men and women. As with any other large group of people, some fail in the task with which they have been entrusted, and such failures often have very serious consequences indeed. These days one often hears about police brutality and corruption and, indeed, such things do take place, but it is important to remember that they are very much the exception rather than the rule – they would not make the headlines otherwise. During my twenty-five years in forensic work, I have known police officers to fail seriously on many occasions, but I have never known a case in which an officer was motivated by sheer malice or a desire to harm someone whom he knew or believed to be innocent. I do not say that this does not happen, merely that it is outside my experience. On the other hand, I *have* known cases in which innocent people, or at least people against whom the evidence was very weak but whom the police officers involved firmly believed were guilty, were pursued with such relentless ferocity that they eventually broke down and 'confessed'. The police officer's belief in the person's guilt may be quite genuine but the reason for it is often prejudice of one kind or another.

Police work is often unpleasant and always difficult. Two kinds of activity are expected of police officers: the prevention of crime and the apprehension of criminals when crimes have been committed. Unfor-tunately, one of the currently fashionable notions in society is that peo-ple can be judged by measuring 'results'. The belief that people's general abilities and qualities (such as patience, commitment, kindness and intelligence) can be measured, like the temperature of an invalid, is a pseudo-scientific fiction propagated by some scientists and, per-versely, by some non-scientists as well. The ability and effectiveness of a police officer is, therefore, now 'measured' by the number of success-ful convictions he secures. The same applies to a police force as a whole. However, even committed 'metricians' as we may call them cannot measure, or at any rate count, the number of crimes that *could* have happened but which did not happen due to the efforts of a conscientious policeman. Other kinds of police service, especially what may be termed social activities, are also effectively unmeasurable. Consequently, there is pressure on police forces to give such activities less importance since they cannot earn them any 'brownie points'. In order to establish and maintain their credibility, police forces are now under pressure to secure large numbers of convictions; in other words, to produce results that the metricians can measure, in spite of the fact that such 'measurements' must be a poor indication of the forces' real effectiveness.

There are now league tables for police forces just as there are for schools. Those forces that submit high 'clearing-up rates' score higher than those that do not. The 'rate' is, in fact, the percentage of reported and recorded crimes that have been satisfactorily resolved. Unfortunately, reported crimes are not always recorded, since a police officer may feel that some are unlikely to be solved and so would lower the percentage of successfully solved cases. I have no idea how common this practice is, but it certainly does happen. The natural consequence is that some forces can make their record look better than it really is. A far more serious consequence is that some police officers who sometimes feel that they 'know' who committed a crime, may try to secure the conviction of an innocent party in order to improve the 'rate'. Again it is impossible to know how often this occurs, but there is no doubt that it does.

The damaging effect of this attitude to policing cannot be overemphasized. However much one may condemn the actions of over-zealous police officers in their attempts to secure convictions 'at any price', one cannot deny that the pressures under which the police are made to work must encourage such actions. I am not for a moment arguing that police officers cannot help it and that they *have* to do these things – quite the opposite, but I do believe that by applying unnecessary pressure of the wrong kind we are effectively ensuring that a perverse result will follow. It is no use denying justice to people and then lamenting that they are behaving badly. I am firmly convinced that these kinds of pressures on police forces should be lifted. I do not mean that there should be no supervision of their work or that they should not be held accountable for their actions – again, quite the opposite, but the treatment of police forces as though they were commercial businesses must be brought to an end if the police are to give society of their best. So long as convictions are treated as though they were commercial 'products', there will be pressure to produce more of them. The inevitable result is a greater risk that innocent people will be convicted.

I do not wish to give the impression that police corruption is someone else's fault. It is not. Although I have liked most police officers I
have met, there are some whom I regard with great suspicion. There is
much ignorance, arrogance and bigotry in many sections of the police
and those officers who suffer from these attitudes are among the most
dangerous people in society.

Once a person has been charged with a crime he is usually brought
to trial. Surely here the truth should be revealed and the true culprit
identified. Experience shows that this does not always happen. What
many people do not realize is that the purpose of a trial is not to discover what happened as *such*, but rather to discover whether the
accused committed the crime or not. In other words it is not the purpose of the trial to find out *who* committed the crime but simply
whether the person in the dock did. This is perfectly reasonable, since
a trial is not a police investigation, which is the procedure of discovering who might have committed the crime, but a public investigation of
an individual person's guilt or innocence.

In Britain, criminal trials are conducted according to the adversarial
system in which one barrister attempts to prove the guilt of the accused
while another barrister attempts to prove his innocence. The two barristers in a case are *adversaries* and the dictionary definition of the word
'adversary' is *opponent* or *enemy*. Barristers are said to *fight* cases and
they *win* or *lose* them. A successful barrister is one who has won many
cases. It follows that a clever barrister may, in theory at least, secure the
release of someone who is actually guilty and a less skilled barrister may
fail to secure the release of someone who is innocent. Many people feel
that a system in which two opposing points of view are argued in court
simply for the sake of winning a case must result in some damage to the
truth and, inevitably, to an unjust verdict and sentence.

Can such a system be a good one? The answer is yes *if* the barristers
involved are genuinely interested in the truth. Often the procedure of
a court-room trial may give the onlooker the impression that each side
is out to win at all costs. While this is undoubtedly sometimes the case,
this is not how the system is intended to work. Barristers are not meant
to do all they can to secure the release of someone whom they know to
be guilty.

The purpose of the exercise then is this. Say a defence barrister is
convinced of the innocence of an individual. Naturally, he will do all
he can to secure that person's release. He will present the evidence in
support of his belief and will do his best, quite scrupulously, to argue
his case in such a way that it will show his client in the best light. When
one holds a point of view strongly and honestly, it is often difficult to

see that there may be a perfectly valid alternative opinion on the matter. This is why playing 'Devil's Advocate' is such a valuable exercise even if one is convinced of the opinion that one is trying to demolish. It is an exercise that clears the mind, and the truth will often unfold clearly and unequivocally. The adversarial system provides each barrister with just such a 'Devil's Advocate' in the person of the opposing barrister. If the same evidence is presented and argued clearly, ably and conscientiously by two intelligent minds, the probability that the truth will emerge is very great. Indeed, the best and most conscientious barristers do not believe that their role is to secure a conviction (or an acquittal) come what may; rather, they feel that their function is to argue their case with as much rigour and fair-mindedness as possible and to leave it to the jury to decide. Winning or losing is not the purpose of the exercise. To them being a successful barrister means that they should present their interpretation of the evidence as honestly as possible, not that they should present the evidence in such a way as to influence the jury into delivering a verdict that is favourable to their client. I am sure that a fair trial must take place when barristers approach their task with the right attitude. In the words of Sir Eric Hallinan, a former Chief Justice of the Windward and Leeward Islands (the italics are his):

> ' ... It is the duty of the prosecutor to present the evidence for the Crown as cogently and *at the same time as fairly as possible*. It is not the function or duty of a prosecutor to try and obtain a conviction by every means in his power or to make the case appear stronger than it is. On the other hand he must lead the evidence for the Crown even though he may consider it weak; he must leave it to the jury to assess its value ... [The barrister] is not 'out to win' ... At the end of a criminal trial where I was prosecutor, I never felt that the Crown had 'lost' its case, if the accused person was acquitted. If the Crown's case had been cogently and fairly presented, then I was satisfied – whatever the outcome.'

Unfortunately, trials do not always proceed in this objective and even-handed manner. When barristers do not live up to the spirit and ideals of the adversarial system, miscarriages of justice are very likely to happen.

But what of forensic scientists; what errors do *they* commit to the detriment of the Criminal Justice System?

One day I received a visit from a senior police officer who wished to consult me about a murder that was being investigated by his force. I agreed to examine the evidence and, eventually, produced my report and sent it to him. He telephoned back, thanking me for my report which, he said, was very helpful to their enquiries. It appeared that they had a suspect and that my report supported their view that he was guilty. The officer, very flatteringly, was full of praise of my technical abilities. Some time later however, I received another call from him. This time he did not sound so happy. He said that further evidence had shown, quite clearly, that their original suspect was innocent. Moreover, they now had another suspect of whose guilt they were 'certain'. Unfortunately, my report did not support their belief in his culpability. Clearly, he said, I was mistaken. After all, my field of investigation was not an exact science, was it? It is not as though it were nuclear physics, a subject widely believed, erroneously, to be 'exact'. It was abundantly clear, he went on, that my report was of little value in this case and that other, 'more important', evidence showed that my findings were incorrect. Would I be prepared, perhaps, to 'modify' my original conclusions in the light of this latest, 'very impressive' evidence? Naturally, I declined to do so, since the new evidence did not remotely affect the kind of evidence that I had examined. The officer was not pleased and did not contact me again.

This little story has a moral; the scientific specialist is not looked upon kindly if his findings fail to satisfy the preconceived notions of those who consult him. People who consult forensic specialists frequently have a sincere and honest desire to arrive at the truth, but all too often the motive is a need to support a strongly-held belief or, if not a belief, then a particular position that they choose, for whatever reason, to defend. Such an attitude always gives rise to problems, because 'clients' of this sort feel that, since they are paying the consultant a fee, they ought to be given what they want.

A forensic scientist can make one of two responses to such an attitude. He can tell the client the truth regardless of whether his findings support or refute his (i.e. the client's) position, or he can compromise himself and produce a report that would serve the client's interests, regardless of the truth. Clearly, if he were to do the latter, he would be acting immorally and illegally. If he did the former, he would risk losing his living since fewer people would consult him in the future; he will have acquired the reputation of being 'difficult'.

In real life some specialists will compromise themselves and others will not. The questions this statement raises are obvious and very important. Are those who compromise themselves only a small minority, or are they a more substantial portion of the forensic community? What damage do such people do? Why are such people tolerated and not exposed? How, and at what stage in the administration of justice, is forensic evidence misrepresented?

Obviously, the simplest way in which evidence can be misrepresented is by the specialists stating things that are not true – straightforward lying. Shocking though this may be to many people, this does often happen in court. A more subtle approach is taken when errors of omission are made, in other words, when the truth, *but not the whole truth*, is stated. Although I do not for a moment condone what happened, I believe that miscarriages of justice, like the much-publicized cases of Judith Ward and the Maguire Seven which involved partial truth-telling, are often – but not always – the result of weakness of character, rather than active malice.

New and unhealthy pressures have been brought to bear on forensic scientists in recent years, with dire results. In order to understand how these changes came about, it is necessary to say a few words about the past and present organization of forensic science in Britain. For many years the Home Office, the government department responsible for law and order, administered six forensic science laboratories in England and Wales.* Until 1989, English and Welsh police forces could make use of this Home Office Forensic Science Service without the payment of a fee for each case, although each force made an annual financial contribution to the Service, the size of which was fixed according to the size of the force in question and not on the basis of the amount of work undertaken for that force in a particular year. In 1989, all this changed. The HOFSS was given agency status (in other words, it was, to all intents and purposes, privatized) and it became known simply as the Forensic Science Service (FSS). Since then, police forces requiring forensic work have been obliged to pay the full costs of the work at a time when their budgets were being cut back. It is interesting that one member of the Commons Home Affairs Committee, which recommended the change to agency status, disagreed with his colleagues and prepared an amendment stating that the marketplace approach was inappropriate to forensic science. Unfortunately, he was unable to make his views prevail.

* The situation in Scotland is, in many ways, different from that in the rest of Britain; Scottish law differs from English law in certain respects and Scottish police are part of the remit of the Scottish Office, not the Home Office. In Wales, it is the Home Office, not the Welsh Office, that has responsibility for the police.

Two consequences followed from this change. First, in order to husband their resources, police forces have been obliged to become more selective with regard to the kind of physical evidence that they would ask the FSS to examine (fees are charged item by item) to the extent that some cases, which would have been investigated forensically in the past, are now no longer investigated in this way at all. Secondly, police forces now feel that they have to find cheaper sources of forensic advice; in other words, they may consult practitioners outside the FSS. While this is not necessarily a bad thing, especially when such practitioners are specialists in areas of science not available within the FSS, the pressure on the police to consult cheaper consultants has led to a fall in standards in forensic science as a whole, because many such consultants are of a very low calibre indeed. Of course, defence lawyers have employed such people since long before the 1989 changes were implemented, having rarely consulted the HOFSS or its successor.

All forensic scientists, including those in the FSS, are now obliged to function like hard-nosed businessmen. Many independent (i.e. non-FSS) scientists are honest, hard-working people, but they, too, are subject to financial pressures that could affect their conduct. Consider, for example, the following scenario. A police officer goes to a consultant, struggling to make a living through his consultancy, and asks him to carry out a particular investigation, for example the determination of the time of death of a murder victim. The officer will explain the background to the case, while the consultant takes notes and asks questions for clarification. So far, so good. However, at the end of the discussion, the consultant may realize that in this particular case the problem could be solved in a much cheaper way, or that another consultant with a different expertise might be able to answer the question more effectively. Should the scientist tell the police officer this or should he simply hold his tongue and carry out the desired work, albeit conscientiously and to the best of his ability?

I have no doubt that the scientist should be honour-bound to inform the police of the best way for them to spend their money and time. Nevertheless, this does not always happen, with the result that justice is ill-served, since its limited resources are squandered for personal gain. Again, the motive in this kind of situation is not malice but a weakness born of a need to survive financially. The culprit – for such a person is culpable – will often justify his actions by telling himself that, if he did not take on all the cases that came his way regardless of whether his services were really required, his valuable expertise would be lost to the police. He can easily make a self-serving action appear morally justifiable in his own eyes. The first step on the road to corruption will have been taken.

At this point it is necessary to introduce the real villain of the piece: the 'muddy-water' consultant. It is a fact well known to many forensic scientists and lawyers that some forensic consultants exist purely for the purpose of assisting the defence by muddying the waters and by refuting evidence presented by the prosecution. Let no one doubt that such practitioners – 'experts' as they style themselves – exist in some numbers. They are usually totally unqualified, or are qualified in one specialism but are ready, indeed eager, to give evidence in areas that lie far outside their competence.

The malign influence of these consultants is a natural consequence of the way in which forensic evidence is handled in court. Normally, the police and crown barristers have more funds than the defence to pay for the necessary forensic investigations in a case. Formerly the crown (or prosecution) was legally obliged to disclose all its evidence to the defence but there was no requirement for the defence to disclose its evidence to the prosecution, although nowadays forensic evidence is usually disclosed by the defence. Recently, the law in this matter has been changed, so that the crown may withhold evidence that it considers might be helpful to the defence. It used to be said that the prosecution had to fight its case with one hand tied behind its back; nowadays, this is more true for the defence.

If the defence is able to obtain the prosecution evidence, it can consider ways in which to counter it, as for instance by retaining a 'muddy-water' consultant. Such a person will produce, for a fee, a report that will satisfy the defence but may confuse the issue so much that the evidence as a whole appears useless to a jury. After all, if a jury listens to two so-called experts in court, one saying day and the other saying night, one saying black and the other saying white, they will have to conclude that, if the specialists themselves disagree so fundamentally, they the jury members cannot possibly evaluate the evidence. The result is that they will probably ignore it completely. Thus, a combination of lack of funds and secretiveness produces a totally distorted picture of the evidence.

I have known a number of 'muddy-water' consultants. At the end of a particular court case in which one such had done his best to cloud the issue, a colleague of mine went up to him and rebuked him for his unprofessional behaviour, telling him that the facts did not support his testimony. Our man was totally unabashed and declared that he was 'uninhibited by facts'! He is still very widely consulted by defence lawyers.

The man who must be awarded first prize in 'muddy-water' consultancy is an 'expert' I came across during the investigation of a particularly brutal murder. I had completed my work on the victim's time of death and submitted my report to the police. Some time later, the inspector in charge of the case telephoned and said that my report had been disclosed to the defence, who had engaged their own consultant. This person, after simply reading my report, declared that everything I had written was incorrect. He arrived at conclusions that were the exact opposite to mine on every point. He stated that some of the things that I 'claimed' to know were, in fact, unknown and unknowable. All this, without ever having examined the evidence.

I told the inspector that this man's comments should not be taken seriously unless he produced a report after studying the evidence. The inspector naturally agreed and arranged for the man to examine the evidence, in my presence, at one of the FSS laboratories. I duly arrived at the venue with the inspector and another officer and we met the defence consultant at the entrance. We were shown by a member of the FSS staff into a large laboratory. Our host offered the 'expert' a range of equipment that he could use, including an electron microscope if necessary. To my surprise, he declined all her offers and picked up one of the test-tubes containing preserved evidence. He looked at it and turned it over and over in his hands, seemingly uncertain what to do next. The forensic scientist repeated her offer of the use of microscopes, but he waved his hand and said that he had all he needed in his pocket and, producing a small, plastic-framed magnifying glass, he proceeded to look at the minute specimens floating around in the alcohol inside the tube. His examination, if one could call it that, lasted for a few seconds, after which he placed the tube on the laboratory bench and announced that the evidence was too stale to be of any use. He then turned to me and said, with the utmost insolence, 'You can't do much with this. A maggot's a maggot, isn't it?'. I made no answer. He tried again to engage me in conversation, but I replied that my instructions from the police were to attend his examination and not to engage in debate with him over the evidence. Quite unbelievably, he became angry. He said that he knew what he was doing and that his livelihood depended upon his knowing all about such matters. He was no academic like me, he said, he had down-to-earth knowledge gained from real life, whereas I had got all my knowledge 'from books'. Clearly, we were getting nowhere, so I turned to the inspector saying that there was no point in my remaining, and rose to leave. The man then had the audacity to offer me a lift to the railway station but I declined and the officers and I left the room.

A few weeks later Mr X, as I shall call him, produced a report for the defence who agreed to let me see it. I read it and, were it not for the fact that I was dealing with a very serious crime, I would have found it highly entertaining. Essentially, his was a report on my report, not a report on the evidence which, of course, he had not really examined. It contained statements that were totally untrue and other statements that revealed a complete ignorance of insect physiology, anatomy and ecology. It even included fictitious names of insect species; he had simply made them up as he went along. The police asked me to respond by writing a report on his report on my report, which I duly did, describing the errors – I should say, more accurately, nonsensical assertions – in Mr X's report. This report was disclosed to the defence but, brass-necked as ever, Mr X stood by his conclusions.

Eventually, a date was fixed for the trial. The prosecution barrister was worried about the diametrically opposed nature of Mr X's report and mine, and he invited me to discuss the whole matter with him. While convinced of Mr X's incompetence, the barrister wanted to know how his evidence could be shown up in court for the nonsense it was. I travelled to the north of England with a suitcase of books and scientific papers so that I could support every statement I had made in my two reports. I spent a long time going over every point of the evidence with the barrister and his assistants, invoking the support of published research results. By the time we finished, counsel was confident that Mr X's testimony would be discredited in the court room. I hoped he was right, but one can never be sure of the effect of such contradictory conclusions by two scientific witnesses on a jury. I left all the books and papers with the barrister and returned to Cambridge.

The day of the trial finally dawned and I went up north again. I sat in court, listening to the pathologist's evidence on how the victim had been killed. He was describing in gory detail the nature of the fatal wounds and how they had been inflicted. He also referred to some of my findings (this is quite normal), where they impinged on the pathology evidence. It was a horrific murder and the accused, sitting in the dock, was in torment. I watched him as he swayed back and forth, put his face in his hands, ran his hands through his hair and looked, with twisted features, up at the ceiling. The pathologist continued, quite nonchalantly, with his testimony, in the soft voice of a kindly gentleman addressing a meeting of the local Women's Institute: 'We then packed the samples in bubbly-wrap. You know, the transparent plastic stuff with bubbles, which children like to pop ... There were so many flies, I kept doing this [shooing motion of the hand] all the time ... ' When the judge adjourned for lunch the accused appeared to be on the verge of collapse. As I left the court room I saw Mr X who greeted me affably, but I fear I responded with a curt nod of the head.

After lunch I made my way back to the Crown Court and went to see the prosecuting barrister. He was not in the barristers' waiting room, so I sat down with the junior barrister and I mentioned my concern that the evidence might be weakened by Mr X's testimony. As we were discussing this, the senior barrister appeared. He thanked me for my help in the case, but said that I was now released and would not be asked to give evidence. Utterly astounded, I asked him why I was no longer needed. He permitted himself a little smile. The accused, he said, had broken down completely during the lunch break. He had admitted to the murder and changed his plea to 'guilty'. The trial had come to an abrupt end.

So, the trial had a satisfactory outcome. Mr X did not have the opportunity to talk nonsense in court, confusing the jury and jeopardizing the administration of justice. Nevertheless, matters could easily have taken a different course had the accused not changed his plea. Later, when I met the police officers in the case, I asked them whether Mr X had, indeed, been consulted by the defence in other cases; they confirmed that he had.

It is not generally known that anyone can claim to be a forensic scientist (but not a forensic pathologist) and can practice as such quite legally. In fact, the very concept of forensic science is not recognized under English or Scottish law. There is nothing to prevent a person who is totally unqualified as a scientist from practicing as a forensic consultant, although his credentials (or lack of them) may, of course, be questioned by barristers in court. Nevertheless, anyone, whether he be a charlatan or a distinguished scientist, may put a brass-plate on his door proclaiming himself a forensic scientist, an authority on DNA fingerprinting, ballistics, toxicology, forged documents, glass fragments, blood analysis, textiles and fibres, or any other forensic discipline – in other words an 'expert' in any subject other than medicine – without fear of legal retribution. (Medicine, including forensic medicine, is a legally-recognized concept and no-one may practice in these fields unless they hold legally-recognized qualifications.) The success or failure of such a person's enterprise will depend solely on whether people decide to consult him frequently enough. If he becomes known as the kind of practitioner who will give the desired answer for a fee, he may do very well indeed.

Consider for a moment the following hypothetical situation. You go to a doctor as you are not feeling well. He prescribes certain drugs and advises you to take this or that measure. Some time later, you discover that the doctor actually has no medical qualifications whatsoever and has never even studied medicine. In this situation, I imagine you would feel that you had been monstrously deceived. We consider our health to be a matter of such importance that it cannot be left in the hands of amateurs and dilettantes. Yet, in another area of supreme human importance, justice, totally unqualified people are permitted to influence the course of events. In order to remedy this quite absurd state of affairs it is absolutely essential for the concept of forensic science to be recognized in law and then for first degree courses in forensic science to be instituted at universities. At the present time, there is much more control over the standards of manufacture of toy soldiers, for example, than there is over the standards of scientific evidence in criminal cases.

The survival, nay 'thrival' (to use a word coined by someone of my acquaintance), of dishonest forensic practitioners is largely due to the existence of dishonest solicitors and police officers. Not so long ago, I was consulted by a solicitor in a case concerning the death of two young people. After studying the evidence I had to tell him that it was inconclusive: it neither supported his opinion of what had happened, nor did it refute it. He was not satisfied with this answer. He asked me whether I could give him any indication as to whether his version of events could be supported in any way. I was unable to do so. He then asked: 'Can you make a wholly unscientific guess about what happened?' Naturally, I said that I was not in the business of making wholly unscientific guesses. He did not consult me again.

This situation is not an isolated one in my experience. On another occasion I was approached by a forensic scientist working for the defence. He arrived one evening, reeking of alcohol, and asked me whether I could confirm the time of death in a case involving the murder of a twelve-year-old boy. I asked to see the evidence, but he requested me to tell him first whether I would be able to confirm the date on which he and his clients believed the boy had died. I could only repeat that it was impossible for me to answer his question before I examined the evidence. In a light-hearted way, I reminded him of Sherlock Holmes' dictum that one should never theorize in advance of the data. Not amused, he looked at me fixedly for a few seconds and then rose, snatched his papers from my hands telling me that I was being 'unhelpful', and left.

The misrepresentation of evidence is not confined only to corrupt forensic scientists and solicitors. Police officers are also capable of this, although it is my belief that the police have taken great strides in eliminating this kind of malpractice from their ranks in recent years, probably as a consequence of considerable adverse publicity during the 1980s. Nevertheless, the problem still exists.

Police manipulation of forensic results not only involves bringing pressure to bear on forensic scientists, as we have seen, but, perhaps more seriously, it also includes interference with the evidence itself and, in some cases, its destruction. When police officers decide to alter the evidence, the consequences can be very serious; indeed, they can be far more serious than the consequences of manipulation of evidence by lawyers. The reason for this is that the evidence is damaged at source and it is extremely difficult to rectify this at a later stage in the investigation. If the evidence reaches the forensic scientist or the lawyer already changed, or if it is completely concealed or destroyed, then there is little that they can do. On the other hand, if the evidence is correctly handled at the outset and is presented to scientist and lawyer in a pristine condition, any subsequent tampering with it would be easier to reveal, because the earlier police records would be available.

Moreover, police manipulation of evidence can take place at different stages. I was once involved in the investigation of a murder and drug-dealing case in which the determination of time of death was of particular importance. When I sent my report to the investigating officers, I asked them in my covering letter to send someone to Cambridge to take possession of the samples that I had examined. This is normal practice, since the physical evidence is, legally, police property. A few weeks later, a junior police officer telephoned to thank me for my report, which had been considered very helpful, as my conclusion about the time of death exactly coincided with the expectations or suspicions of the investigating officer. I then asked him when someone would come to repossess the samples. He replied that they did not want the samples and that he had been instructed to tell me to destroy them.

The enormity of this suggestion may not be immediately apparent. What I was being asked to do was to destroy crucial evidence, so that the defence would not have the opportunity to submit it to their own specialist who might well have arrived at a different conclusion from mine and one that might not have suited the police. Moreover, the *police* did not recover the evidence and then destroy it but asked *me* to destroy it, not in writing, but by word of mouth. There would therefore be no record of the request having been made. The implication of all this is clear. If the case had come to trial and the defence barrister or the judge had asked to see the exhibits, they would have been told that they had been destroyed. 'Destroyed by whom?', would have been the inevitable question, 'By the police?'. 'No, my lord, by the forensic scientist; *he* destroyed the evidence after his examination', would have been the answer. Thus, the police would not only have got rid of the evidence, but would also have absolved themselves of all responsibility for its destruction.

What is even more disturbing is that the officer who made this request – in fact, it was more in the nature of a command – did so in a very cheerful voice. He did not sound as if he felt that he was doing something wrong or unusual; it was all in a day's work. Clearly, he was used to doing this and, far more sinister, he sounded as if *he was used to scientists complying readily with his request*. In other words, the destruction of evidence, unwanted for whatever reason, was commonplace and was carried out by agreement between police officer and forensic scientist.

I will not record in detail my response to the officer in question. Suffice it to say that he was left in no doubt that I would not destroy the evidence and that he would be well advised not to do so either. His manner, swaggeringly confident up to that point, changed abruptly. He said that he agreed with me totally; that it was not his idea; that he had been told by his superiors to do it; that it was the investigating officer's fault ... I asked him to come and collect the samples the following week, which he did. I insisted that he sign a receipt for the samples, which he did very readily. The expenses I incurred in investigating this case were not paid for over a year.

Corruption breeds corruption. We have already seen how some defence barristers will engage consultants of the Mr X type. The police are perfectly aware of this and try to find ways round the problem. One solution is to destroy the evidence before it gets into the hands of the defence. So, in the above case, a desire to ensure that the evidence was not manipulated resulted in a deliberate attempt to destroy it altogether.

It is worth mentioning that the destruction of evidence is not the only police malpractice that can take place. I have had cases in which statements from my report had been deleted when it was copied on to the standard 'Statement Form'. In other cases where my conclusions were not to the liking of the investigating officer, I would receive bullying telephone calls asking me to change my mind. Yet again, subtle pressure can be brought to bear: one is told that all the other experts in the case disagree with one's conclusions, implying that one is not quite competent at one's work. Additionally, there is the underlying threat that one may be discredited altogether if one does not concur with the opinion of the majority.

It may be argued that if I really wanted to expose corruption of this sort publicly I should give full details of these cases and name the individual police officers involved. There are two reasons why I cannot and will not do this. First, by the very nature of many of these cases, there is no documentary evidence providing a permanent record of what happened. This is, of course, intentional, as I explained previously in the murder and drugs case. Therefore, I would not be able to support any accusations against named individuals. Secondly, I have always pursued such matters to their ultimate conclusion and all cases of police corruption that have come to my notice have been dealt with appropriately.

I hope I have shown in this chapter that expert evidence, as it is misleadingly called, can frequently be manipulated and misrepresented by forensic scientists, police officers and lawyers. The very word 'expert' itself is intended to mislead, since being an expert is a matter of opinion, not of fact. A forensic scientist may well be a *specialist* in a particular field of science, but whether or not he is expert at his work is quite another matter. When a forensic scientist appears in court to give evidence and is presented as an 'expert', the impression given is that he is effectively infallible. Needless to say, this can never be the case. I have always advocated the use of the word 'specialist' rather than 'expert', but the latter word continues to be used almost exclusively.

Can anything be done about this state of affairs? If not, how much worse will the situation become?

In 1993, two reports on the state of British forensic science were published, one by the Royal Commission on Criminal Justice, the other by the House of Lords Select Committee on Science and Technology. Both highlighted a number of concerns about the way forensic science was being handled and made recommendations to the government. Both were also critical of many aspects of forensic science practice but I believe they did not go far enough.

Some of the conclusions and recommendations of these reports are worth enumerating. The Royal Commission concluded that whereas concern had been focused in the past on malpractice by individuals, there had been no examination of the system within which such malpractice occurs. Among other things, their Report recommended closer liaison between forensic scientists, lawyers and police officers as a way of reducing misunderstandings.

The House of Lords' Report made a number of very specific proposals. First, it proposed a system of accreditation so that incompetent and dishonest practitioners could be excluded from the Criminal Justice System. As a result, accreditation has become a subject of intense discussion in forensic circles but, so far, little or nothing has actually been done about it. Secondly, it recommended the establishment of a new Forensic Science Research Institute, which could, in the words of the Report, 'provide Ministers and the courts with a source of scientific advice which could be seen to be wholly independent'.

Late in 1993, I was invited by the University of Durham to set up such an institute. Despite great interest in the project from many quarters, the experiment was a complete failure. There were many reasons why the projected institute did not get off the ground, the principal one being the refusal of the government or, to be specific, the Home Office, to provide even the most basic financial assistance. Pump-priming funds were refused. Research funds were refused. Attempts to raise funds from other sources also failed, largely because other funding bodies, including the government research councils, felt that the work of the proposed institute fell within the remit of the Home Office and that it should therefore fund it. But still the Home Office refused to offer any kind of financial backing, in spite of the moral and scientific support received from almost everyone concerned with forensic science in Britain for such an institute. Regrettably, the University of Durham itself felt unable to provide the funds needed, believing that external funding would suffice. The result was that a great opportunity to remedy many of the ills of British forensic science was lost.

The Royal Commission set up to look into miscarriages of justice in recent years recommended the establishment of a Forensic Science Advisory Council that would have a remit to monitor forensic science laboratories and ensure the maintenance of the highest standards of practice. Again, this proposal was not implemented by government, in spite of repeated calls for such a body. There is little doubt that, if such a body had been set up, standards in forensic science would not have fallen so drastically.

At the beginning of 1998, the Report of the Working Group on Forensic Science appeared. It recommended the establishment of a Registration Council which would record the names of reliable forensic scientists. Practitioners who were regarded as being unreliable would not be included, the hope being that fewer police officers and lawyers would consult them but if they did, the fact that they were not on the register would be mentioned in court. Such people would not however be barred from practising. Totally incompetent people such as

Mr X would be easily excluded since, while still harmful, they could be shown to lack qualifications and professional credentials. Such people are more easily discredited in court than the more able but dishonest forensic scientist, who is often suave, self-confident and very plausible. He will have many qualifications and, possibly, a professional title, like Doctor. It would be quite easy to devise a series of questions to test whether an 'expert' knows what he is doing, but it is hard to see how such a test could be devised to determine whether someone is dishonest or not. This is the main problem with the proposed Registration Council. However, I believe it to be a very necessary first step, though not as easy to implement as it may appear.

It is clear that the problems with forensic science, highlighted and emphasized over so many years, have not been recognized by government, which, inexplicably, has refused to take any effective action. Although various bodies have expressed their concerns about forensic science evidence, they have not gone far enough because they have not addressed sufficiently adequately the central issues, namely, the market-place approach to forensic science and the misuse of the subject by lawyers. Certainly, these points were mentioned in the above reports, but they failed to propose any radical solutions, which are absolutely necessary if the problems of forensic science are to be resolved. The House of Lords' Report specifically said that it would not address this point – the point most urgently in need of addressing.

In my opinion the market-place approach to forensic science is an unqualified evil. Whatever the merits or demerits of the market-place approach in other fields, it is wholly out of place in the context of justice. Money should not be allowed to buy justice, which is, in fact, what is happening. It may be objected that lawyers are paid fees for their work and that forensic scientists should be no different. This view does not take into consideration the fact that lawyers represent their clients, whereas forensic scientists do not, or should not, represent anyone and should be totally independent. Not all the players in an adversarial trial belong to one side or the other. The judge does not. He is impartial and does not take sides. His role is to preside over the proceedings and to advise the jury without bias. And so it should be with the forensic scientist. We would rightly consider it totally absurd to employ judges on the market-place principle, and it is equally absurd that forensic scientists should be employed on the same basis.

The reputations of forensic scientists must not rest in the hands of their 'clients', be they police officers or lawyers, because these clients will base their opinions on whether or not the scientist has helped them in their case-work. If a scientist helps a lawyer to win a case or a police officer to apprehend a suspect, he will be considered to be a 'good' forensic scientist, but if he fails to do so, he will be poorly regarded. The real test of a scientist's ability should be his scientific competence and his proficiency in drawing valid conclusions from his results. As it is, competence is not the criterion by which forensic scientists are measured.

For example, not so long ago, the Law Society started to compile a *Directory of Expert Witnesses*, and forensic consultants from many disciplines were invited to submit their names and details of their expertise. To ensure that only the 'right' people were included, references from two satisfied solicitors were required, in other words, solicitors whom the scientist had been able to help win cases. References from other scientists competent in evaluating another's work *were not required*. Having been invited to submit my own name, I told the Law Society that I was not prepared to comply with their request to provide solicitors' names as referees, but would instead give the names of forensic scientists and pathologists with whom I had worked and who could evaluate my competence. Surprisingly, my proposal was accepted but the general requirement for solicitor referees remained in force.

Why is the market-place philosophy such a bad thing for forensic science? After all, those who buy a commodity should be well-qualified to judge its worth. If the service is not up to standard surely no-one would pay for it and the incompetent practitioner would be weeded out. When someone buys a refrigerator from a dealer and it turns out to be faulty, it will become known that the dealer is unreliable and, eventually, no-one will buy refrigerators from him. In any case, the issue is between the customer and the dealer and is nobody else's business. This is not the case with forensic science. The consequences of a forensic investigation are not solely the business of the client (police officer or lawyer) and the consultant (forensic scientist), because those consequences will affect other people, and will affect them more seriously than the parties between whom money has changed hands. If the forensic investigation is incompetently or unscrupulously conducted, it will not be the solicitor or the police officer who suffers the consequences, but the victim or the accused (if innocent). Furthermore, as we have seen, it may be in the interests of a dishonest solicitor deliberately to seek out an unscrupulous forensic scientist who will give him the answers he wants. Thus, what the solicitor (or police officer) wants and what justice demands may often be two very different things. It follows that those who pay for forensic science expertise should not be the ones to evaluate the competence of the practitioners. As I said earlier, the intrusion of money-making into forensic science is an unmitigated evil and a bad influence on practitioners; I was once advised by a forensic science colleague not to examine evidence on behalf of a prisoner who appealed to me for help, because he could not pay. Forensic science should serve justice and nothing else.

Forensic science should be funded by the state but, like the judiciary, be independent of it. The FSS should be an integral part of the judiciary and not simply an extension of the police force, as it is widely, but largely incorrectly, perceived to be. Forensic scientists should not be subject to financial or emotional pressures and their independence must be guaranteed and defined in law, so that, like judges, their neutrality and objectivity can be upheld in every way. Unfortunately at the present time forensic science evidence is paid for by people who are, by the very nature of the system, biased, even if they are sincerely trying to arrive at the truth. Police officers and lawyers are interested but not, with the best will in the world, *disinterested* parties.

Forensic evidence presented at a trial is commissioned by the prosecution or the defence. Rival evidence is presented, which is argued out in court. New evidence may be sprung on a scientist as he stands in the witness box and he may need time to consider whether it will alter his conclusions. Barristers in court do not allow a scientist time to reconsider. He is obliged to do one of two things: either entrench in his original opinion or instantly change his mind. Either course of action may enable a clever barrister to discredit him, even though this would be most unjust. The scientific witness is more often than not treated almost like a criminal when being cross-examined, which discourages many people from entering the profession and encourages those already in it to leave. The manipulation of forensic science has been reduced to an elegant game in many trials. This is utterly disgraceful, notwithstanding the fact that it has now acquired the hallowed nature of a tradition.

The existing system that provides for the presentation of rival forensic evidence is unsound but, so long as it remains in place, it is important that scientific evidence should be discussed by the forensic advisers of both sides together and in the presence of the barristers involved. In that way all or most problems could be resolved before their conclusions are presented in court, so the significance of the evidence can be made perfectly clear to the jury. Under the present system of forensic science provision, the most reasonable and unbiased way for scientific evidence to be presented would be for it to be commissioned by the judge; unfortunately this does not happen.

Much scientific evidence will have had to be collected by the police long before the trial – in other words, before the judge becomes involved – but the judge should have the right to commission practitioners of his own choice. These would be drawn from a panel of reputable and competent scientists who would be subject to a very strict system of accreditation. They would report on the evidence before the trial began, but the judge should have the freedom to seek their advice and obtain opinions at any time during the trial. In this way there would be no financial and other subtle or unsubtle pressures that might accompany instruction by a solicitor or police officer.

Although this would be an improvement on present practices, I believe it to be very inferior to those that would result from the establishment of a totally independent statutory forensic body, as proposed above (see p. 240), that would be answerable only to the judge and would carry out the work from the beginning to the end of a case. There will, of course, be occasions when specific areas of expertise will not be available internally, in which case outside assistance should be sought but, if the forensic body is properly staffed, they would be rare. Moreover, external specialists consulted on such occasions would still be answerable only to the court.

It is worth pointing out that the problem of 'expert' witnesses is not confined to the Criminal Justice System, but extends to the civil courts as well. An issue currently exercising the legal world is the adoption of a 'no win, no fee' system for lawyers – the so-called Conditional Fee Arrangement (CFA). In the world of civil litigation it is now being proposed by the legal profession that CFAs should be the basis for payment of technical advisers too, resulting in their not being paid unless the solicitor and his client won the case, thus reducing the cost for the solicitor. It follows from this that the expert would be under pressure to present the facts and his technical interpretation of them in the most favourable light to those who paid him, since, if the case were lost, he would not be paid. This pressure is very undesirable and CFAs should not be introduced for technical consultants whatever the virtues of this system for the lawyers themselves. The consultants object to CFAs because they stand to make less money under such a system, which strikes me as at most of secondary concern. The very fact that CFAs have been proposed at all reveals that there is more concern about the financial position of the lawyer than the objectivity of the witness.

In 1996, Lord Woolf, the Master of the Rolls, produced a report, entitled *Access to Justice*, on the state of the Civil Justice System in Britain. At roughly the same time, in the late summer of 1996 I published an article in a magazine called *Science & Public Affairs*, which is read mainly by politicians, civil servants and others involved in the formulation of public policy in scientific and related matters. In it I proposed that scientific witnesses in the Criminal Justice System should be answerable to the judge alone, not to either side in an adversarial battle. When I read Lord Woolf's report, I was delighted to see that he had made the same proposal in the context of the civil courts. Unfortunately, once again nothing was done. Later, however, there were rumblings of discontent from the Lord Chancellor's Department. The employment of experts in civil cases was now costing the taxpayer half as much again as the entire county court system. The idea of having one expert answerable to the court was again put forward and Lord Woolf, commenting that the situation was now 'out of control', expressed the view, with which I wholeheartedly agreed, that many experts 'are not necessary and ... rather than assisting justice, impede it.' In April, 1999, Lord Woolf's proposals became law.

While all this is encouraging, I am concerned that, whatever changes are being made in the Civil Justice System, the Criminal Justice System will not automatically follow suit. This is because much of the pressure for change in the civil courts is financial. Certainly, there is concern about the actual conduct of many 'experts', but the driving force for change is governmental concern that too much is being spent on paying their fees. Civil trials are much more common than criminal ones, and often involve large sums of money whereas, in contrast, people involved in criminal cases do not stand to gain or lose very much financially, the gain or loss being of a far more basic kind — their freedom. However, although the expert in a criminal trial does not cost the taxpayer very much, the individual expert may make a great deal of money.

As a result of my experience as a forensic scientist, I am forced to conclude that a number of solicitors and barristers are simply not interested principally in the truth. I was once involved in the investigation of a particular case of murder on behalf of the prosecution. The defence retained a highly disreputable forensic scientist who was well known to be both incompetent and corrupt. His reports, which were eventually copied to me, showed me very clearly that he was trying to support the defence's case by dishonest means. I was asked by the prosecutor to present written commentaries on them, which I did in great detail. My explanations could have left no doubt in anyone's mind that the defence expert's reports were fraudulent and his conclusions insupportable. The defence barrister read my reports, yet persisted in retaining this 'expert', despite the fact that he could hardly have failed to understand that he had consulted a complete charlatan.

One can only conclude that the defence barrister was not interested in either the truth or justice. His sole concern was winning the case. I regret to say that this is not an isolated anecdote. I have explained clearly to lawyers on so many occasions that a particular forensic scientist is untruthful or incompetent, yet those lawyers continued to consult them simply because they supported their own position. Occasionally, however, the basic story is somewhat different from usual.

There was a murder case in which I carried out my part of the investigation late one summer. I heard nothing more until about a year later, when I was told that it was coming to trial and that the barrister would like to have a conference with me. (Barristers never seem to have meetings, only 'conferences'!). Several police officers were present when I explained the evidence and my conclusions to the barrister. He seemed satisfied, feeling the conclusions supported his case, although, as I was at pains to explain, they did leave some room for doubt or, rather, slightly different interpretations. I made clear what these were and why I considered my conclusion to be the most likely. But the barrister wanted his case to be watertight. He asked me, in a chatty sort of way, what kind of evidence would have had to have been found in order to render my conclusion beyond doubt. Unsuspectingly, I explained that, if such-and-such a kind of evidence had been found, then my conclusion could hardly be questioned, but that, in the absence of such evidence, it was not possible to be absolutely certain. All present listened attentively to what I said and, after finishing my cup of coffee, I departed.

A few days later I received a fax from the police force in question. Lo and behold! Evidence of the kind I had said would have been needed to clinch the case had suddenly appeared. A police officer, who had attended the scene of the murder a year earlier, had suddenly 'remembered' that he had seen some very relevant evidence. Part of the fax was a sworn statement from this officer, describing this new evidence. It is hardly necessary to say that I was highly suspicious. Nevertheless, I looked at this statement and considered it in conjunction with the evidence that I had already examined in order to see whether it would fit the whole picture. It did not. For legal reasons I cannot divulge the details of this story, but I can explain what happened by means of an analogy. Let us say that the damning evidence would have been the presence of a certain make of green waxed jacket at the scene. The police officer's sworn statement included the equivalent of the assertion that a lorry-load of green jackets had been found at the scene. In other words, the evidence was not only vastly exaggerated but, precisely because it was so ridiculously embellished, it lost its force completely. In other words, the vast quantity of hypothetical jackets would argue *against* the prosecution's case, not in support of it. The police, misunderstanding its significance, fabricated the new evidence and went too far, shooting themselves in the foot.

I telephoned the police, and the officer in question was obliged to hear my opinion of his conduct. I then contacted the barrister's chambers and asked for another conference which took place a few days later. Taking with me all the relevant papers, including the new 'evidence', I explained to the barrister and the police officers (the culprit officer was not present) why the new information could not possibly be true. The barrister looked strained and uncomfortable and the police officers did not look at all happy. After a long, tense period of silence, the barrister had no option but to agree with my request that this piece of evidence be withdrawn. However, he soon recovered his composure and tried to make light of the whole affair. He treated it as though it were a somewhat embarrassing incident, not a crime. Smiling, he said that 'we had better' not bring this up in court, 'had we?'. This was disgraceful. If such a thing had happened in Germany, the prosecutor would have been legally-bound to order an immediate investigation. In France, the examining magistrate, or *juge d'instruction*, would have had to investigate the case. But the barrister did nothing, other than yield to my insistence that the so-called evidence be ignored.

This incident left a very ugly impression on my mind, not only because of the police officer's conduct, but because I felt that I had left the matter unfinished. As I sat on the train on my way home I realized that, although I could dispose of the fraudulent evidence, I was not able to prevent this malpractice from being covered up and I even began to have uncomfortable feelings that I was, in a sense, colluding with it by not making an even greater fuss. The more I thought about it, the more oppressive the thought became. By the time I arrived home I had taken the decision to write a letter to the Director of Public Prosecutions, asking for advice on what to do if and when, as a forensic scientist, I came across malpractice of this sort. I did not mention the case or the details; I merely made a general request for guidance. I received a reply some weeks later. The gist of this letter was that I should contact the police force in question and tell them what happened, which is, of course, what I had already done. Needless to say, the police force took no action. The barrister was happy to let it pass. In Britain, there is no established mechanism for dealing with this kind of corrupt practice, unlike that in France and Germany.

It may be argued that a public exposure of the police officer would have brought the culprit to justice. In fact, this would not have achieved the desired object. At the conference with the barrister, the police officers present were at pains to point out that they had all had similar memories about the evidence, but that it was such a long time ago that they could be mistaken. One's memory can play tricks on one, they said. Their absent colleague, they said, probably suffered from a faulty memory, like themselves. He was, of course, an excellent officer they said, in whom they had full confidence. The ranks had closed.

I strongly believe that the measures I have proposed above would go a very long way towards improving the present state of forensic evidence. If nothing is done I have to say that the situation is bound to get much worse. Many new and inexperienced people are jumping on the bandwagon of forensic free enterprise. We live in an age in which monetary values and considerations dominate society, and forensic science, the subject that could serve the Criminal Justice System so well, is crumbling under their assault. The pervasive nature of this market-place philosophy has made it all but impossible to argue the case against its adoption in forensic matters.

The flaws in the way that the system is currently organized have yet to become the subject of public debate in Britain. Similar flaws exist in other countries with similar legal systems to the British, such as the USA and Australia, but in those countries there is some kind of public debate, precipitated by some well-publicized miscarriages of justice. In Britain, public attention has focused only on individual trials, but the general underlying problem continues to be ignored.

The concept of justice, perhaps more than any other, distinguishes human beings from animals. But justice cannot exist without objectivity and impartiality, attitudes which themselves cannot exist within a system that is essentially partisan.

Forensic scientists and, more especially, those concerned with the role of forensic science in the Criminal Justice System would do well to reflect upon the words of François Rabelais:

'Science without conscience is but the ruin of the soul'.

Sources and further reading

Chapter 1 – A very simple clue

This introductory chapter is based on my own experiences and views. There are few general introductions to the subject of forensic entomology, but those interested in exploring the subject further might like to consult:

Smith, K. G. V. (1986). *A Manual of Forensic Entomology*. British Museum (Natural History), London.

Greenberg, B. & Kunich, J.C. (due 2002). *Flies as Forensic Indicators – entomology and the law*. Cambridge University Press, Cambridge, UK.

Chapter 2 – The nature of evidence

Again, this chapter is based largely upon my perceptions and experience of case-work, supplemented over the years by the reading of specialist forensic and scientific papers and books, which are too many to list. However, anyone interested in finding out more about the nature of evidence and its interpretation for the courts may like to consult the following book, which is not, however, an introductory text, but a rather advanced one:

Robertson, B. & Vignaux, G. A. (1995). *Interpreting Evidence*. John Wiley & Sons.

Good introductions to forensic science include:

Saferstein, R. (1995). *Criminalistics; An Introduction to Forensic Science*. Prentice-Hall, New Jersey, USA.

White, P. [Ed.] (1998). *Crime Scene to Court: The Essentials of Forensic Science*. Royal Society of Chemistry, Cambridge.

A more detailed reference work is:

Siegel, J., Knupfer, G. & Saukko, P. [Eds.] (2000). *Encyclopedia of Forensic Sciences*. Academic Press, London. (3 vols.).

Chapter 3 – The evidence of nature

There is no general account of the use of living organisms as forensic evidence; indeed, the chapter was written as a way of partly providing such an account. Readers who wish to know more about the natural history of bluebottles and greenbottles may wish to consult:

Erzinçlioglu, Z. (1996). *Blowflies*. Richmond Publishing Company.

An excellent introduction to the biology of flies in general is:

Colyer, C. N. & Hammond, C. O. (1968). *Flies of the British Isles*. Frederick Warne & Co., London.

Chapter 4 – Foul, strange and unnatural

I have relied here on my own experiences. No general accounts of the cases described in this chapter are available, apart from newspaper reports that appeared at the time of each trial. Many newspaper items about the Jason Swift case appeared after the release of Sidney Cooke in 1998.

Chapter 5 – Broken lives

Most of this chapter is based on my own experiences and views. The full story of the 'Babes in the Wood' may be read in:

Clement, H. (1996). *No Justice for the Poor*. Published by the author.

Chapter 6 – A medley of madness

This chapter is based on my own experiences and opinions. The section that discusses the story of the man I have named Henry Nash includes some dialogue. I have always been suspicious of the authenticity of conversations of this sort when given in non-fiction books, so I take this opportunity to point out that I noted down all Mr Nash's comments soon after he said them. The reasons for my desire to keep a record of what happened will be obvious from the content.

For a discussion of the M'Naghten Rules and related matters see:

Hall Williams, J. E. (1986). *Criminology and Criminal Justice*. (Butterworths).

Chapter 7 – Cases of identity

The accounts of the cases in this chapter are based on my own experiences. Those who wish to know more about the identification of human remains may like to consult:

Prag, J. & Neave, R. (1997). *Making Faces*. British Museum Publications.

A more advanced text is:

Iscan, M. Y. & Helmer, R. P. [Eds.] (1993) *Forensic Analysis of the Skull*. John Wiley & Sons, New York.

Good introductions to the use of DNA evidence in human identification may be found in the forensic science books cited under Chapter 2 – 'The nature of evidence' above.

Chapter 8 – Past times

Apart from those parts of the chapters that are based on my own experience, the authorities to which I have referred in the discussion of the historical reconstruction of the natural history of flies are too well known to require detailed referencing here. Essentially, they are the Bible, the works of Herodotus, Josephus, Homer, Aristotle, Pliny and Shakespeare, as well as some other texts. All the sources are given in the chapter. See also the references in the next chapter.

Chapter 9 – Maggots and medicine

There are many accounts of the history of medical entomology. In writing this chapter, I have referred to many sources too numerous to cite here. However, anyone wishing to read more about the history of medical entomology might like to start by consulting the following works:

Cloudsley-Thompson, J. L (1976). *Insects and History*. St Martins Press.
Greenberg, B. (1971, 1973). *Flies and Disease*. 2 vols. Princeton University Press.
James, M.T. & Harwood. R.F. (1969). *Herms's Medical Entomology*. Macmillan.

There are many biographies of Napoleon and his campaigns. The reader might like to read about Baron Larrey in the following works:

Dible, J. H. (1970). *Napoleon's Surgeon*. Heinemann.
Memoirs of Baron Larrey. (1997). Worley Publications.

Chapter 10 – The ends and the means

The views expressed here are my own. Those interested in a more formal presentation of the arguments may wish to read the following article:

Erzinçlioglu, Z. (1998). British forensic science in the dock. *Nature* **392**: 859–860.

Lord Woolf's Report on the Civil Justice System is:

Access to Justice by the Right Honourable the Lord Woolf, Master of the Rolls (1996). HMSO.

Index